# Special Topics in Multimedia, IoT and Web Technologies

Valter Roesler • Eduardo Barrére • Roberto Willrich
Editors

# Special Topics in Multimedia, IoT and Web Technologies

 Springer

*Editors*
Valter Roesler
Department of Computer Science
Federal University of Rio Grande do Sul
Porto Alegre, Rio Grande do Sul, Brazil

Eduardo Barrére
Department of Computer Science
Federal University of Juiz de Fora
Juiz de Fora, Minas Gerais, Brazil

Roberto Willrich
Department of Computer Science
Federal University of Santa Catarina
Florianopolis, Santa Catarina, Brazil

ISBN 978-3-030-35104-5      ISBN 978-3-030-35102-1   (eBook)
https://doi.org/10.1007/978-3-030-35102-1

This Springer imprint is published by the registered company Springer Nature Switzerland AG.
The registered company address is: Gewerbestrasse 11, 6330 Cham, Switzerland

# Foreword

I was working with hypertext before the birth[1] of the Web... in fact, I happened to enjoy Sir Tim Berners-Lee demonstration in the Hypertext'91 Conference! *live*, of course... that was 1991! 8-)

This road led me to studying Web/document engineering, human–computer interaction, information retrieval, ubiquitous computing ... and to contributing to many Web-ambient-mobile-collaborative-based interactive multimedia applications... >:)

I was lucky: my work evolved in consonance with the Web, as in the recent paper[2] "Promoting Social Connection and Deepen Relations in Older People: Design of Media Parcels Towards Facilitating Time-Based Media Sharing"...

We are fortunate: this book brings fundamental and advanced concepts as well as hands-on examples on must-know Web and multimedia topics, from research to

---

[1]Check a little history in https://www.w3.org/History.html.
[2]http://dx.doi.org/10.2196/14112.

applications, from data extraction to data analysis, from context awareness to IoT, from modeling to authoring to learning ... and a lot more as shown by the chapter titles word cloud[3] ... ;-)

Readers will learn a lot from the nine chapters in the book: the 37 contributing authors have in-depth experience in the subject they present. Moreover, I know firsthand how demanding the three editors can be :) and, in this book, you can experience yourself the result of their excellent job in orchestrating the authors' hard work. As a result, we can use the chapters not only as introduction or reference material for classes, but also to solving problems in the wild by taking advantage of Web and multimedia data and infrastructure!

As I say to my students: there are plenty of real life problems to be solved and a lot of opportunities to make the world a better place: with the right tools and learning with each other, we can do a lot (more)...I am sure you will get inspired by this book...

Best

University of São Paulo, São Carlos, Brazil                    Maria da Graça Pimentel
September 2019

---

[3]Thanks to https://www.wordclouds.com/.

# Preface

This book presents up-to-date information about a series of hot topics on multimedia and Web. The focus of the book is on practical examples teaching how to use platforms related to these topics. The book has a didactic approach, aiming to show how these concepts relate to solving real problems in computer science, mainly in the area of multimedia and Web.

The main intended audience for this book is students (postgraduates and undergraduates) and lecturers on these specific topics. Professionals can also benefit from the book since some chapters work with practical aspects relevant to the industry. In this context, the book is not a textbook, but can be used as a reference in special topics courses, or parts of disciplines as "Special Topics in multimedia" for example.

Many multimedia applications are already part of life for many of us and will continue to be for generations to come. If we consider the great advance of the Web and the rapid growth of mobile devices, we see that today it is increasingly simple to produce, share, and consume media and multimedia applications. As a consequence, the field of multimedia has encountered new challenges and possibilities in scenarios such as IoT, IPTV, and Web.

The chapters are grouped into three parts: System Architectures and Environment (Chaps. 1 through 4), Tools and Application Development (Chaps. 5 and 6), and Data Collection and Analysis (Chaps. 7 through 9). The chapters in the first part (System Architectures and Environment) aim to introduce Web systems architectures and Fog of Things (FoT) and to discuss the use of deep learning and context-aware computing technologies in the multimedia/hypermedia area, all in a practical and applied way.

Chapter 1 presents the evolution of Web-based software architectures and the current software architectural styles, patterns, and development platforms based on client-side and server-side technologies. In addition, this chapter discusses Web 3.0 requirements such as communication protocols, microservices, MV* browser-based frameworks, boilerplates client-side code, asynchronous programming, and integration with cloud computing infrastructures. Chapter 2 presents the Fog of Things (FoT) paradigm, describing the main characteristics and concepts from the sensor and actuator communication to gateways, local and cloud servers.

Additionally, this chapter presents SOFT-IoT platform as a concrete implementation of FoT, which uses microservice infrastructure distributed along with devices in the IoT system. The final two chapters change the focus to multimedia systems. Chapter 3 aims at presenting main concepts, solutions, and technologies related to the integration of mobile cloud computing (MCC) and context-aware applications, which are research topics with growing interest. MCC seeks to leverage cloud computing features to improve the performance of mobile applications and reduce the energy consumption of mobile devices, while the latter seeks effective ways to build applications that react to changes in its context environment. This chapter presents also a practical guide to the development of a context-aware multimedia Android application using the framework CAOS. Chapter 4 takes into consideration the recent deep learning research that allowed significant advances in several areas of multimedia, especially to build applications that are sensitive to its media content semantics. However, the development of such applications is usually done from scratch, and moreover, the current hypermedia standards do not fully support such kind of development. To support such development, this chapter proposes that a hypermedia language can be extended to support such features. This chapter proposes an extension of the nested context language (NCL) and the model behind it. In the second part of the book (Tools and Application Development), chapters 5 and 6, we introduce selected tools and techniques applied in the development of ubiquitous applications and multimedia learning objects.

Chapter 5 presents the theoretical and practical basics of model-driven engineering (MDE) aiming at the construction of ubiquitous applications. MDE is an approach that considers models as the main artifacts in software development. These models are generally built using domain-specific languages, such as UML and XML, which are defined by their own metamodel. In this context, this chapter presents some key frameworks and languages available to assist in building models in accordance with a particular metamodel. Models built in this environment can then be used to document and maintain systems from different domains. Chapter 6 discusses both the pedagogical and technological recommendations involved in the authoring of multimedia learning objects (LOs). LOs are entities that can be used, reused, or referred during the teaching process, allowing students to individualize their learning experience with nonlinear browsing mechanisms and content adaptation.

Finally, in the third and last part of the book (Data Collection and Analysis), chapters 7 to 9, we aim to deliver a comprehensive view to collect data from different sources and present different approaches for extracting and processing information.

Chapter 7 presents different approaches for extracting and processing information from Twitter using Natural Language Processing and Machine Learning techniques, examining tools and methods to collect and analyze semantic information from tweets. Understanding these approaches is worthwhile because Twitter emerges as a valuable data source to get information about what people think and feel about the most different subjects. Chapter 8 presents three important issues to deal with data from multiple sources with a focus on practical strategies and research questions. These issues are considered important because data from the

Web are increasingly heterogeneous and unstructured, representing challenges for data crawling, integration, and preprocessing. There are studies that are "data-oriented," i.e., based on the available data, but their results are restricted to the respective data. In contrast, there are various problems prior to identifying what data is needed to solve them, and often multiple data sources are needed. Finally, Chap. 9 aims to discuss game development for researchers who wish analyze game user experience. In the first part of chapter 9 the authors introduce the theory of game design, highlighting definitions and examples about data collection involving guidelines and usability. The second part discusses multimedia data collection and variable analysis.

The organization of the book in three parts allows a formative and at the same time punctual study on each theme. This division assists teachers to organize their disciplines, focusing only on one, two, or even three parts. Students can use the book to gain a broad understanding of multimedia architectures and environments, tools and techniques for application development, or even how to collect and analyze data from the Web or multimedia applications.

Postgraduate students, professionals, and other researchers can read the book to treat a specific topic (chapter), or even know/update one of the three parts of the book.

This book was originated from the short courses of the Brazilian Symposium on Multimedia and Web (WebMedia). Promoted by the Brazilian Computer Society (SBC), WebMedia is the main event of the theme in Brazil and an excellent opportunity for scientific and technical exchange among students, researchers, and professionals in the areas of multimedia, hypermedia, and Web. Briefly, there were 36 proposals submitted for short-course chapters in 2017 and 2018. Of these, 12 were selected to be presented during both symposia. Of these 12 short courses accepted, 9 themes were selected to be extended in order to compose this book.

Porto Alegre, Brazil                                    Valter Roesler
Juiz de Fora, Brazil                                    Eduardo Barrére
Florianopolis, Brazil                                   Roberto Willrich
September 2019

# Acknowledgments

We would like to thank the effort of all the authors of this book, who did their best to create this excellent didactic material. We would also like to thank the members of the Special Committee of Webmedia (CE-Webmedia) and the Brazilian Computer Society (SBC). A special mention to Maria da Graça Pimentel, author of the foreword of this book and a great influence in the area of Multimedia and Web.

# Contents

# Contributors

**Andressa Andrade**  Federal University of Bahia (UFBA), Salvador, Brazil

**Leandro Andrade**  Federal University of Bahia (UFBA), Salvador, Brazil

**Eduardo Barrére**  Department of Computer Science, Federal University of Juiz de Fora, Juiz de Fora, Minas Gerais, Brazil

**Natércia A. Batista**  Federal University of Minas Gerais (UFMG), Minas Gerais, Brazil

**Michele A. Brandão**  Federal Institute of Minas Gerais (IFMG), Belo Horizonte, Brazil

**Antonio José G. Busson**  Pontifical Catholic University of Rio de Janeiro (PUC-Rio), Rio de Janeiro, Brazil

**Sergio T. Carvalho**  Informatics Institute, Federal University of Goiás, Goiânia, Brazil

**Sérgio Colcher**  Pontifical Catholic University of Rio de Janeiro (PUC-Rio), Rio de Janeiro, Brazil

**Antonio Coutinho**  State University of Feira de Santana (UEFS), Feira de Santana, Brazil

**Daniel H. Dalip**  Federal Center of Technological Education of Minas Gerais (CEFET-MG), Minas Gerais, Brazil

**André Luiz Brandão Damasceno**  Pontifical Catholic University of Rio de Janeiro (PUC-Rio), Rio de Janeiro, Brazil

**Claudiomar Pereira de Araújo**  Federal University of Paraiba (UFPB), João Pessoa, Brazil

**Matheus Lima Moura de Araújo**  Federal University of Paraiba (UFPB), João Pessoa, Brazil

**Brenno de Mello** Federal University of Bahia (UFBA), Salvador, Brazil

**Marcelo Fernandes de Sousa** Institute of Higher Education of Paraiba (IESP), Cabedelo, Brazil

**José Neuman de Souza** Federal University of Ceará (UFC), Fortaleza, Brazil

**Leandro Agostini do Amaral** University of São Paulo (USP), São Paulo, Brazil

**Aguinaldo Macedo Filho** Audit Office of Paraiba (TCE/PB), João Pessoa, Brazil

**Renata Pontin Mattos Fortes** University of São Paulo (USP), São Paulo, Brazil

**Márcio Maestrelo Funes** University of São Paulo (USP), São Paulo, Brazil

**Francisco Gomes** Federal University of Ceará (UFC), Fortaleza, Brazil

**Rudinei Goularte** University of São Paulo (USP), São Paulo, Brazil

**Álan Livio V. Guedes** Pontifical Catholic University of Rio de Janeiro (PUC-Rio), Rio de Janeiro, Brazil

**Edward Hermann Haeusler** Pontifical Catholic University of Rio de Janeiro (PUC-Rio), Rio de Janeiro, Brazil

**Raoni Kulesza** Federal University of Paraiba (UFPB), João Pessoa, Brazil

**Thacyla Sousa Lima** Federal University of Maranhão (UFMA), Maranhão, Brazil

**Cleber Lira** Federal Institute of Bahia (IFBA), Salvador, Brazil

Federal University of Bahia (UFBA), Salvador, Brazil

**Ruy Luiz Milidiú** Pontifical Catholic University of Rio de Janeiro (PUC-Rio), Rio de Janeiro, Brazil

**Mirella M. Moro** Federal University of Minas Gerais (UFMG), Minas Gerais, Brazil

**Michele B. Pinheiro** Federal University of Minas Gerais (UFMG), Minas Gerais, Brazil

**Cássio Prazeres** Federal University of Bahia (UFBA), Salvador, Brazil

**Paulo A. L. Rego** Federal University of Ceará (UFC), Fortaleza, Brazil

**Lincoln Rocha** Federal University of Ceará (UFC), Fortaleza, Brazil

**Valter Roesler** Department of Computer Science, Federal University of Rio Grande do Sul, Porto Alegre, Rio Grande do Sul, Brazil

**Carlos Salles Soares Neto** Federal University of Maranhão (UFMA), Maranhão, Brazil

**Marlo Souza** Institute of Mathematics and Statistics, Federal University of Bahia (UFBA), Salvador, Brazil

**Fernando Trinta**  Federal University of Ceará (UFC), Fortaleza, Brazil

**Windson Viana**  Federal University of Ceará (UFC), Fortaleza, Brazil

**Marcos Alves Vieira**  Goiano Federal Institute, Iporá, Brazil

**Roberto Willrich**  Department of Computer Science, Federal University of Santa Catarina, Florianopolis, Santa Catarina, Brazil

**Clarissa Castellã Xavier**  Institute of Mathematics and Statistics, Federal University of Bahia (UFBA), Salvador, Brazil

# About the Editors

**Valter Roesler** is an associate professor at the Federal University of Rio Grande do Sul (UFRGS), Brazil. He has a PhD degree (2003) and Master degree (1993) in Computer Science, and graduation in Electrical Engineering (1988). He coordinates the PRAV laboratory (Projects in Audio and Video) since 1998, and his interest areas are Multimedia, Computer Networks and eHealth.

**Eduardo Barrére** is a professor at the Federal University of Juiz de Fora (UFJF), Brazil. He has Ph.D. degree (1996) and Master degree in Systems Engineering and Computing (UFRJ). He coordinates the LapIC laboratory (Applications and Innovation in Computing), developing research in developing and use multimedia applications and information retrieval in video.

**Roberto Willrich** received the B.S. and M.Sc. degrees in electrical engineering from the Federal University of Santa Catarina (UFSC), Florianopolis, Brazil, in 1988 and 1991, respectively, and the Ph.D. degree from Université Paul Sabatier, Toulouse, France, in 1996. Also, he was a visiting researcher at LAAS-CNRS in 2005–2006. He is currently a full professor of Computer Science with the UFSC. His research interests include recommender systems, knowledge systems, semantic Web, and annotation systems.

# About the Authors

**Andressa Andrade** received B.S. (2018) in Computer Engineering from Federal University of Bahia (UFBA). She has acted as a monitor in the subject of Robotics Intelligent at UFBA and currently works with database management. Since 2015, she has been a member of the Web, Internet and Intelligent Systems Research Group (WISER). Her research interests are in the Perception Layer technologies, working mainly on the development of physical devices based on IoT architecture.

**Leandro Andrade** is a Ph.D. candidate at Federal University of Bahia (UFBA) and received M.S. (2014) and B.S. (2012) in Computer Science at UFBA. He is researcher of the Web, Internet and Intelligent Systems Research Group (WISER) where he works in projects related to Internet of Things, Fog Computing and Big Data. In 2017, Andrade has done a Ph.D. internship at Insight Centre for Data Analytics (former DERI) at the National University of Ireland, Galway (NUIG). Leandro is a member of the Brazilian Computer Society (SBC) and IEEE Communications Society, and he has publications in international and national conferences. He is a substitute lecturer at the Department of Computer Science in UFBA and his research interests are Web Semantic, Web Services, Internet/Web of Things, Fog Computing, Machine Learning, Education and Free Software.

**Natércia A. Batista** is a graduate student in Computer Science at the Federal University of Minas Gerais, with Bachelor in Information Systems from the Federal University of Minas Gerais (2017). She is currently working at the CS+X Interdisciplinary Computing Laboratory and her main interests are in the areas of data analysis and management, and social network analysis.

**Michele A. Brandão** is a Professor at IFMG and recently finished her postdoctoral in the Graduate Program in Computer Science at the Federal University of Minas Gerais (UFMG), PhD and MS in Computer Science at UFMG, Bachelor in Computer Science at the Universidade Estadual de Santa Cruz (UESC, Bahia). Her main research interests are in the areas of data mining, data management, recommendation systems, link prediction, social networks and digital forensics.

**Antonio José G. Busson** is Ph.D. candidate working under the guidance of Prof. Sergio Colcher at Pontifical Catholic University of Rio de Janeiro (PUC-Rio). He received a B.S. (2013) and M.S. (2015) in Computer Science from the Federal University of Maranhão (UFMA) on Brazil. His research interests are in multimedia systems, working mainly on the following topics: Coding and Processing of multimedia data; Hypermedia Document models, Pattern Recognition, and applications such as Web, iDTV and Games. Currently, he is working on the official Ginga Middleware development project, which is the middleware of the Japanese-Brazilian Digital TV System (ISDB-TB) and ITU-T H.761 recommendation for iPTV services. He also is working on the VideoMR project, one of the selected projects in the Microsoft and RNP A.I. challenge, which aims to detect improper content in videos.

**Sergio T. Carvalho** is a professor at the Institute of Informatics, Federal University of Goiás (UFG), Brazil, since 2006, where he works in the Postgraduate Program in Computer Science (Master and Doctoral Advisor) and teaches courses in Computer Science, Information Systems and Software Engineering. He has taught in various colleges and university centres in Computer Science area. For several years he served mainly as software project coordinator, and held positions such as Director of the Information Systems, responsible for the development and maintenance of systems, and Director of Technology Support, responsible for hardware and software infrastructure. For over seventeen years, he served as IT professional on various public and private companies, exercising activities on software development, database management and network and systems management. He holds a BSc. in Computer Science from the UFG, a MSc. and a PhD. in Computer Science, both from the Fluminense Federal University (UFF). He has experience in Distributed Systems and Software Engineering areas, and his main fields of activity are ubiquitous computing, with focus on health care applications, software architecture and self-adaptive architectures.

**Sérgio Colcher** received B.S. (1991) in Computer Engineer, M.S. (1993) in Computer Science and Ph.D. (1999) in Informatics, all by PUC-Rio, in addition to the postdoctoral (2003) at ISIMA (Institute Supérieur d'Informatique et de Modélisation des Applications—Université Blaise Pascal, Clermont Ferrand, France). Currently, he teaches in Informatics Department at Pontifical Catholic University of Rio de Janeiro (PUC-Rio). His research interests include computer networks, analysis of performance of computer systems, multimedia/hypermedia systems and Digital TV.

**Antonio Coutinho** is a Ph.D. candidate at UFBA and received a M.S. (2000) and B.S. (1998) in Computer Science from Federal University of Campina Grande (UFCG). Since 2004, he has been assistant professor of the Department of Technology (DTEC) at the State University of Feira de Santana (UEFS). Since 2016, he has been a member of the WISER and GAUDI research groups at UFBA. His research interests are in Fog Computing, working mainly on its integration with distributed ledger technologies. Particularly in the SBRC 2016, he authored and taught the minicourse "Fog Computing: Concepts, Applications and Challenges". At SBRC 2018, he authored and taught the minicourse "Blockchain and the Revolution of Consensus on Demand".

**Daniel H. Dalip** is a Professor at CEFET-MG and his research areas are Information Retrieval, Natural Language Processing and Databases. He has a PhD and MSc degrees in Computer Science from Federal University of Minas Gerais and a BSc degree in Computer Science from University Center of Belo Horizonte (UniBH). During his PhD and MSc, he researched the use of machine learning to assess the quality of collaborative content and his thesis has awarded important prizes.

**André Luiz Brandão Damasceno** is Ph.D. candidate working under the guidance of Prof. Simone Diniz Junqueira Barbosa at Pontifical Catholic University of Rio de Janeiro (PUC-Rio). He received a B.S. (2013) and M.S. (2015) in Computer Science from the Federal University of Maranho (UFMA) on Brazil. He is researcher member at IDEIAS & DASLab – PUC-Rio. His research interests include Multimedia Systems, Data Science and Machine Learning, working mainly on the following topics: Educational Data Mining and Learning Analytics. Currently, he is working on models to develop dashboards to support instructors understand logs from Virtual Learning Environment in order to predict the students' performance and identify behavior patterns. He also took part on the development of the GT-VOA in partnership with RNP, the National Research and Educational Network in Brazil, which was developed in the context of the RNP Working Groups program, during the cycles of 2012–2013, 2013–2014, and 2015. This work resulted in publications on conferences and symposiums such as CBIE 2014, SBGames 2016, WebMedia 2015 and 2016, ACM Hypertext 2017 and HCI 2017.

**Claudiomar Pereira de Araújo** is a software developer with 2+ years of professional experience and bachelor's degree (2018) in Computer Science at UFPB. He was a researcher at LAVID, where contributed to multimedia and Web systems. Currently, he works at Indra Company providing solutions for Web systems.

**Matheus Lima Moura de Araújo** is a MSc. candidate and received a degree in Computer Science (2018) from UFPB. He is a researcher member at the LAVID. His research interests are in the development of the client side, mainly web and mobile applications.

**Brenno de Mello** is a MSc. candidate at Federal University of Bahia (UFBA) and received a degree in Systems Analysis and Development (2016) from the Federal Institute of Bahia (IFBA). He has experience in the area of Computer Science, with emphasis on Information Systems and Software Engineer. Currently, Mello is participant in the Web, Internet and Intelligent Systems Research Group (WISER) and his research interests are in Internet of Things, Data Stream Mining, Fog Computing and Smart Water.

**Marcelo Fernandes de Sousa** is PhD in Computer Science at Federal University of Pernambuco (UFPE), MSc and B.S. in Computer Science at Federal University of Paraiba (UFPB). He is professor and coordinator of computer graduation courses at Institute of Higher Education of Paraiba (IESP). He is currently a researcher at the Digital Video Applications Laboratory (LAVID), having worked on the GIGA-VR, Ginga Middleware and RH-TVD CAPES projects. He is mainly interested in the following subjects: Software Engineering, Digital Television, Interactivity, Ubiquitous Computing, Multimedia, MulSeMedia and Web Systems.

**José Neuman de Souza** holds a PhD degree at Pierre and Marie Curie University (PARIS VI/MASI Laboratory), France, since 1994. He is currently working as a researcher full professor at the Federal University of Ceará in the Computer Science Department, and is IEEE senior member. Since 1999, he has been the Brazilian representative at the IFIP TC6. His main research interests are Cloud Computing and Network Management.

**Leandro Agostini do Amaral** is Ph.D. candidate at University of São Paulo (USP), received M.S. (2014) and B.S. (2010) in Computer Science at USP. Responsible Researcher in a PIPE / FAPESP project that uses games for cognitive training aimed at the public over 50 years. Since 2010 research subjects related to Human-Computer Interaction, prioritizing accessibility issues.

**Aguinaldo Macedo Filho** MSc., is Accounts Auditor and Special Technical Advisor of the Intelligence Division of Paraiba Audit Office (TCE-PB). He is B.S. in Computer Science at UFCG and MSc in Computer Networks at UFPE. He has experience in project management of Web systems developments for the Brazilian Credit Protection Service, ANATEL, Ministry of Justice and TCE-PB.

**Renata Pontin Mattos Fortes** is professor at the Department of Computer Sciences at the University of São Paulo, São Carlos campus. Graduated in Bachelor of Computer Science from the University of São Paulo (1982), Master's degree in Computer Science and Computational Mathematics from the University of São Paulo (1991) and PhD in Physics from the University of São Paulo (1996). Currently associate professor at the University of São Paulo, consultant at the Ministry of Education and ad hoc consultant at the São Paulo State Research Support Foundation. Has experience in Computer Science, focusing on Software Engineering, acting on the following subjects: web engineering, free software projects, web accessibility and software process.

**Márcio Maestrelo Funes** is senior researcher at Lenovo, received M.S. (2018) in Computer Science at University of São Paulo. Currently conducts research in user data collection with games, Virtual Reality and accessibility. Works on the following subjects: Human-Computer Interface, Ubiquitous Computing, Natural Interfaces and Virtual Reality.

**Francisco Gomes** holds a Master degree from the Federal University of Ceará. He is currently a PhD student and an assistant professor at UFC Crateús. He works in the area of Software Engineering applied to Ubiquitous Computing, Mobile Computing and MCC.

**Rudinei Goularte** is associate Member of the Brazilian Computer Society (SBC) and the Association for Computing Machinery (ACM). Graduated in Computer Science from the Federal University of Mato Grosso do Sul (1995). Master's degree (1998), a doctorate (2003) and a teaching degree (2011) from the University of São Paulo [São Carlos], all in Computer Science. Currently an associate professor at ICMC / USP under full dedication to teaching and research and a full masters and doctoral advisor. Ad hoc consultant to the São Paulo State Research Support Foundation (FAPESP) and the National Council for Scientific and Technological Development (CNPq). Develops Multimedia research in the following lines: Digital Video Coding, 3D Video, Content Based Retrieval, Multimodal Analysis, Multimedia Big Data Analytics.

**Álan Livio V. Guedes** holds a Ph.D. (2017) from the PUC-Rio, where he acts as post-Phd Researcher in TeleMídia Lab. He received his Bachelor (2009) and M.Sc. (2012) degrees in Computer Science from the UFPB, where he worked as researcher in Lavid Lab. In both labs, Álan worked in interactive video and TV research projects, and acquired experience in C++/video development and research writing/publication. At Lavid, he worked in awarded projects such Ginga Store and Brasil 4D. At TeleMídia, he contribute to the Ginga and NCL specifications which today are standards for DTV, IPTV and IBB. His research interests include Multimedia, Interactive Video, Immersive Media, and Deep Learning for Multimedia.

**Edward Hermann Haeusler** received B.S. (1983) in Mathematics from University of Brasilia. He also received a M.S. (1986) and Ph.D. (1985) in Computer Science from Pontifical Catholic University of Rio de Janeiro (PUC-Rio), he teaches in Informatics Department at. Currently, he teaches in Informatics Department at PUC-Rio. He has experience in Computer Science, focusing on Computability and Computational Models, acting on the following subjects: Proof Theory, Category Theory, Natural Ceduction and Formal Semantics.

**Raoni Kulesza** is an adjunct professor at the Federal University of Paraiba/ Informatics Center (UFPB/CI) and researcher of Digital Video Applications Laboratory (LAVID) where he teaches and coordinates multimedia systems projects, including Web systems. Ph.D in Computer Science at Federal University of Pernambuco (UFPE), MSc in Electrical Engineering at USP and B.S. in Computer Science at Federal University of Campina Grande (UFCG). He has been working with Web systems development for 20 years in projects for e-commerce, multimedia content management, digital TV and video transmission management, social networks and intensive data processing systems integrated with mobile devices.

**Thacyla Sousa Lima** received a B.S. (2016) and M.S. (2019) in Computer Science from Federal University of Maranhão (UFMA). She is researcher member at Telemidia Lab – UFMA. Her research interests are in multimedia systems, working mainly on the following topics: Hypermedia Document models, authoring and applications such as Web and iDTV. She took part on the development of the GT-VOA in partnership with RNP, the National Research and Educational Network in Brazil, which was developed in the context of the RNP Working Groups program, during the cycles of 2012–2013, 2013–2014, and 2015. This work resulted in publications on conferences and symposiums such as CBIE 2014, SBGames 2016, WebMedia 2015 and 2016, and ACM Hypertext 2017.

**Cleber Lira** is a Ph.D. candidate at Federal University of Bahia (UFBA) and received M.S. (2015) in Computer Systems at UNIFACS. He is a researcher of the Web, Internet and Intelligent Systems Research Group (WISER) and Nucleus of Mathematics in Computational Environment (NUMAC), where he works in projects related to Microservices, Internet of Things, Semantic Web Services and Education. Santana is a member of IEEE Communications Society and he has publications in international and national conference. Since 2013, he has been a professor of the Federal Institute of Bahia (IFBA) and his research interests are Web Semantic, Web Services, Internet of Things, Fog Computing, Artificial intelligence and Education.

**Ruy Luiz Milidiú** received B.S. (1974) in Mathematics and M.S. (1978) in Applied Mathematics from Federal University of Rio de Janeiro. He also received a M.S. (1983) and Ph.D. (1985) in Operations Research from University of California. Currently, he teaches in Informatics Department at Pontifical Catholic University of Rio de Janeiro (PUC-Rio). He has experience in Computer Science, focusing on Algorithmics, Machine Learning and Computational Complexity.

**Mirella M. Moro** is an Associate Professor in the Department of Computer Science (DCC) of the Federal University of Minas Gerais (UFMG). She holds a Ph.D. in Computer Science from the University of California in Riverside (2007), and a Master's Degree in Computer Science from the Federal University of Rio Grande do Sul (UFRGS). She is a member of the Education Council of ACM (Association for Computing Machinery). She was Director of Education at SBC (Brazilian Computing Society, 2009–2015), editor-in-chief of the electronic magazine SBC Horizontes (2008–2012), associate editor of JIDM (Journal of Information and Data Management, 2010–2012) and coordinator of Special Commission on Databases (CE-BD) of SBC (2015). Her research interests are in the Database area, including topics such as query processing, social networks, recommendation, bibliometry, and NoSQL.

**Michele B. Pinheiro** is a PhD student in Computer Science at the Federal University of Minas Gerais (UFMG). She has a master (2016) and Bachelor (2013) degrees in Computer Science, UFMG. She has worked with active crowdsourcing/crowdsensing in the context of geographic data. She currently works in interdisciplinary projects at the research group CS+X (Department of Computer Science—UFMG) and the Indisciplinar Group (School of Architecture—UFMG).

**Cássio Prazeres** has been an assistant professor at Federal University of Bahia (UFBA) since 2010, where he leads research activities and projects in the Web/Internet area, teaches undergraduate and postgraduate courses, and is advisor for Ph.D, M.Sc. and B.Sc. students. Also at UFBA, Prazeres is a co-founder and leader of Web, Internet and Intelligent Systems Research Group (WISER). He received a Ph.D (2009) in Computer Science from University of Sao Paulo (USP). He has several publications in international conferences and journals. Prazeres is member of: Brazilian Computer Society (SBC); IEEE Communications Society; IEEE Computer Society Technical Committee on Services Computing; IEEE Smart Cities Technical Community; IEEE Internet of Things Technical Community; ACM SIGWEB (Special Interest Group on Hypertext the Web); W3C Web of Things Community Group. He is interested in research involving topics of Internet of Things, Web of Things, Web Services, Semantic Web, Microservices, Fog Computing, Fog of Things, Web of Data, and Linked Data. Prazeres has coordinated projects in the Internet/Web of Things themes in the last years and has participated in other related projects such as Digital TV, crowdsourcing and e-learning. Recently, Dr. Prazeres had a sabbatical year as a Postdoctoral Researcher at Insight Centre for Data Analytics (former DERI) at the National University of Ireland, Galway (NUIG).

**Paulo A. L. Rego** holds a PhD in Computer Science from the Federal University of Ceará (UFC) since 2016. He is currently an adjunct professor at Computer Science Department—Federal University of Ceará, and is a member of the IEEE. He works in the area of Computer Science, with emphasis on Computer Networks and Distributed Systems. His main research interests include MCC and IoT.

**Lincoln Rocha** holds a PhD in Computer Science from Federal University of Ceará (2013). He is currently an adjunct professor at UFC Computer Science Department since 2014. He works mainly in the area of Software Engineering. Currently, his main research interests include MCC, Context-Aware Computing, and IoT.

**Carlos Salles Soares Neto** received a B.S. (2000) in Computer Science from Federal University of Maranhão (UFMA), M.S. (2003) and Ph.D (2010) in Computing at Pontifical Catholic University of Rio de Janeiro (PUC-Rio). He is currently an adjunct professor at the UFMA where he is coordinator of TeleMidia Lab – UFMA and is associate researcher at the TeleMidia Laboratory of PUC-Rio. He has experience in Computer Science area, with emphasis on Hypermedia, working mainly in multimedia applications, iDTV and Hypermedia Document models. He also took part on the development of the GT-VOA in partnership with RNP, the National Research and Educational Network in Brazil, which was developed in the context of the RNP Working Groups program, during the cycles of 2012–2013, 2013–2014, and 2015. This work resulted in publications on conferences and symposiums such as CBIE 2014, SBGames 2016, WebMedia 2015 and 2016, ACM Hypertext 2017 and HCI 2017.

**Marlo Souza** received his doctoral degree in 2016 at Federal University of Rio Grande do Sul (UFRGS) and currently is adjunct professor at Federal University of Bahia (UFBA). His teachings and research activities focus on theoretical computer science, knowledge representation, applied logic and NLP. He started working with NLP in 2007 in the context of CoGROO project—Free Grammatical Broker for OpenOffice, moving thereafter to Pontifical Catholic University of Rio Grande do Sul (PUCRS) NLP Research Group where he studied entity identification methods and opinion mining on Twitter. Integrates UFBA FORMAS research group working with semantic information extraction from text.

**Fernando Trinta** holds a PhD degree from Federal University of Pernambuco (2007). He is an adjunct professor at Computer Science Department—Federal University of Ceará since 2011. He works mainly in Multimedia, Software Engineering and Distributed Systems. Currently, his research is focused on MCC, Context-Aware Computing and Fog Computing.

**Windson Viana** is Associate professor at Federal University of Ceará. He has obtained his Ph.D. degree in February 2010 from the University Joseph Fourier (Université de Grenoble) in Grenoble, France. He received his BS degree (2002) and his MS degree (2005) in Computer Science from the Federal University of Ceará, Brazil. His research interests include context-awareness, ubiquitous computing, multimedia management, and serious games.

**Marcos Alves Vieira** is a professor at the Federal Institute of Education, Science and Technology Goiano—Campus Iporá, where he teaches Computer Science subjects in technical and higher education courses. He holds a Bachelor degree in Informatics from the Federal Institute of Education, Science and Technology of Goiás (IFG) and a Master's degree in Computer Science from the Institute of Informatics (INF) of the Federal University of Goiás (UFG), where he developed research focusing on Ubiquitous Computing Smart Spaces and Model-Driven Engineering. He is currently a PhD student in Computer Science from INF/UFG.

**Clarissa Castellã Xavier** started to work with Natural Language Processing (NLP) in 1999 at Catholic University of Rio Grande do Sul (PUCRS) NLP Research Group and received her doctoral degree in 2014 in the same institution. Since then, she worked for multicultural companies around the world, developing language-processing tools for social media and networks. She accomplished a postdoctoral fellowship with focus on semantic data extraction from social networks for urban traffic analysis at the Federal University of Rio Grande do Sul (UFRGS) in 2018. Her current research focuses on semantic data extraction from social networks and multilingual Open Information Extraction. She is also guest researcher at Federal University of Bahia (UFBA) FORMAS research group.

# Acronyms

| | |
|---|---|
| 6LOWPAN | IPv6 over Low power Wireless Personal Area Networks |
| AJAX | Asynchronous Javascript and XML |
| AMQP | OASIS Advanced Message Queuing Protocol |
| API | Application Program Interface |
| ARM | Architectural Reference Model |
| ASD | Autism Spectrum Disorders |
| BFS | Breadth-First Search |
| CAC | Context Acquisition Component |
| CAM | Context Acquisition Middleware |
| CAMCS | Context Aware Mobile Cloud Services |
| CAOS | CAD as an Adaptive Open Platform Services |
| CARMiCLOC | Context Awareness in Reflective Middleware Cloud Computing |
| CGI | Common Gateway Interface |
| CNN | Convolutional Neural Network |
| CoAP | Constrained Application Protocol |
| CPA | Cloud Personal Assistant |
| CRUD | Create/Read/Update/Delete |
| CSS | Cascading Style Sheets |
| CSV | Comma-Separated Values |
| DFS | Depth-First Search |
| DITV | Digital TV |
| DOM | Document Object Model |
| DSML | Domain-Specific Modeling Language |
| DTLS | Datagram Transport Layer Security |
| EE | Entity Extraction |
| EMF | Eclipse Modeling Framework |
| EOL | Epsilon Object Language |
| ESB | Enterprise Service Bus |
| ETL | Extract, Transform, Load |
| EVL | Epsilon Validation Language |
| FOAF | Friend of a Friend |

| | |
|---|---|
| FoT | Fog of Things |
| GMF | Graphical Modeling Framework |
| HCI | Human–Computer Interface |
| HTML | Hypertext Markup Language |
| HTTP | Hypertext Transfer Protocol |
| HTTPS | Hypertext Transfer Protocol Secure |
| ICIDH | International Classification of Impairments, Disabilities, and Handicaps |
| ICT | Information and Communication Technologies |
| IDE | Integrated Development Environment |
| IGDA | Independent Game Developers Association |
| IIC | Industrial Internet Consortium |
| IIoT | Industrial Internet of Things |
| IIRA | Industrial IoT Reference Architecture |
| IISF | Industrial Internet Security Framework |
| IM | Identity Management |
| IoT | Internet of Things |
| IP | Internet Protocol |
| JCoAP | Java Constrained Application Protocol |
| JEE | Java Enterprise Edition |
| JSON | JavaScript Object Notation |
| JSON-LD | JSON-Linked Data |
| JSX | JavaScript Syntax eXtension |
| KEM | Key Exchange and Management |
| K-NCM | Knowledge-Based Nested Context Model |
| LCDS | Microsoft Learning Content Development System |
| LMS | Learning Management Systems |
| LO | Learning Object |
| LoCCAM | Loosely Coupled Context Acquisition Middleware |
| LOD | Linked Open Data |
| M2M | Model-to-Model |
| M2T | Model-to-Text |
| MCC | Mobile Cloud Computing |
| MDE | Model-Driven Engineering |
| ML | Machine Learning |
| MOF | Meta-Object Facility |
| MpOS | Multiplatform Offloading System |
| MQTT | Message Queuing Telemetry Transport |
| MVC | Model–View–Controller |
| MVP | Model–View–Presenter |
| MVVM | Model–View–Viewmodel |
| NCL | Nested Context Language |
| NCM | Nested Context Model |
| NER | Named Entity Recognition |
| NFC | Near Field Communication |

| | |
|---|---|
| NLP | Natural Language Processing |
| NLTK | Natural Language Toolkit |
| OCL | Object Constraint Language |
| OGC | Open Geospatial Consortium |
| OKF | Open Knowledge Foundation |
| OMG | Object Management Group |
| openHAB | open Home Automation Bus |
| OSGi | Open Services Gateway initiative |
| PD | Participatory Design |
| PERSIST | Personal Self-Improving Smart Spaces |
| PGASS | Brazilian General Program of Health Actions and Services |
| PHP | Hypertext Preprocessor language |
| PLC | Programmable Logic Controller |
| PSS | Personal Smart Space |
| RA | IoT Reference Architecture |
| RDF | Resource Description Framework |
| REE | Remote Execution Environment |
| REST | Representational State Transfer |
| RFID | Radio-Frequency IDentification |
| RM | IoT Reference Model |
| RNN | Recurrent Neural Network |
| SBC | Brazilian Computer Society |
| SCORM | Shareable Content Object Reference Model |
| SDI | Spatial Data Infrastructure |
| SDK | Software Development Kit |
| SMIL | Synchronized Multimedia Integration Language |
| SMQTT | Secure Message Queue Telemetry Transport |
| SMS | Short Message Service |
| SOA | Service-Oriented Architecture |
| SOAP | Simple Object Access Protocol |
| SPA | Single Page Application |
| SPO | Subject-Predicate-Object |
| SQL | Structured Query Language |
| SSL | Secure Sockets Layer |
| SSM | SceneSync Model |
| SUS | Brazilian Health System |
| SVM | Support Vector Machine |
| TATU | The Accessible Thing Universe |
| TF-IDF | Term Frequency-Inverse Document Frequency |
| TLS | Transport Layer Security |
| TPI | Thing Protocol for Internet |
| TRA | Trust and Reputation Architecture |
| UI | User Interface |
| UML | Unified Modeling Language |
| URI | Uniform Resource Identifier |

| | |
|---|---|
| URL | Uniform Resource Locator |
| VDOM | Virtual Document Object Model |
| VM | Virtual Machine |
| VNC | Virtual Network Computing |
| W3C | World Wide Web Consortium |
| WAI | Web Accessibility Initiative |
| WCAG | Web Content Accessibility Guidelines |
| WHO | World Health Organization |
| WLAN | Wireless Local Area Network |
| WoT | Web of Things |
| WPAN | Wireless Personal Area Network |
| WWW | World Wide Web |
| WYSIWYG | What You See Is What You Get |
| XML | Extensible Markup Language |
| XMPP | Extensible Messaging and Presence Protocol |

# Part I
# System Architectures and Environment

# Chapter 1
# Evolution of Web Systems Architectures: A Roadmap

Raoni Kulesza, Marcelo Fernandes de Sousa, Matheus Lima Moura de Araújo, Claudiomar Pereira de Araújo, and Aguinaldo Macedo Filho

## 1.1 Introduction

Web systems have become popular because of the Web browsers ubiquity. This characteristic allows us to conveniently install and maintain software systems on a server without changing client-side software, even if it is accessed by millions of browsers [15]. Currently, Web systems are used for all kinds of applications, such as e-commerce, audiovisual content access, email, social networks, searches, corporate portals, etc. [13].

Web systems can be considered a kind of client–server architecture model. In this scenario, the Web browser represents the client that interprets HTML, CSS, and JavaScript code. Besides, it communicates with the server using a URL and the HTTP protocol [7]. In the beginning, each Web page was delivered to the browsers as static documents and the server's responsibility was only to receive requests for locating and sending files. However, servers can now generate a dynamic page for each request by running software, accessing the database, or integrating with other systems. In addition, a Web page can also execute code on the client-side. These characteristics led to the creation of different software development platforms

R. Kulesza (✉) · M. L. M. de Araújo · C. P. de Araújo
Federal University of Paraiba (UFPB), João Pessoa, Brazil
e-mail: raoni@lavid.ufpb.br; matheus.lima@lavid.ufpb.br; claudiomar.araujo@lavid.ufpb.br

M. F. de Sousa
Institute of Higher Education of Paraiba (IESP), Cabedelo, Brazil
e-mail: marcelo@iesp.edu.br

A. M. Filho
Audit Office of Paraiba (TCE/PB), João Pessoa, Brazil
e-mail: amfilho@tce.pb.gov.br

© Springer Nature Switzerland AG 2020
V. Roesler et al. (eds.), *Special Topics in Multimedia, IoT and Web Technologies*,
https://doi.org/10.1007/978-3-030-35102-1_1

(languages, libraries, APIs, frameworks), both server-side and client-side [25, 26]. Such solutions are mainly written using Java, C#, Python, Ruby, or JavaScript, and there are hundreds of options [26].

Another important issue is that several Web systems have quickly become very important and have gained worldwide access. For example, Facebook has one billion hits every day and Netflix has 81.5 million customers in 80 countries [13]. These kind of systems need to meet increasingly demanding requirements, such as high availability and performance, scalability, security, multiple failure points, disaster recovery, transaction support, and integration with other systems [23]. Consequently, the client–server architecture has evolved in this software category and there are several models currently presented as a solution [5].

This chapter aims to study the main options of web-based software platforms, both on the client-side (React JS, Angular JS, and Vue JS) and the server-side (Spring and Node.js). In addition, we present the history and evolution of Web System's architectural models, such as 3 layers, n layers, RESTFul [30], and microservices [3]. Finally, we present solutions developed at the Paraiba Audit Office (TCE/PB) in partnership with the Digital Video Applications Laboratory (LAViD) of the Federal University of Paraiba (UFPB) in order to illustrate the practical use of technologies and architectural models in a real project. The main contribution of this work is the dissemination of the history of Web systems and the understanding of the technologies and architectures used today, as well as the trends for the future.

## 1.2 Fundamentals of Web Systems

### 1.2.1 History and Evolution of the Web

The Web—also known as the WWW or World Wide Web—was created by Tim Berners-Lee in the early 1990s and can be understood as a distributed and weakly coupled system for document sharing. Actually, Tim originally conceived the Web as a collaborative space where people could communicate through shared information [2]. However, the emergence of new technologies, such as cloud computing [24] mashups [31], among others, has boosted Web development. Thus, what was once a distributed system of interlinked documents became a platform for open, interactive, and distributed applications and services [21]. In order to understand the evolution of the Web, [1] proposed a taxonomy that was adapted by [4] that divides the story into three waves: (1) read only, (2) read/write Web, and (3) programmable Web. As we can see in Fig. 1.1, the so-called waves are not divided by time necessarily, but by the appearance of new functionalities and, in this way, they can overlap and coexist in certain periods.

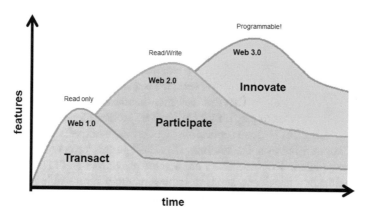

**Fig. 1.1** Web evolution: adapted from [4]

The first wave of the Web (read only Web) is called Web 1.0 and has applications capable of providing information in a single direction, being limited in terms of communication and interaction between users. Therefore, applications that allow the realization of transactions of goods and knowledge such as search engines and e-commerce services belong to this first wave. The second wave of the Web (the read/write Web) is called Web 2.0 and has as its main characteristic the interaction in communities through participation, collaboration, and co-creation. In this way, social networks, blogs, etc., are representatives of this second wave. Finally, the third wave of the Web (programmable Web) is called Web 3.0 and has the feature of allowing anyone to create a new application or service from a web-supplied infrastructure. This wave is driven by the advent of cloud computing which allows the Web to take on the role of a platform for an ecosystem of people, applications, services, and even objects (Internet of Things—IoT).

## 1.2.2 URL and HTTP

To better comprehend the modern Web systems, it is necessary to understand the following fundamental concepts: resources and their representations; URIs; and actions (verbs). In the Web context, resources are data and information, such as documents, videos, or any device that can be accessed or manipulated through Web-based systems. Many real-world resources can be represented on the Web, requiring only the proper information abstraction to do so. This strategy makes the Web a heterogeneous and accessible platform, since practically anything can be represented as a resource and made available on the Web [30]. To identify, access, and manipulate resources published on the Internet, the Web provides the Uniform Resource Identifier (URI), which establishes a way to identify resources through a one-to-many relationship. This means that a URI identifies only one resource, but one resource can be identified by many URIs. For example, a resource such as a Playlist can be represented by the HTML markup language and interpreted by Web browsers. In a similar way, the Playlist can also be represented in XML/JSON format, which is usually used by other systems and machines. Figure 1.2 exemplifies the representation of a resource with several URIs and representations. The Uniform Resource Locator (URL) is a URI that identifies the mechanism by which a resource can be accessed. For example, HTTP [9] (HyperText Transfer Protocol) URIs are examples of URLs. HTTP is an application layer protocol of the TCP/IP stack model used for data transfer over the Internet. It is through this protocol that resources can be manipulated. To do so, there are actions provided by HTTP. The original HTTP specification provides a series of request methods responsible for indicating the action to be performed on the representation of a given resource. These methods are also known as HTTP verbs. The HTTP verbs used for interaction with Web resources are GET: is used to request a representation of a specific resource and should only return data; HEAD: similar to the GET method, however, it does not have a body with the feature; POST: is used to submit an entity to a specific resource, possibly causing a change in resource state, or requesting server-side changes; PUT: requests data load replaces all current representations of your resource; DELETE: removes a specific resource; CONNECT: establishes a tunnel for connection to the server from the target resource; OPTIONS: describes communication options with the target resource; TRACE: runs a loopback call as test during the connection path to the target resource; PATCH: applies partial modifications to a specific feature.

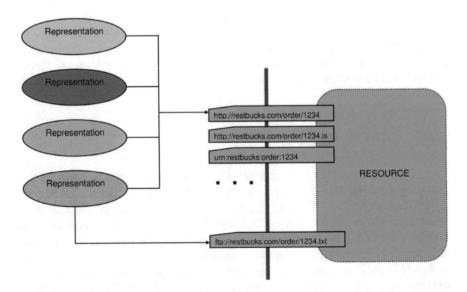

**Fig. 1.2** Web principles [30]

## 1.3   Client Technologies for Web Systems Development

The success of the Web increased its access, as well as the complexity of the available content, that evolved from static pages to applications with the capacity to behave in a similar way to desktop applications. In this context, in 1995, Netscape Communications introduced JavaScript, a client-side scripting language that allows programmers to enhance user interface and interactivity with dynamic elements. A few years later, in 2005, Jesse James Garrett proposed an approach to Web application development called AJAX (Asynchronous JavaScript + XML). Until then, user interactions (client-side) in a Web application submitted HTTP requests to a server that returned a new HTML page. Garrett's proposal brought a significant change to this traditional method, adding a layer responsible for requesting data from the server and performing all processing without the need to update the entire HTML document structure, thus making the communication between client and server asynchronous [14] HTML pages have become more user friendly with the advent of AJAX, since it allows to update parts of a web page without reloading the whole page. However, the JavaScript language had to face the competition between Web browsers that developed specific solutions for their products that were often incompatible with rival Web browsers. This scenario motivated the JavaScript community to implement libraries and frameworks, such as jQuery, to mitigate this problem, offering uniform behavior and productivity. Following the success of AJAX, the consolidation of both HTML5 and the tools used to improve the user interface development, the concept of Single Page Application (SPA) has emerged. This is a type of application that loads a single HTML page along with its JavaScript and CSS resources. After that, the browser becomes responsible for dynamically rewriting the current page instead of loading whole new pages from a server, minimizing client–server traffic. Thus, the browser supports more programming logic, being able to perform tasks such as HTML rendering, validation, UI changes, and so on [22]. JavaScript has grown a lot over the years and has an active community. Nowadays, developers have several modern alternatives for developing user interface with JavaScript based frameworks. For example: AngularJS, Ember, ReactJS, VueJS. In the Sect. 1.3.2, we will introduce you to ReactJS.

### 1.3.1   Single Page Application

The single page application, or SPA, is based on the idea that the entire application runs as a single web page designed to provide a user experience similar to that of a desktop application. The presentation layer that was previously handled by the server was factored to be managed from the browser. As a result, single page applications are able to update parts of an interface without necessarily sending or receiving a full page request from the server, thus improving performance and user experience in most cases [28]. In a SPA, browser updates are not required until the initial page load all the tools needed to create and display previews are downloaded and ready to use. If a new view is needed, It will be generated locally in the browser and dynamically attached to the DOM (Document Object Model) via JavaScript.

In a SPA, we can use different approaches to rendering server data. An example of this is partial server-side rendering, where we can combine HTML snippets with server response data. One of the most used approaches is to let the client render and only data is sent and received during business transactions. Commonly, one of the data-exchange formats for this type of data is JavaScript Object Notation (JSON), but other types of formats can be used, such as Extensible Markup Language (XML).

### 1.3.2   ReactJS

Throughout the history of the Web, several JavaScript libraries have been developed to address the problems of dealing with complex user interfaces. However, these libraries still maintained the classic separation of responsibilities that divides style (CSS), data, structure (HTML), and dynamic interactions (JavaScript). ReactJS is a JavaScript library for the development of user interfaces created and maintained by Facebook [8]. Unlike other approaches, ReactJS follows a component-based development approach. Thus, instead of defining a single model for the interfaces, they are divided into small reusable components, so the principle is to reduce complexity through component separation [19]. Therefore, ReacJS facilitates reuse, in addition to other benefits such as maintenance and distributed development, and easily promote integration with the development process. It is worth noting that the development of componentized user interfaces (UIs) is not a new approach, however, React was the first to do so from pure JavaScript without the use of models. In React, you can focus on your view layer before introducing more aspects to your application. React is not a complete JavaScript front-end framework and does not establish a specific way to develop modeling, style, or routing of data. React acts as the "V" of the MVC architecture model. Therefore, developers use React along with a routing or modeling library. The developer is free to choose which libraries to use, but there is a React Stack widely adopted to develop a complete front-end application [19]. This stack consists of data and routing libraries designed to be used specifically with React. For example, the RefluxJS, Redux, Meteor, Flux are used for the data model. The React Router is recommended for routing library. Finally, for user interface styling the React component collection that consume the Bootstrap Twitter library, the React-Bootstrap can be used.

To facilitate development in ReactJS, JavaScript Syntax eXtension (JSX) was developed. JSX is a syntax extension for writing JavaScript as if it were XML. It does not run in the browser, but is used as the source code for compilation. It is transpiled in regular JavaScript. It is optional but is recommended by Facebook for React application development. Although it sounds like a model language, JSX has the same power as JavaScript and produces React elements.

In a React application you need to think about using the component-based architecture, which allows you to reuse code by separating functionality into loosely coupled parts. By adopting this strategy, code becomes scalable, readable, reusable, and simple to maintain. This abstraction allows reuse of user interfaces in large and complex applications as well as in different projects. Standard HTML tags (div, input, p, h1, etc.) can be used to compose React component classes as well as other components. This allows for flexibility in creating robust and potentially reusable components. Theoretically, the components in React are like JavaScript functions. It is possible to provide data entries called "props," and they return React elements that describe what should be displayed on the screen. You can define a component in several ways, the simplest one being through a JavaScript function.

In addition to ReactJS, other client-side frameworks have been created those have also become famous among developers, namely Angular and Vue.js. Angular is popular web framework, from Google, built and based on Typescript. In addition, Angular uses well-known concept for components, DOM and virtual models. Code for templates can also be placed in a separate HTML template file. Like ReactJS, Vue.js is also based on Virtual DOM, but its implementation is different from ReactJS. Its implementation is optimized for efficiency, which means it only updates those DOM elements if really need it. Instead of using JSX, Vue uses its templates. These feature easy-to-use and readable syntax for creating your UI.

### 1.3.2.1  Single Page Application and ReactJS

React makes it possible to develop a SPA, although it also allows other alternatives. Code written in React can coexist with markup rendered on the server by something like PHP or other client-side libraries. For example, assuming SPA uses an MVC architecture, the application navigator acts as the "C" of the MVC architectural standard, and determines which data to fetch and which model to use. It also performs requests for data collection and populates the views from the data obtained to render the user interface. The UI sends actions back to the SPA, such as mouse events, keyboard events, etc. [19].

### 1.3.2.2  Virtual DOM

A fundamental concept that makes ReactJS applications different is the Virtual Document Object Model (VDOM). This is a programming concept in which a virtual representation of the user interface in pure JavaScript is created, kept in memory and synchronized with the actual DOM (Document Object Model) by a library such as ReactDOM [8]. Therefore, the application interacts with VDOM instead of the DOM. The main reason for this is to avoid performance issues, because if DOM updates its structure directly, several unnecessary updates would be executed, causing performance issues, especially in cases where the user interface is complex [19]. Thus, with each change in the VDOM, an algorithm first calculates the difference between the VDOM and the real DOM and, from this analysis, the library is able to identify the change in the rendering, updating only the change in the real DOM [6].

## 1.4 Architectural Patterns for Implementing SPA

It is essential in a SPA to keep code segregated based on its functionality. Taking this approach, application code is easier to design, develop, and maintain if segmented based on the type of responsibility each layer has. The SPA can be broken into multiple application layers, both server and client-side. Architectural patterns have emerged to help developers build robust and scalable applications [28]. This section details some of the most successful patterns in client-side approaches to building SPAs, namely: MVC, MVP, MVVM, Flux, Redux.

MVC is one of the oldest standards. This pattern is based on the idea of separating the application into three layers called data, logic, and presentation. The MVC pattern includes the Model, the View, and a Controller. The model contains data, business logic, and validation logic. The model notifies the view of state changes but never cares about how data is presented [28]. The controller is responsible for user interactions and sending commands to the model to update its state. The view is aware of the model in this pattern and is updated when changes are observed.

In MVP, the role of the controller is replaced with a Presenter. The MVP is a variation of MVC. The purpose of this pattern was to increase dissociation between the model and the other two components of MVC. The view delegates actions to the presenter. The Presenter has direct access to the model for any necessary changes and calls methods on the view to notify it to update itself [28]. So, the presenter is responsible for mediate the actions between the model and the view.

The MVVM is based on MVC and MVP, which tries to make UI development even more isolated from behavior and business logic in an application. The MVVM pattern includes Model, View, and ViewModel. As in MVP, the view itself is the point of entry. The ViewModel is a model or representation of the view in code, in addition to being the middleman between the model and the view [28]. It changes Model information into View information, passing commands from View to Model.

Flux is an architectural pattern that was developed as an alternative to traditional MVC architectures or their derivatives. Basically, it is an architecture designed to avoid the concept of multidirectional data flow and linking, which is common in typical MVC structures. The components that make up this architectural pattern are Actions, Dispatcher, Store, and View [8]. The Action is a simple object containing the new data and an action ID type property that is dispatched to the Store. Dispatcher is responsible for managing the entire data flow in a Flux system. It is important to note that it is not the same as the MVC Controller, as Dispatcher does not usually have much logic inside it. The Store contains all the logic and state of an application. Dispatcher, Store, and Views are independent nodes with distinct inputs and outputs. The View observes state changes emitted by the store.

Redux comes up with the idea of enhancing the original design of the Flux pattern by creating a single global singleton Store that stores state for each existing View in the application. Redux, like Flux, emphasizes the importance of unidirectional data flow. Redux is based on three principles. The first is that the entire state of the application is contained in a centralized repository, a single store, acting as the only source of truth of the system, which differs from the Flux model, where it is possible to have different stores, each responsible for its own logical domain. The second principle of Redux is that the state of the application is immutable, that is, the object representing the state should not be directly modified [20]. The third principle says that all functions that calculate a new state, in this case Reducer functions, must be pure functions. Pure functions are functions that have no side effects and are deterministic, that is, for a given set of inputs, the output will be the same. In Redux, this state is modified by Reducers that modify bits and pieces of the global app state.

## 1.5 Web Systems Architecture

Web system architectures have evolved considerably since the beginning of the Internet. At first, the systems were developed using the CGI (Common Gateway Interface) architecture. CGI gave a lot of power to the servers, since it started to offer the ability to execute code scripts—usually Perl—when processing HTTP requests, making Web systems able to process requests in a more dynamic way [18]. Another problem at the beginning of the Web was the difficulty in developing the interface code and the business logic code of the Web applications in a separate way. In order to do so, the template systems emerged, which allowed executable codes of a programming language to be injected directly into the files responsible for presenting the system. Thus, the 2 layers (presentation and logic) were better divided [10]. After that, a number of architectures emerged, such as MVC's "Model 2" architecture, which later became one of the main Web systems model [29] and pushed technologies such as Struts, Tapestry, and Java Server Pages (JSF). Also at that time, frameworks were developed to facilitate the mapping between object-oriented models and relational models, such as Hibernate, which served as the basis for 3-tier architecture (presentation, business logic, and data) [10]. Figure 1.3 presents a typical 3-tier architecture for enterprise applications with a view layer, a controller layer, and a model layer. As we can see, a request is realized by the user through the browser defining which view of an application will be presented. So, the view triggers the controller that can retrieve the information directly in the model or call business services in order to aggregate data from different sources. Finally, the model classes provide the mapping onto the data storage and are passed back up through the layers [11].

Due to the growing use of systems in a corporate environment with global access, it was necessary to divide the processing from 3 to n layers [12]. So, distributed execution platforms such as Java Enterprise Edition (JEE), .NET, and Spring emerged.

**Fig. 1.3** Typical enterprise
application architecture:
adapted from [11]

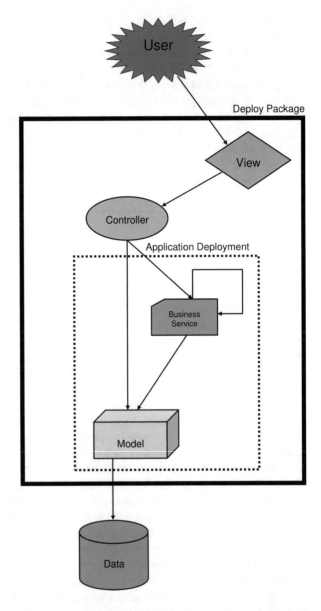

Communication protocols (SOAP, REST, etc.) also appear, allowing systems to communicate regardless of the programming language, facilitating the integration of heterogeneous and legacy systems. As a result, developers were no longer just developing applications that served content to browsers; but rather complex systems that involved multiple layers of internal and external communication (with other systems) [17]. Besides, real enterprise applications usually diverged from the clean architecture presented in Fig. 1.3 that presents clear boundaries between functionality within a layer. This situation happens because of a number of reasons, such as deadlines pushing the development team, changes in development team over time, difference of architecture preferences by the developers, etc. In this context, the boundaries between functionalities become blurred, resulting in components in each layer no longer having a well-defined purpose [11]. From then on the systems grew a lot, and the number of users increased considerably, causing these systems to become too large, turning them into giant monolithic systems [23].

A monolith, according to [11], is an application that has all its components contained within a single deployable, usually does not respect boundaries between functionalities and has a release cadence of 3–18 months. It is also a common characteristic multiple deploy packages that are part of a single deployment. These systems have many scalability and performance issues when many users use it, but it is worth mentioning that the concept is more related to the coupling of dependencies between components, leading to a problem when updating a single component is necessary. The ideal scenario is to perform this task without needing to cascade updates across many components, which allows a faster release cadence [11]. The solution was found in less monolithic and more distributed architectures, such as service-oriented architecture (SOA), using the concept of microservices and polyglot persistence [27]. These models have a better distribution of each system service, making the request load better distributed, greatly improving scalability requirements such as load balancing and high reliability [23].

Figure 1.4 demonstrates a typical microservices architecture for enterprise applications. We can understand a microservice as a single deployment executing within a single process, isolated from other deployments and processes, responsible to do one thing well. In other words, a microservice accomplishes a specific business functionality, which is a logical way to separate the domain models of an enterprise. A microservices architecture becomes useful when containing many microservices loosely coupled communicating with each other and working together [11].

As mentioned, major breakthroughs have also been achieved at the client-side presentation layer through frameworks that enable Web systems to have performance and usability comparable to traditional desktop systems [28]. These frameworks use SPA architectures [28], updating only what is needed through the use of newer versions of JavaScript (e.g., ECMAScript versions 5 and 6) and AJAX server communications [28]. This model removes the responsibility for generating the view of servers, making systems lighter and faster [28]. In this context, in [26] we can find that there are currently numerous options for development platforms (languages, APIS, libraries, frameworks, etc.) for systems. The next section describes a case study that demonstrates a set of state-of-the-art options regarding the use of technologies (client and server) and the application of modern architecture concepts to Web systems.

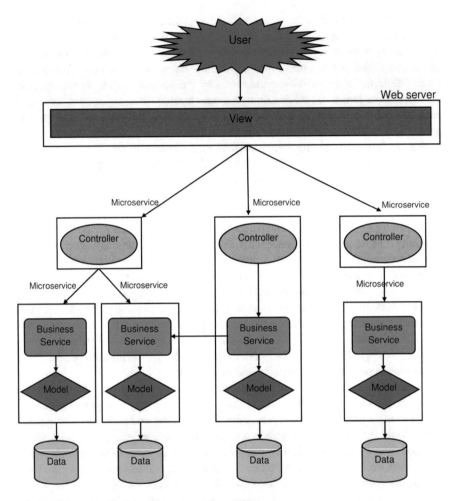

**Fig. 1.4** Enterprise microservices: adapted from [11]

## 1.6   Case Study: *Você Digital*

*Você Digital*[1] is a research and development project conducted by the Paraiba
Audit Office (TCE/PB) in partnership with the Digital Video Applications Laboratory (LAViD) of the Federal University of Paraiba (UFPB) for modeling and
development of a collaborative computing platform for electronic government (e-
government). The main objective is to improve political engagement by automating
popular compliments and complaints, which enables a better interaction and
communication between society and public administration. In addition, the platform

---

[1] Available at: http://controlesocial.tce.pb.gov.br/.

aims to exploit the collective intelligence present in the networks, promoting citizen participation that can help reduce TCE/PB operating costs, increase transparency, reliability, and efficiency of services promoted by the virtual and democratic communication channel of society's demands through the proposal tool. In addition, as a digital public management tool, the idea is to evaluate part of public services, as well as to encourage popular participation in the decision-making process of public auditors and managers. In order to evaluate the platform, a mobile application has been developed that will use new methods capable of increasing citizen involvement in the context of problem diagnosis in different areas of public service (e.g., education, health, and safety).

## 1.6.1 Vsocê Digital *Architectural Project*

Figure 1.5 presents the high-level architectural design of the *Você Digital* platform with its subsystems highlighted in blue. Possible TCE/PB internal systems are highlighted in orange and external systems are represented in the upper corner of

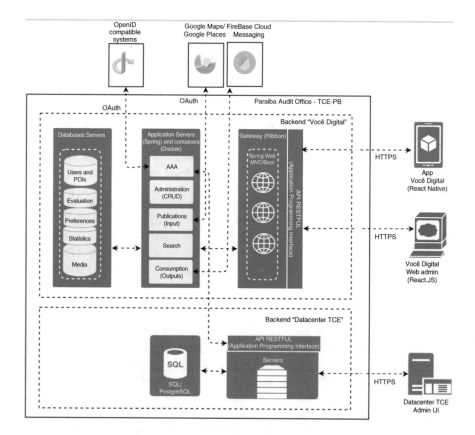

**Fig. 1.5** *Você Digital* architectural design overview

the illustration ("Systems with OpenID," "Google Maps and Google Places"). Both parts of the *Você Digital* system and TCE-PB internal systems will use the data center and virtualization infrastructure currently available on TCE/PB. The *Você Digital* system consists of two large subsystems: (1) 2 (two) client software systems (front end) and (2) 1 (one) back-end system. The first (1) set has a mobile app built with React Native technology (see Fig. 1.5 *Você Digital* App) available for download from Apple and Google Web Stores. In addition, there is also a client software system (see Fig. 1.5, *Você Digital* Administration) that allows to manage the *Você Digital* system through tasks such as data management, registration management, user permissions, statistical reports, etc. This application is based on the Single Page Application (SPA) approach and React technology to enable it to run on any web browser (desktop or mobile device). The second set (2) is responsible for the processing of data registers available in the system, as well as inferring through this data information for users. This subsystem is divided into three parts: (I) **Controller**: Responsible for load balance, high availability, and secure access to data and information available to applications through a RESTful API; (II) **Application servers** (containers based on Docker platform and technologies for the development of microservices architectures) responsible for handling the integration and processing of internal and external data and partitioning of the functionalities available for client software and (III) **Database Systems**: responsible for storing data using polyglot persistence (this module uses SQL and/or NoSQL technologies). Communication between applications (1) and servers (2) is accomplished through HTTPS protocol and RESTFul APIs.

Regarding the integration requirements of the *Você Digital* system with external systems, APIs available on OpenID-compliant systems were used to allow external authentication (e.g., social networks) so no registration is required on the *Você Digital* system to access application services. Similarly, the Google Maps APIs were used to obtain geolocation information (Google Maps) and geo-localized points of interest registered by individuals and legal entities (Google Places). For the integration with the internal systems of the TCE/PB, a mapping was made of what data and/or information would be needed. Thus, the TCE/PB team offered a RESTful API for communication between systems. Similarly, the *Você Digital* system offers APIS RESTFul for TCE /PB to access data. According to Fig. 1.5, the application server subsystem has been organized into the following components: **AAA** (Authentication, Authorization, and Accounting): these are the procedures related to authentication, authorization, and auditing. As is well known, authentication verifies the identity of users, authorization handles permissions, that is, it ensures that an authenticated user only has access to the resources authorized for their profile and, finally, the audit is related to the action of collecting data on user behavior in relation to the system. It is noteworthy that this module communicates with external authentication services and is responsible for managing the sections; **Administration** (CRUD): is the module that manages all entities of the class model, being responsible for performing the four basic operations of creation, query, update and destruction in database; **Publications** (Inputs): this module is the main source of data input of the *Você Digital* system and it is responsible for receiving all user-generated information such as ratings, comments, video and photo recordings. In addition, it also has the responsibility to handle data security. Due to the nature of the system, it is necessary to apply text filters to comments to identify inappropriate posts, as well as to sanitize data to prevent HTML injection attacks. Another competency for this module is to provide application authentication mechanisms to prevent fraud through artificial intelligence programs (robots) that can be used for information manipulation; **Search**: handles low granularity searches, such as miscellaneous database queries; and finally, **Consumption** (Outputs): this module uses the Search module to perform Data Analytics in order to generate statistical data, data transformation, graphs, reports, and other analyzes. Continuing to detail the architecture, the database server subsystem was organized in the following bases: **Users and POI**: this base stores the user registration information and their points of interest; **Evaluation**: this database stores information related to the history of evaluations performed by users; **Preferences** (profile): this database stores dynamic information related to users, such as: IP, Latitude and Longitude, among others; **Statistics**: this database stores persistent statistics that can be used by the Consumption module of the application server subsystem; and lastly, **Media**: which is a base that stores all user-generated media, such as text, images, videos, and audios. From a technology standpoint, the Spring ecosystem was adopted for the implementation of the Application Server subsystem. The Spring framework is a tool used to increase productivity in writing enterprise applications by exploring concepts such as dependency injection and inversion of control. In addition to Spring technology in the development of business logic and data access on the server, the Spring Cloud Suite Solutions also has been adopted on the Controller subsystem, which provides functionality for configuration, routing, load distribution, and high availability for implemented services.

### 1.6.2 Você Digital *Frontend Architectural Project*

The *Você Digital* frontend application architecture, as shown in Fig. 1.6, follows the Redux architectural pattern. In Fig. 1.6 the Views are composed of the components of React. Actions will be triggered from interactions in Views by the user, following to Reducers, in case of synchronous requests. Asynchronous requests will be handled in the Redux Thunk Middleware,[2] which will query the APIs used in the system, in this case the *Você Digital* API, the Google Maps API, and the Google Places API. After the API result returns, the result goes to the Reducers along with the current state of the application. The Reducer responsible for the dispatched Action will update and return the new state of the application, updating the Listener Views.

---

[2]Available at: https://github.com/reduxjs/redux-thunk.

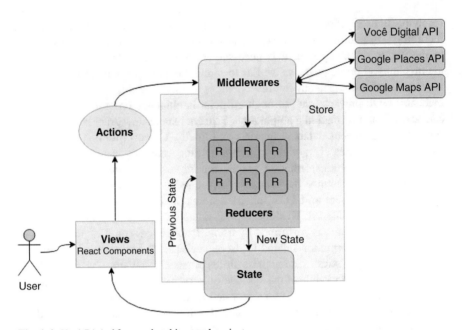

**Fig. 1.6** *Você Digital* frontend architectural project

The main architectural difference between the mobile application architecture (React Native) and the web application architecture (ReactJS) is how to render Views. While React.js uses Virtual DOM React Native uses native iOS or Android APIs.

ReactJS uses the virtual DOM. DOM building takes time because DOM trees are big today. But ReactJS can perform this procedure faster using a virtual DOM. ReactJS then uses an abstract copy of the Document Object Model and distributes the changes into one component without influencing the rest of the UI.

React Native uses native APIs to render parts of the UI that can be reused on iOS and Android platforms. So what it really does is use Java APIs to render Android components and Objective-C APIs to write iOS components. JavaScript is not a language that runs natively on the mobile device, it is executed on an interpreter known as JavaScript Core Engine and communicates with native APIs via a JavaScript bridge [16]. It then uses JavaScript to compose whatever remains of the code, individualizing the application for each platform. This gives React Native mobile applications maximum component reuse and code coding capability.

## 1.7 Final Remarks

This chapter was a brief roadmap of Web technologies related both client and server-side software development platforms. It presented the history of architectural models evolution of Web systems. It also presented a case study through the solutions developed at the Paraiba Audit Office (TCE/PB) in partnership with the Digital Video Applications Laboratory (LAViD) of the Federal University of Paraiba (UFPB). The Você Digital solution has adopted the technologies and architectural models discussed in a real project. The main contribution of this work is to disseminate the history of Web systems and to elucidate the technologies and architectures used today and trends for the future.

# References

1. Benioff, M.: Welcome to Web 3.0: Now Your Other Computer is a Data Center. TechCrunch. http://techcrunch.com/2008/08/01/welcome-to-web-30-now-your-other-computer-is-a-data-center-2/ (2008). Cited 16 Jul 2019
2. Berners-lee, T.: WWW: past, present, and future. Computer (1996) https://doi.org/10.1109/2.539724
3. Boner, J.: Reactive Microservices Architecture. Pearson Education, Sebastopol (2016)
4. Buregio, V.A.A.: Social machines: a unified paradigm to describe, design and implement emerging social systems. Doctor of Computer Science (PhD): Computer Science, Federal University of Pernambuco, Recife, Brasil (2014)
5. Burns, B.: Designing Distributed Systems: Patterns and Paradigms for Scalable. O'Reilly Media, Sebastopol (2018)
6. Chedeau, C.: React's diff algorithm. Performance Calendar. https://calendar.perfplanet.com/2013/diff/ (2013). Cited 16 Jul 2019
7. Deitel, P., Deitel, H., Deitel, A.: Internet e World Wide Web: How to Program. Pearson Education, Boston (2012)
8. Facebook (2018): React – A JavaScript library for building user interfaces. ReactJS. https://reactjs.org. (2019). Cited 23 Jul 2019
9. Fielding, R., Reschke, J.: Hypertext transfer protocol (http/1.1): semantics and content. Internet Engineering Task Force (IETF) (2014). https://tools.ietf.org/html/rfc7231. Cited 23 Jul 2019
10. Fields, D.K., Mark, A.: Web development with JSP. Manning, Shelter Island (2002)
11. Finnigan, K: Enterprise Java Microservices. Manning Publications, Shelter Island (2019)
12. Fowler, M.: Patterns of Enterprise Application Architecture. Addison Wesley, Boston (2002)
13. Fox, R., Hao, W.: Internet Infrastructure. Taylor & Francis Group, New York (2018)
14. Garrett, J.J.: Ajax: a new approach to web applications. semanticscholar. https://pdfs.semanticscholar.org/c440/ae765ff19ddd3deda24a92ac39cef9570f1e.pdf (2005). Cited 23 Jul 2019
15. Groef, W.: Client- and Server-Side Security Technologies for JavaScript Web Applications. Doctor of Engineering Science (PhD): Computer Science, Faculty of Engineering Science, Ku Leuven, Leuven (2016)
16. Hansson, N., Tomas, V.: Effects on Performance and Usability for Cross-Platform Application Development Using React Native (2016)
17. Holdener, T.: AJAX the Definitive Guide. 1st edn. O'Reilly Media, Sebastopol (2008)
18. Hunter, J., Crawford, W.: Java Servlet Programming, 2nd edn. O'Reilly Media, Sebastopol (2001)
19. Mardan, A.: React Quickly: Painless Web Apps with React, JSX, Redux, and GraphQL. Manning Publications Co., Shelter Island (2017)
20. Masiello, E., Jacob, F.: Mastering React Native. Packt Publishing Ltd., Birmingham (2017)
21. Maximilien, E.M., Ranabahu, A., Gomadam, K.: An online platform for web APIs and service mashups. IEEE Internet Comput. (2008) https://doi.org/10.1109/MIC.2008.92
22. Mikowski, M., Powell, J.: Single page web applications: JavaScript end-to-end. Manning Publications Co., Shelter Island (2013)

23. Newman, S.: Building Microservices. Pearson Education, Sebastopol (2015)
24. Patterson, D., Fox, A.: Engineering Long-Lasting Software: An Agile Approach Using SaaS and Cloud Computing. Strawberry Canyon LLC (2012)
25. Raible, M.: Comparing Hot JavaScript Frameworks: AngularJS, Ember.js and React.js. Raible Designs. https://raibledesigns.com/rd/page/publications (2015). Cited 16 Jul 2019
26. Raible, M.: Front End Development for Back End Developers. Raible Designs. https://raibledesigns.com/rd/page/publications (2017). Cited 16 Jul 2019
27. Sadalage, P.J., Fowler, M.: Nosql Distilled: A Brief Guide to the Emerging World of Polyglot Persistence, 1st edn, Addison Wesley, Boston (2013)
28. Scott, Jr. E.A.: SPA Design and Architecture Understanding Single-Page Web Applications, 1st edn. Manning Publications, Shelter Island (2016)
29. Sommerville, I.: Software Engineering, 10th edn. Pearson Education, London (2015)
30. Webber, J., Parastatidis S., Robinson I.: REST in Practice: Hypermedia and Systems Architecture. O'Reilly Media, Sebastopol (2010)
31. Yu, J., Benatallah, B., Casati, F., Daniel, F.: Understanding mashup development. IEEE Internet Comput. (2008). https://doi.org/10.1109/MIC.2008.114

**Raoni Kulesza**, DSc., is an adjunct professor at the Federal University of Paraiba/ Informatics Center (UFPB/CI) and researcher of Digital Video Applications Laboratory (LAVID) where he teaches and coordinates multimedia systems projects, including Web systems. Ph.D in Computer Science at Federal University of Pernambuco (UFPE), MSc in Electrical Engineering at USP and B.S. in Computer Science at Federal University of Campina Grande (UFCG). He has been working with Web systems development for 20 years in projects for e-commerce, multimedia content management, digital TV and video transmission management, social networks and intensive data processing systems integrated with mobile devices.

**Marcelo Fernandes de Sousa**, DSc., is Ph.D. in Computer Science at Federal University of Pernambuco (UFPE), MSc and B.S. in Computer Science at Federal University of Paraiba (UFPB). He is professor and coordinator of computer graduation courses at Institute of Higher Education of Paraiba (IESP). He is currently a researcher at the Digital Video Applications Laboratory (LAVID), having worked on the GIGA-VR, Ginga Middleware and RH-TVD CAPES projects. He is mainly interested in the following subjects: Software Engineering, Digital Television, Interactivity, Ubiquitous Computing, Multimedia, MulSeMedia and Web systems.

**Matheus Lima Moura de Araújo**, B.S., is a MSc. candidate and received a degree in Computer Science (2018) from UFPB. He is a researcher member at the LAVID. His research interests are in the development of the client-side, mainly web and mobile applications.

**Claudiomar Pereira de Araújo**, B.S., is a software developer with 2+ years of professional experience and bachelor's degree (2018) in Computer Science at UFPB. He was a researcher at LAVID, where contributed to multimedia and Web systems. Currently, he works at Indra Company providing solutions for Web systems.

**Aguinaldo Macedo Filho**, MSc., is Accounts Auditor and Special Technical Advisor of the Intelligence Division of Paraiba Audit Office (TCE-PB). He is B.S. in Computer Science at UFCG and MSc in Computer Networks at UFPE. He has experience in project management of Web systems developments for the Brazilian Credit Protection Service, ANATEL, Ministry of Justice and TCE-PB.

# Chapter 2
# Fog of Things: Fog Computing in Internet of Things Environments

**Leandro Andrade, Cleber Lira, Brenno de Mello, Andressa Andrade, Antonio Coutinho, and Cássio Prazeres**

## 2.1 Introduction

The Internet of Things (IoT) has matured in recent years allowing market solutions to emerge using the technology in different directions. Several domain scenarios such as Smart City, Smart Transportation, Connected Vehicles, Smart Health, Smart Building, Industrial Internet, Smart Farming, Smart Supply Chain, and others have been the focus for products and applications. The increasing demand for more local processing and more ways to protect the data before it goes to the cloud has made Fog Computing more relevant.

In a typical implementation of IoT, the data collected from sensors is stored and processed in cloud servers. Although this type of approach is commonly used, it has some limitations according to Abdelshkour [2]: connectivity to the cloud is a precondition and some IoT systems need to be able to work even when connection is temporarily unavailable; high demand for bandwidth, as a result of sending every bit of data over cloud channels; and slow response time (high latency) and limited scalability as a result of dependency on remote servers hosted in centralized data centers.

L. Andrade (✉) · B. de Mello · A. Andrade · C. Prazeres
Federal University of Bahia (UFBA), Salvador, Brazil
e-mail: leandrojsa@ufba.br; brenno.mello@ufba.br; dsandrade@dcc.ufba.br; prazeres@ufba.br

C. Lira
Federal Institute of Bahia (IFBA), Salvador, Brazil

Federal University of Bahia (UFBA), Salvador, Brazil
e-mail: cleberlira@ifba.edu.br

A. Coutinho
State University of Feira de Santana (UEFS), Feira de Santana, Brazil
e-mail: acoutinho@uefs.br

© Springer Nature Switzerland AG 2020
V. Roesler et al. (eds.), *Special Topics in Multimedia, IoT and Web Technologies*,
https://doi.org/10.1007/978-3-030-35102-1_2

23

In order to overcome the aforementioned Cloud Computing limitations, Bonomi et al. [7] proposed a Fog Computing paradigm which brings some operations of computing and storage close to the edge of the network. The adoption of Fog Computing does not exclude Cloud Computing and brings characteristics such as low latency, location awareness, support for mobility, a strong presence of streaming and real-time applications, and scalability for a large number of fog nodes. Based on the Fog Computing paradigm for IoT systems, Prazeres and Serrano [21] introduced the Fog of Things (FoT) paradigm. It proposes the cooperative use of network edge processing capability with Cloud servers to perform data processing and service delivery on devices, small local servers, and gateways (very small servers).

The SOFT-IoT platform is a concrete implementation of the FoT paradigm [21], that uses microservice infrastructure distributed along devices (gateways, local servers and cloud servers) in the IoT system. The microservices of SOFT-IoT are deployed on an Enterprise Service Bus (ESB) infrastructure based on the OSGi, which is a specification for middlewares that combines the functionality of a Service-Oriented Architecture (SOA) and modularity [22]. This chapter presents the Fog of Things paradigm and the SOFT-IoT platform. In addition, it describes the characteristics and architecture of FoT and the technologies used to implement SOFT-IoT.

The chapter is organized as follows. Section 2.2 describes FoT paradigm. Section 2.3 presents FoT implementation following IoT architecture divided in different layers. Section 2.3 introduces the SOFT-IoT platform in a conceptual perspective. Section 2.5 introduces some topics of research related to SOFT-IoT platform. Lastly, we present final remarks and future works in Sect. 2.6.

## 2.2   Fog of Things (FoT)

The FoT was proposed with the objective of taking advantage of the benefits that Fog Computing can bring to the IoT. In the FoT paradigm part of the data processing capacity and service delivery operations are processed locally on small servers. The Fog of Things paradigm goes beyond Fog Computing in the following aspects: (1) using all the edge processing capabilities of the network through data processing and service delivery on devices; (2) defining IoT services at the edge network; (3) distributing the IoT services on the edge of the network through a message and service-oriented middleware.

IoT platforms based in FoT paradigm can be deployed in a hybrid fog in which some of the IoT services will be deployed in the gateways and others in one or more servers. These implanted in the servers will be responsible for the self-organizing management of system, security management (authentication and identification), and storage. These deployed at gateways will be responsible for the basic services of an IoT platform, such as device access, discovery, composition, location, and others.

Some of the concepts used in FoT are based on the Architectural Reference Model (ARM) [5] for the IoT. The ARM was developed by the partners of the European FP7 Research Project IoT Architecture (IoT-A) with the technical objective of creating a generic architecture reference that could be useful to build a real IoT system. The IoT-A project was ran between 2010–2013, providing several resources (models, views, best practices, etc.) and bridging existing developments in the IoT domain.

As shown in Fig. 2.1, the FoT paradigm is composed of components, such as applications, devices, gateways, servers, messaging-oriented middleware, and security providers. In Prazeres and Serrano [21], the FoT is presented with the following organization characteristics:

- **FoT-Device:** identified as "D" in Fig. 2.1 reuses the concept proposed by ARM IoT [5] in which "devices are technical artifacts that perform real-world integration with the digital world of the Internet." Thus, Bassi et al. define three types of IoT devices: sensor (e.g., temperature sensor), actuator (e.g., switch), and label (e.g., RFID). They also transform raw data into structured content following Linked Data guidelines;

- **FoT-Gateway:** the gateway ("G" in Fig. 2.1) is the basic communication node in the network managed by FoT. Its basic aim is to translate communication layer protocols (Ethernet, WiFi, ZigBee, Bluetooth, etc.) to the HTTP protocol and to the rest of the IoT system. FoT offers access to FoT-Devices and other IoT services. Therefore, the applications can abstract the protocol of communication with the devices and access them in a standardized way for each type of device, as happens in most Web applications;

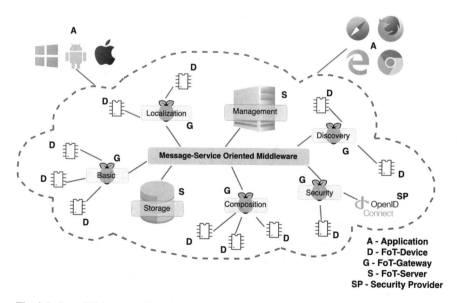

**Fig. 2.1** Fog of Things paradigm

- **FoT-Server:** the server "S" in Fig. 2.1 can be two types: a special type of gateway that has platform management features or a special feature type (see definition of feature below) that provides specific information such as historical device data that is not supported by the gateways. It is important to note, as shown in Fig. 2.1, that FoT-Gateways can provide storage features, such as data transformation, but in general they have a lower capacity of storage and processing than FoT-Servers. FoT-Server is called a server with the name of the main functionality it offers in FoT. For example, "management server," "storage server," "authorization server," etc.;
- **Enterprise Service Bus (ESB):** an ESB is a distributed infrastructure based on open standards which combines messages, Web Services, data transformation, intelligent routing, invocation, and service mediation to facilitate the integration of securely and reliably distributed applications and services [9];
- **Application:** identified as "A" in Fig. 2.1, it is any type of application based in HTTP, which is provided by the FoT-Gateways or FoT-Servers to access the FoT-Devices and provide interaction with these devices for the user. Thus, applications can be Web, mobile (Android, iPhone, or Windows Phone), or even traditional desktop applications.
- **Security Provider:** a security provider ("P" in Fig. 2.1) is a FoT-Server and is treated separately given the importance of the security aspect for an IoT platform.

In addition to the previously described components, for a better understanding of the operation of the FoT, some concepts are defined below.

- **Resource:** reuses the concept of the IoT-A ARM [5], where resources are software components that provide data to or from devices. In the IoT-A ARM, there is a distinction between "on-device resources" and "network resources." The first, as the name suggests, are software components which are deployed on the device to provide access to it. The second are resources available somewhere on the network. For example, a database for storing historical data of the FoT-Devices;
- **IoT Service:** it is based in the concept of IoT ARM [5], where IoT service provides an open and standardized interface, which offers all the necessary functionality to interact via network with IoT resources or devices. On the FoT, all IoT services will be implemented as RESTful Web Services;
- **User:** is someone who uses IoT services of the FoT. In this way, a user can be, among other things, a person, an application, or another service;
- **Profile:** as can be seen in Fig. 2.1, each node in the FoT has a label: basic, discovery, composition, management, etc. These labels are the names of the node profiles which define a set of functionalities that the node must offer, via an IoT Service, to the platform as a whole or to external applications/services. The purpose of profiles is to facilitate and optimize platform management dynamically and in a self-organizing way.

Profiles were defined to guarantee the functionalities of the FoT to support dynamic, self-organizing capabilities. Other profiles can be defined and deployed even after the platform development and deployment. The Basic Profile implements

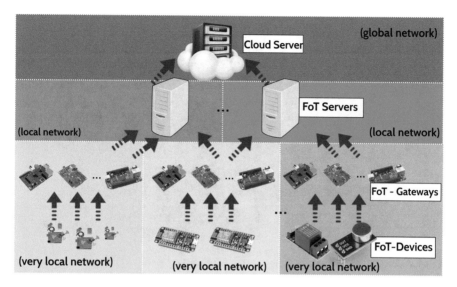

**Fig. 2.2**   Fog of Things paradigm, based in [4]

the basic functionalities that are: communication protocol mapping for HTTP; access to devices (for example, provide access to device features such as getting temperature, turning on/off a lamp, and changing the temperature of the air conditioner); automatic device configuration; and automatic publishing (exposing device features such as a RESTful Web Service). The FoT-Gateway which has only the basic features belongs to the Basic Profile. However, if necessary, this gateway can receive new features to incorporate one of the other profiles such as Discovery, Composition, Localization, Storage, Security, and Management.

Figure 2.2 presents the flow of transition of data in a FoT architecture, from the IoT devices to the cloud server. It shows that the flow of data ascends from very local networks (from IoT Devices to FoT-Gateway) to a global network in cloud servers. This structure is suitable to support mobility in devices, faster answers in layers of local network, and autonomy to keep the IoT system in operation when there is no communication with the cloud server.

## 2.3   IoT Architecture with Fog of Things

IoT development depends on the design of new applications and business models. In recent studies, Khan et al. [15] and Al-Fuqaha et al. [3], divided the structure of IoT into five layers: (1) Perception Layer, (2) Network Layer, (3) Middleware Layer, (4) Application Layer, and (5) Business Layer. Figure 2.3 shows IoT Architecture following the FoT paradigm. In the remainder of this section, we explain each one of these layers and some security aspects under development in the FoT.

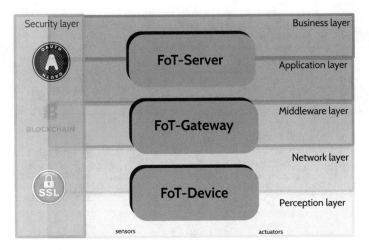

**Fig. 2.3** IoT architecture with FoT

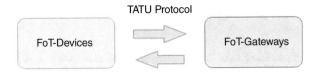

**Fig. 2.4** Communication between FoT-devices and FoT-gateways

### 2.3.1 Perception and Network Layers

The Perception Layer contains the FoT-Devices. These devices can be categorized, as described by Bassi et al. [5], as actuators, identifiers, and sensors. Actuators can change the environment, for example, devices with relays (electrically operated switches) that can turn other devices on/off. Identifiers can identify people and collaborate with the system to allow people access. Sensors can collect data from the environment, for example, devices with a DHT11 sensor able to collect the temperature and humidity of the environment. The FoT-Devices interact with the other elements in the FoT through the Network layer. This layer transfers the information from the Perception Layer to the Middleware Layer. On SOFT-IoT the transmission can be wireless or wired. Also, we can use technology 4G, Bluetooth, and infrared depending on the device.

Figure 2.4 is based on the Fig. 2.3, but with a focus on the communication between FoT-Devices in the Perception Layer, the FoT-Gateways in the Middleware Layer, and the use of The Accessible Thing Universe (TATU) protocol through the Network Layer to connect these layers.

TATU[1] arose from the need to develop a messaging pattern so that communication between devices was facilitated even for devices that did not use Message
Queuing Telemetry Transport (MQTT), it functions as an extension of MQTT,[2]
developed as a set of solutions to make the Perception Layer simpler and more
intuitive. We call this protocol TATU Thing Protocol for Internet (TATU TPI). This
protocol follows the JavaScript Object Notation (JSON) format.

### 2.3.1.1  TATU Methods

In the FoT, as the IoT, there are many types of data flow, generally used to meet data
analysis demands and real-time data presentation, e.g., temperature and luminosity
by a dashboard.[3] TATU protocol offers two methods for data requisition, GET and
FLOW [6].

The traditional GET requisition pattern (see Fig. 2.5a) is useful when the FoT-
Gateway or application needs to collect some data in real-time, so either the
application or the FoT-Gateway triggers the communication by sending a GET
request. Then, the FoT-Device collects the required data and returns its value to
whoever demanded it.

The FLOW requisition pattern (see Fig. 2.5b) was proposed to avoid continuous
communication between FoT-Gateway/application and an FoT-Device, in this data
flow pattern, the FoT-Gateway/application sets up a time range and sample amount
(one array with multiple values) which it expects to receive periodically. So, the FoT-
Device will behave proactively, sending the arrays automatically to the requester as
soon as the parameters are set up. The time between requisitions can be changed at
any time as a request from either application or FoT-Gateway.

The GET pattern can perform the same functions provided by the FLOW data
flow pattern. However, when compared to FLOW, the GET pattern tends to demand
more network utilization to transfer the samples, this is due to the GET data flow
pattern being based on request and responses, whereas the FLOW pattern is mostly
based on responses.

**Fig. 2.5**  TATU's methods GET and FLOW. (**a**) GET requests. (**b**) FLOW requests

---

[1]TATU is available on: https://github.com/WiserUFBA/TATUDevice.

[2]MQTT Protocol: http://mqtt.org/.

[3]A tool for management and monitoring of metrics and indicators, projected to ease the
comprehension and decision-making.

## 2.3.2  Middleware Layer

The Middleware Layer provides an interface between FoT-Device (sensors and actuators) and the rest of the IoT system through FoT-Gateways. In the FoT paradigm the Middleware Layer is divided in two parts with different functionalities and orientations: the message-oriented part, and the service-oriented part.

The message-oriented part provides communication between the FoT-Devices using the TATU protocol. This functionality implements a virtual communication between FoT-Devices through TATU protocol and offers uniform access to the sensor data for FoT-Gateways in the Middleware Layer.

The service-oriented part provides access to the collected sensor data for the Middleware and Application Layer in the FoT based IoT systems. It is also responsible for gathering the sensor data obtained from the message-oriented part and storing it in a local database. The service-oriented part offers an interface for the other modules in the application layer to have access to the collected data.

## 2.3.3  Application and Business Layers

The Application Layer is responsible for providing the services requested by the users. Applications can be deployed on devices with limited capacity (e.g., Raspberry Pi FoT-Gateways) and servers that are located on the edge network (FoT-Server) or servers located in the cloud (cloud server). In FoT paradigm an application is any kind of application that uses the HTTP-based REST API to access IoT services and offer interaction with services to the user.

In FoT, applications run on a service bus. The service bus enables the dynamic deployment of software through a base infrastructure, which supports communication between applications. Applications in the FoT paradigm adopt the Microservice architectural style. Microservices enable the creation of a system from a collection of small and isolated services capable of managing their own data [13].

The academic interest in Microservices for the development of IoT applications is recent [10]. Newman [19] lists some benefits, discussed below, when adopting Microservices as a solution in the development of applications.

- **Technology Heterogeneity:** each part of the application can be implemented with different technologies. So if a part of the application needs to improve its service quality it is possible to decide to use a different technology stack that is more adequate to achieve the required Quality of Service (QoS) levels. For example, in Fig. 2.6 (side b), each application can be built with different technologies to meet each objective.
- **Scaling:** with Microservices it is possible to scale parts of the application according to the need. Thus, it is possible to execute other parts of the application on a device with less computational power.
- **Ease of Deployment:** with Microservices it is possible to make a change to a single service and deploy it independently of the rest of the system. If a

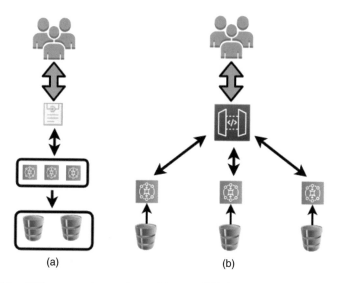

**Fig. 2.6** Monolithic versus microservices architecture [13]. (**a**) Monolith. (**b**) Microservices

problem does occur, it can be isolated quickly to an individual service, making fast rollback easy to achieve.

- **Organizational Alignment:** with Microservices, it is possible to better align the application architecture with the organizational structure.
- **Composability:** One of the key issues in service-oriented architectures and in distributed systems is the possibility of improving application reusability. With Microservices, it is possible for a functionality to be consumed in different ways for different purposes.

The Business Layer manages the general activities and services of an IoT system. The responsibilities of this layer are to build a business model, graphs, flowcharts, etc., based on data received from the Application Layer. In the FoT paradigm, the aim of the Business Layer is to enable the creation of different data visualizations that take into account the hierarchical levels in an architecture involving fog and cloud. In this context, Pinto [20] presents a model for data visualization that organizes the presentation at different levels of abstraction. This model intends to provide multiple forms of visualization over the same dataset from its generation in the FoT-Devices until its storage in the cloud, passing through the FoT-Gateways and FoT-Servers.

## 2.3.4 Security Layer

Current IoT systems integrate physical objects, sensor data, and computing resources into a large network over the Internet. IoT security is an area that aims to guarantee the privacy, confidentiality, and availability offered by an IoT ecosystem.

In such environments, potential security vulnerabilities and privacy violations need to be addressed based on trust and suitable mechanisms which developers can use to build secure, scalable, and reliable distributed solutions. It involves ensuring the security of IoT infrastructure components such as data, network, services, and devices.

Each layer of the IoT architecture with the FoT paradigm shown in Fig. 2.3 can employ mechanisms for addressing related security issues. In the following sections, general models, security threats, and examples of mechanisms used to improve trust, security, and privacy at every level of the IoT architecture are discussed.

### 2.3.4.1   Security Models and Concepts in IoT

Major reference architectures such as the Architectural Reference Model (ARM) [5] and the Industrial Internet Reference Architecture (IIRA) [18] offer standards-based architectural templates which enable IoT system architects to design solutions based on a common framework and concepts. Also, these architectural models: (1) define essential concepts and properties such as trust, security, and privacy; (2) discuss potential security issues and approaches for IoT architecture; and (3) define security models and functionality for IoT systems that serve as solid foundations upon which it is possible to build complex solutions that guarantee those properties.

The ARM consists of three interconnected parts: the IoT Reference Model (RM), the IoT Reference Architecture (RA), and a set of guidelines or best practice. The RM provides a set of models that are used to define certain aspects of the architectural views such as IoT domain model, information model, communication model, functional model, and finally models for security, trust, and privacy.

Based on the RM, the RA consists of a set of views that represent structural aspects of the system and perspectives that focus on the quality of the system. Figure 2.7 shows the IoT-A ARM functional view that proposes a layered model of functional groups which maps the concepts introduced in the ARM domain model together with a set of essential functional components that an IoT system should provide [8].

The following functional components were proposed in the RA security group:

- **Authorization (AuthZ)**—The AuthZ component is a front end for managing policies and performing access control decisions based on access control policies. This access control decision can be called whenever access to a restricted resource is requested. For example, this function is called inside the IoT service resolution component to check if a user is allowed to perform a look-up on the requested resource. This is an important part of the privacy protection mechanisms.
- **Authentication (AuthN)**—The AuthN component is involved in both user and service authentication. It checks the credentials provided by a user, and, if valid, it returns an assertion as a result, which is required to access the IoT services.

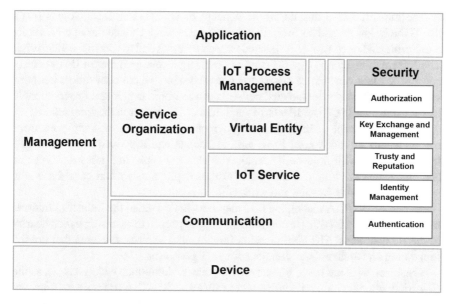

**Fig. 2.7** IoT-A ARM functional view and security components

Upon checking the correctness of the credentials supplied by a newly joining node, it establishes secured contexts between this node and other entities.

- **Identity Management (IM)**—The IM component addresses privacy questions by issuing and managing pseudonyms and accessory information to trusted subjects so that they can operate (use or provide services) anonymously.
- **Key Exchange and Management (KEM)**—The KEM component is involved in enabling secure communications between two or more IoT-A peers that do not have initial knowledge of each other or whose interoperability is not guaranteed, ensuring integrity and confidentiality.
- **Trust and Reputation Architecture (TRA)**—The TRA component collects user reputation scores and calculates service trust levels. Its functions can be invoked at a given remote entity to request or provide (recommendations or feedback) reputation information about another entity.

The Industrial Internet of Things (IIoT) has to consider safety more heavily than in the standard IoT. Information leaks in IIoT can cause not just a loss of reputation and money but also the loss of human lives. Critical incidents can be a result of system operations that do not occur in a timely and correct manner.

The IIRA model was first published in 2015 by the Industrial Internet Consortium (IIC), an open membership organization founded by AT&T, Cisco, General Electric, IBM, and Intel to accelerate the IIoT technology adoption. It focuses on the industrial sector where cyber-physical systems and other objects have fast become Internet-enabled, and security is an overall critical problem.

The industrial area introduces the concept of Operational Technologies (OT), that is the hardware and software that detects or causes a change through the direct monitoring and or control of physical devices processes and events in the enterprise. The Information Technology (IT) and OT convergence are critical in IIoT security because it has given remote access to control systems where conventional control systems usually are on an isolated network. An example is giving a Programmable Logic Controller (PLC) an IP address and then connecting it to the Internet.

Also, the concept of brownfield deployments is prominent in factory environments, where solutions need to be able to coexist and interoperate with existing legacy systems with no security features. Instead of replacing industrial types of equipment that are tough to change, industrial deployments often have these new and old systems side-by-side and work with each other.

As part of the IIRA model, the ICC members have defined the Industrial Internet Security Framework (IISF), a common security approach to assessing cybersecurity in the IIoT systems. The IISF presents fundamental security concepts that lay the foundation and architectural decisions for IIoT platforms.

These concepts are based on three main security definitions widely known as the CIA triad: confidentiality, integrity, and availability. The CIA triad is a well-known model designed to guide policies for information security within an IT organization. In this context, confidentiality is a set of rules that limits access to information, integrity is the assurance that the information is trustworthy and accurate, and availability is a guarantee of reliable access to the information by authorized people.

However, IoT systems pose extra challenges to the CIA triad due to the large amount of transmitted data, the variety of data formats, the heterogeneity of devices and network technologies, and the continuously growing number of data sources. This new computer scenario demands a high level of privacy, which is related to the right of an individual or group to control who can access or manage system components and information. This concept ties with confidentiality, as individual entities should be able to see specific data while others should not. It can have stakeholder specific requirements based on different commercial markets. Also, it should be clearly defined to users, so they know how their data is being used.

The IISF model also emphasizes safety, reliability, and resilience as essential and related concepts. In industrial environments, where system failures can lead to different types of security risks, safety concerns the necessity of a cyber-physical system to operate without directly or indirectly causing damage to the health of users. Reliability is the ability of a system to perform its required functions at a needed time, and the guarantee that security protocols do not interfere with system functions. Resilience is the ability of a system to avoid, absorb, or manage dynamic adverse conditions, keeping their state under control.

Figure 2.8 presents the related security concepts in IoT. All these related concepts lead to the central concept of trustworthiness, which is the degree of confidence that the system will perform as intended concerning all key system characteristics.

The IISF also defines functional and other concepts involved in the development of a security framework which can also apply to generic IoT systems. The application of these functional concepts into practical ideas involves providing

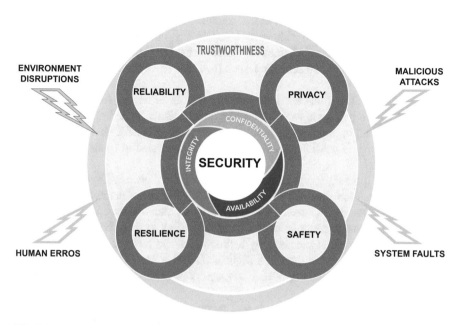

**Fig. 2.8** Security concepts in IoT

seamless mechanisms to endpoint protection, communications protection, security monitoring, and security management. Other concepts employed in the proposed framework, such as public key infrastructure and change control are a driving force for providing security in real-world IoT platforms.

### 2.3.4.2 Security in Perception and Network Layer

The Perception Layer may involve different devices that perform actions on the physical environment based on collected data. There are several kinds of sensors and actuators, sensing technologies and types of data transmission. All these possibilities could also be a target of cybersecurity threats at the Perception Layer.

The IoT devices are vulnerable to a variety of attacks that may try to capture or replace it with a malicious node and to compromise the security of the IoT application [16]. Most of the current IoT literature treats the IoT security from the network or software perspective. However, embedded IoT systems are designed to perform specific applications based on a mix of hardware and software components. In the Perception Layer perspective, the root of trust coming from hardware is always the best and most reliable solution. If the edge devices are compromised, then the entire system may be compromised. Dedicated security modules in the microcontroller/SoC used in the IoT edge devices can help in designing better protection mechanisms [16].

The connection to the Internet in IoT is mandatory, where several heterogeneous devices can communicate with each other in the ubiquitous network. Tamper resistance and encryption schemes to protect sensitive data are used to deal with a range of communication security issues from the Perception Layer to the cloud data center.

MQTT and COAP are the most used protocols to access IoT edge devices. Neither of these protocols use any security mechanisms by default. Although the option to add an optional security layer in the form of TLS/SSL for MQTT and DTLS for COAP is possible, it creates additional overhead in terms of processing and bandwidth.

In the FoT paradigm, the primary function of the Network Layer is transmitting the information received from the FoT-Devices at the Perception Layer for processing in the FoT-Gateways, FoT-Servers, or cloud datacenters. To enable this, there are many communication standards, such as 5G, WiFi, WPAN, and Bluetooth. Also, several connectivity technologies can be used at different levels in the same IoT application, such as Zigbee, 6LOWPAN, NFC, and RFID. Each of these edge network technologies may or may not provide security features for data transmission.

Due to the different technologies and number of network channels used in the IoT infrastructures, the Network Layer is highly vulnerable to different types of attacks [14], and there are several security challenges that the IoT deployments are currently facing. In this sense, digital certificates and authentication protocols are fundamental to provide secure and reliable communication between the involved entities. Concerning the risk of different attacks, paradigms such as Fog Computing and Blockchain can provide different solutions to overcome those security threats.

### 2.3.4.3 Security in Middleware Layer

The Middleware Layer includes different components, such as brokers, persistent data stores, and machine learning processing. Although the Middleware Layer is suitable for providing a reliable and robust IoT application, it is also susceptible to security threats. Different attacks can take control of the entire IoT application or damage the environment by corrupting middleware security. The security of databases and FoT nodes is a critical challenge in the Middleware Layer. A well-defined reference framework and standard for an end-to-end IoT application is not yet available.

In the Middleware Layer, the gateway is a broad component that has an essential role in connecting devices, services, and applications. It accomplishes security functions such as decrypting and encrypting IoT data and translating security protocols for communication between different layers. Also, IoT constrained devices do not have the capabilities to download and install the firmware updates. In this regard, gateways are used to download and apply the firmware updates.

This procedure permits different forms of attack that can be avoided by checking the hash of downloaded code and validity of the signatures for secure firmware updates. Therefore, security challenges for IoT gateway involve protecting encryption keys. Services and functionalities should be restricted for unauthorized users to avoid backdoor authentication or information breach.

### 2.3.4.4  Security in Application and Business Layers

The Application Layer has specific security issues that are not present in other layers, such as data theft and privacy issues. Also, the security issues in this layer are specific to a domain of applications. A combination of techniques and protocols such as data encryption, data isolation, privacy management, user and network authentication can be used to protect IoT applications against data thefts.

In the Application and Business Layer, access control and authorization mechanisms are critical security functions since the access is compromised, then the complete IoT application becomes vulnerable. Due to potential security issues present in the lower layers, the industry-standard protocols still focus on providing specific security authorization flows for end-to-end cloud-based applications that run in desktop, mobile phones, and living room devices.

The access to constrained resources remains a blocking concern, where conventional solutions already accepted for both Web and cloud applications cannot be directly used in this context. The generic HTTP is a heavyweight protocol and incurs a significant parsing overhead. There are many alternate protocols accessible at the Application Layer that have been deployed for IoT environments such as MQTT, SMQTT, CoAP, XMPP, AMQP, M3DA, and JavaScript IoT. However, as discussed in Sect. 2.3.4.2, these protocols have limited security and authentication features.

OAuth [17] is an example of a protocol that allows users to have access to resources on a website without exposing their credentials. It is an authorization framework, currently in version 2.0, that allows applications to reach user accounts over an HTTP, such as Facebook and GitHub. It works by delegating the authentication of users to the service that hosts the user account and authorizing third-party applications to access the user account. The OAuth-IoT [24] can be an alternative for a flexible authentication and authorization framework for the IoT.

### 2.3.4.5  Blockchain-Based Security Solutions for the IoT

Currently, IoT trust, security, and privacy services such as identity management, access control, and authentication focus on a client–server architecture [27]. These services are based on the assumption that IoT users have to put all trust in their so-called trusted third parties which possess personal data of users and can see all transactions between users and service providers.

The advance of Blockchain presents an approach to ensure trust, security, and privacy solutions in decentralized systems [1] such as IoT. However, the integration of IoT with Blockchain is recent and needs further research. In [14], a review of Blockchain-based solutions for IoT systems is presented. In Sect. 2.5.3, the Blockchain-related initiatives being taken within the SOFT-IoT project are discussed.

## 2.4   SOFT-IoT Platform on Fog of Things

The Fog of Things paradigm and its concrete implementation in the SOFT-IoT platform supports deployment in several domains such as sensor networks, smart homes, autonomous vehicles, and medical assistance. In addition, SOFT-IoT allows for the use of different architectures in Fog Computing and/or Cloud Computing [4]. It enables the following computational architectures: personal area sensor networks; personal area sensor network combined with gateway management, thus creating a local area network; personal area sensor network with gateways and servers, thus creating a more robust local area network infrastructure; cloud servers managing local devices; deployment of all infrastructure from the global network to the personal area network. Thus, the SOFT-IoT architecture is flexible and configurable to meet specific or generic infrastructure and application requirements.

In SOFT-IoT, the FoT-Devices are sensor nodes or actuators embedded with a driver (TATUDevice). It is implemented from a lightweight protocol TATU defined by Fog of Things. The gateway in SOFT-IoT has the function of providing sensor data, perform data processing and transformation, or indicating actions to the actuators. These actions are obtained by a communication protocol, in the form of Web Services, making the access to the devices transparent. On the other hand, a SOFT-IoT fog server provides specific information, such as historical device data, that is not supported by the gateways.

SOFT-IoT has as the main component for the implementation of its applications a service bus. ServiceMix, based on the OSGi specification, is used as a service bus on the SOFT-IoT platform. Apache ServiceMix[4] is open source software, implemented in Java, where native ESB/OSGi architecture services provide all the infrastructure necessary to support SOFT-IoT. ServiceMix allows services (also called bundles) to be deployed at run time, also allowing services to share data and objects through relationships and dependencies.

Figure 2.9 introduces Apache ServiceMix and its main modules. ServiceMix is lightweight and portable, with a basic requirement for Java 1.7 support. Also, it supports Spring Framework[5] and Blueprint[6] and is compatible with Java SE or with a Java EE application server. Karaf is the core of ServiceMix and offers the concept of features where package collections can be installed as a group in a running

---

[4]http://servicemix.apache.org/.

[5]https://spring.io/.

[6]https://aries.apache.org/modules/blueprint.html.

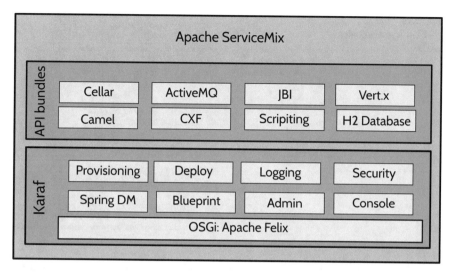

**Fig. 2.9** Apache ServiceMix components

OSGi environment. ServiceMix uses ActiveMQ to provide messaging service, CXF to support RESTful services, Cellar for communication, and interactions between different ServiceMix and Camel installations for integration and exchange of data through routes. Finally, ServiceMix contains additional modules such as the H2 Database, which manage the file-based relational database system.

## *2.4.1  SOFT-IoT Devices*

FoT-Devices in the SOFT-IoT platform are sensors/actuators that use the TATU driver. These devices can have low processing and cost, such as Arduino boards.[7]

This type of board does not have a communication module directly soldered to the board, but there are additional options that allow this device to be categorized as sensors or actuator, as set out in Sect. 2.3.1.

The devices also have a semantic description based on ontology. The Zeroconf[8] protocol is implemented in devices and is responsible for enabling devices to have their functionality exposed by RESTful Web services. The TATU driver allows for the communication of the devices with the gateways, allowing the use of the TATU protocol by the gateways through a RESTful Web service. Also, the transformation from raw data to Linked Data content is carried out on devices with an extension

---

[7]Arduino: https://www.arduino.cc/.

[8]Zeroconf: http://www.zeroconf.org/.

**Fig. 2.10** Gateway
SOFT-IoT technologies

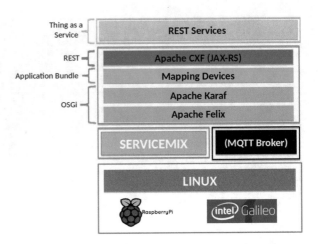

to TATU protocol. Therefore, that data messages between devices and gateways are using JSON-LD3 format, which is a size-reduced format for representing Linked Data content (Fig. 2.10).

### 2.4.2   SOFT-IoT Gateway

The SOFT-IoT gateway implements the message and service-oriented middleware. Service-oriented middleware provides communication between applications and services deployed at gateways. On the other hand, the message-oriented part provides communication between gateways and devices. To allow communication between gateways and devices using the TATU protocol, the MQTTDriver was developed. The MQTTDriver helps the developer in the task of implementing communication with the devices by enabling virtual communication between the service and the device. Some of the features implemented in the MQTTDriver are: change the value of an actuator; read the value of a sensor; obtain device properties such as IP; and edit the device properties. Figure 2.11 shows the Middleware Layer, its modules, and interactions.

The gateway on the SOFT-IoT platform is generally a low-cost device with limited processing and memory resources. The gateway uses a reduced version of the Linux operating system, a Java virtual machine, an implementation of the OSGi (service-oriented part) specification, and an MQTT server (message-oriented part). The technologies used in the gateway are shown in Fig. 2.10. As shown in this figure, the service-oriented Middleware Layer provides interfaces for applications to access devices via RESTful Web Services (TaaS) using Apache CXF technology. The MQTT broker aims to provide communication through messaging between the gateway and the devices and also between the various gateways. Finally, there is the Mapping Devices component that aims to intermediate the communication between

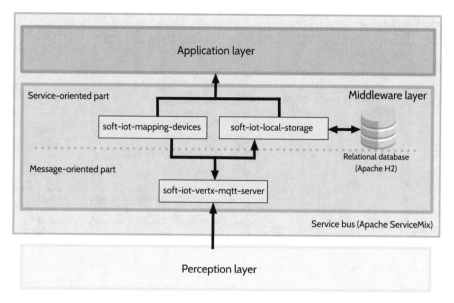

**Fig. 2.11** SOFT-IoT middleware layer components and interactions

the devices and the gateways, being implemented following the OSGi specification and deployed to the Apache Karaf server.

The SOFT-IoT platform has a specific module for mapping the devices and translating the TATU communication messages between the FoT-Device and FoT-Gateway. The module **soft-iot-mapping-devices**[9] implements the virtual interfaces of sensors and actuators connected to the platform. This module also works as a translator of TATU messages exchanged between sensors/actuators devices (FoT-Device) and FoT-Gateway, which allow request and response to requests for sensor data and actuator interactions.

Soft-iot-mapping-devices instantiate a set of objects that represent FoT-Devices. These objects contain information related to devices such as unique identifier, device type (sensor and/or actuator), and geolocation data. In addition, they are available for access by the other modules of the platform, serving as interface for accessing the sensors and/or actuators connected to the platform.

The MQTT Broker component provides a server that is capable of handling connections, communication, and message exchange with remote MQTT clients. In the SOFT-IoT platform the MQTT broker is implemented in the module **soft-iot-vertx-mqtt-broker**,[10] an OSGI-based implementation, as a ServiceMix bundle. This module is responsible for enabling communications with remote MQTT clients, which in the case of the SOFT-IoT platform are connected devices. In

---

[9]https://github.com/WiserUFBA/soft-iot-mapping-devices.

[10]https://github.com/WiserUFBA/soft-iot-vertx-mqtt-broker.

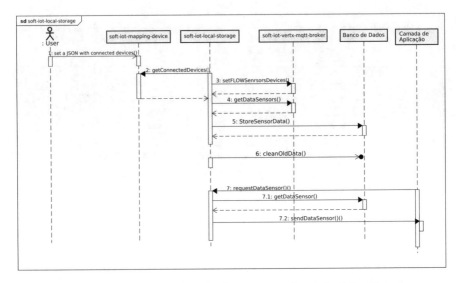

**Fig. 2.12** Sequence diagram with soft-iot-local-storage operations and relationships

addition to the advantages of using a modular architecture, using the Vert.x MQTT Server API makes it possible to scale the reactive MQTT agent according to, for example, the number of cores in the system and thus enables horizontal scalability.

The **soft-iot-local-storage**[11] module is responsible for promoting the collection, storage, and internal access of data produced by FoT-Device sensors. This module concentrates the functionalities related to the internal storage of the sensors data, as well as the access to this data by the other SOFT-IoT platform modules.

With soft-iot-mapping-devices support for translation of TATU messages and identification of platform-connected devices, soft-iot-local-storage requests data flow from each sensor connected to the platform in a user-defined period. The request and response messages are exchanged in the MQTT broker implemented by the soft-iot-vertx-mqtt-broker module to be finally stored in the Apache H2 relational database.

Figure 2.12 presents a sequence diagram of the main operations of soft-iot-local-storage with their relationships. With the devices connected to the platform, through user configuration (1. *set a JSON with connected devices*, Fig. 2.12), the soft-iot-local-storage obtains from the module soft-iot-mapping-devices the connected sensors and their respective collected data flow (2. *getConnectedDevices()*, Fig. 2.12) in order to publish in the soft-iot-vertx-mqtt-broker the sensor data requests (3. *setFLOWSenrsorsDevices()*, Fig. 2.12). With the data request, the sensors will publish in the soft-iot-vertx-mqtt-broker information collected at the configured period. The soft-iot-local-storage will in turn collect this data

---

[11] https://github.com/WiserUFBA/soft-iot-local-storage.

(4. *getDataSensors()*, Fig. 2.12) and store them in the Apache H2 database (5. *StoreSensorData()*, Fig. 2.12). Soft-iot-local-storage also implements a procedure for removing old data, whose period can be configured by the user (6. *cleanOld-Data()*, Fig. 2.12) and application layer modules can request data from the sensors through soft-iot-local-storage (7. *requestDataSensor()*, Fig. 2.12).

The soft-iot-web-service module[12] exposes the sensor data of the IoT system through a RESTful Web service. It accesses the data stored in the local database, managed by the module soft-iot-local-storage, allowing users to obtain JSON data and information about the sensors.

### 2.4.3   SOFT-IoT Server

The SOFT-IoT platform implements three types of FoT-Servers, management server, storage server, and server security provider. The first is a server that acts as a special type of gateway and implements all services related to the dynamic self-organization of the SOFT-IoT platform. The latter two are servers that act as a special type of resource and implement services related to storage and security aspects, respectively. The SOFT-IoT platform implements self-organizing features that must be deployed on servers, for example, the management server must implement all services related to the SOFT-IoT platform self-organization.

The SOFT-IoT platform, based on services, is a sufficiently flexible platform for dynamic deployment of new types of FoT-Servers that can offer their services for specific purposes. For example, IoT services for large data analysis (Big Data Analytics) can be developed and implemented on servers for data analysis locally (at the edge of the network).

The SOFT-IoT platform also proposes self-organizing features that must be deployed on fog servers. For example, management servers must implement all services related to the SOFT-IoT platform self-organization. The main services that can be implemented in the management servers are [22, 26]: self-organized monitoring service; gateway deployment service; disaster recovery service; profile management and balancing service.

### 2.4.4   SOFT-IoT Applications

The SOFT-IoT architecture implements the following modules (see Fig. 2.3, Application Layer). The **soft-iot-data-aggregation** module is responsible for aggregating data in FoT-Gateways. The **soft-iot-semantic-enrichment** module enriches sensor data, in the FoT-Gateway, with Semantic Web descriptions. The **soft-iot-semantic-**

---

[12]https://github.com/WiserUFBA/soft-iot-iot-service.

**data-aggregation** module provides data aggregation from semantic data. The **soft-iot-web-service** application provides services such as RESTful API for accessing IoT devices. These modules enable the Data Interplay which provides the definition and deployment of data operations in regards to the life cycle of data: collection, processing, storage, and access between edge, fog, and cloud infrastructures.

In addition, other modules with the SOFT-IoT platform (see Fig. 2.3, Application Layer) for the construction of rules aiming to create Smart Spaces through FoT were implemented. The **soft-iot-semantic-model** module obtains information semantically described by RDF triples deployed in the FoT-Server. The **soft-iot-semantic-reasoner** module performs semantic reasoning over the RDF data. When the Semantic Reasoner executes the rule and infers that a condition was satisfied, it performs an update on the model. The **soft-iot-semantic-observer** module is responsible for observing changes that are made in the model and notifies the **soft-iot-rules** module which is responsible for informing the actuator and activating the device (for instance, turn on an air conditioner).

Finally, in the Business Layer, the SOFT-IoT architecture implements a Data Visualization model. The aim is to enable the creation of different data visualizations that take into account the hierarchical levels in an IoT architecture involving fog and cloud.

## 2.5 SOFT-IoT Related Research Topics

In this section, some works related to the SOFT-IoT architecture are presented. The aim is to introduce practical examples that serve as a basis for learning the concepts and inspiration for new projects.

### 2.5.1 Reactive Microservices

Santana, Alencar, and Prazeres proposed an architecture and platform [11] to enable the implementation of reactive applications in IoT scenarios by the implementation of Reactive Microservices whose objective was to enable the construction of applications that are performative, resilient, and scalable.

According to Escoffier [12] Reactive Microservices have four features:

- **Autonomy**, this characteristic enables a system to adapt to the availability of the services surrounding them.
- **Resilience**, this characteristic applies to systems that require high availability. A resilient system responds even in the presence of failures.
- **Elasticity**, this characteristic refers to the ability of a system to react appropriately to load variations. Therefore, increasing or decreasing resources will depend on the number of requests to the system.

- **Asynchronous**, to have these characteristics (i.e., Autonomy, Resilience, Elasticity), the system must use asynchronous messages in order to guarantee low coupling, isolation, and location transparency communication pattern.

Thus, Santana, Alencar, and Prazeres compared the architecture and platform proposal with a FOG-based platform [21, 22]. The results showed that the use of a reactive approach resulted in better performance when compared to the same scenarios without a reactive approach.

### 2.5.2   IoT Stream Analytics in Fog Computing

IoT systems, in general, use Fog Computing, which helps solve some issues and improve some aspects of cloud-centric applications such as: achieving low latency; improving quality of service; enabling devices to operate in Fog Computing even without Internet connectivity; Data processing and applications within the boundaries of the local network. In addition, a new area of research has emerged, its biggest challenge is to process and analyze the large amount of data generated by IoT environments in Fog Computing, aiming to take advantage of the benefits of an architecture in fog. This area is described in the literature as part of the more general concept called IoT Stream Analytics [25].

IoT Stream Analytics aims to process data from various sources and domains produced by IoT, such as temperature, humidity, air pressure, luminance, gas, electricity, air quality, and motion sensor data. Common data streams generally follow a statistical distribution over a long period. However, IoT data is produced in large quantities and in a short time. They may also exhibit a variety of sporadic distributions over time [23]. Therefore, IoT Stream Analytics is a new area of research with some issues that should be further investigated.

### 2.5.3   Blockchain-Based Distributed Fog Solutions

As discussed in Sect. 2.3.4, the lack of intrinsic security measures makes IoT systems vulnerable to different privacy and security threats. Also, the Cloud Computing model has drawbacks in terms of high delays, which harm the IoT tasks that require a real-time response. Together, Blockchain and Fog Computing paradigms can help in addressing significant security and performance requirements in IoT platforms [14].

Blockchain capabilities such as immutability, transparency, auditability, data encryption, and operational resilience can solve most architectural shortcomings of IoT. Also, it provides a decentralized way to share information between IoT applications.

However, nontrivial challenges associated with integrating Blockchain technologies to IoT networks need be overcome [14]. One of the critical challenges is the scalability and latency of IoT Blockchain networks since each entry on the Blockchain requires consensus among all network nodes.

Fog and Edge Computing are complementary and useful paradigms to develop IoT solutions with low latency and QoS guarantees. In Edge Computing, data is processed directly by the device itself (data source) or by a local node rather than being transmitted to the cloud data center. Fog Computing spreads the concept of the edge in a scalable and integrated way with network devices such as switches, routers, and IoT gateways. The fog and edge distributed approach reduces the amount of data going through the core network and reduces latency issues.

The integration of Blockchain and Fog Computing technologies allows the development of responsive, secure, interoperable IoT solutions. The SOFT-IoT project has been investigating a strategy for managing these aspects by exploiting the eventual consistency and security guarantees of distributed ledger technologies.

The development of a Blockchain-as-a-Service (BaaS) model, following a fog architecture, can offer better managed Blockchain environments, resulting in higher uptake, better deployment times, and low latency services. Also, a Blockchain-based distributed fog architecture may lead to improvements in the QoS guarantees for clients, in particular fairness.

## 2.6   Final Remarks

This Chapter presented the Fog of Things paradigm, which proposes a definition of IoT infrastructure based on Fog Computing. It also relates the FoT paradigm with IoT architecture, describing the components of FoT in each layer of IoT architecture. Furthermore, the Chapter presented the SOFT-IoT platform that is an implementation of the Fog of Things model. The SOFT-IoT is a distributed IoT platform that uses Fog of Things infrastructure to deploy modules on FoT-Gateways, FoT-Servers, and cloud servers. Furthermore, the SOFT-IoT is an agnostic IoT platform and provides a flexible and configurable infrastructure. Lastly, some related research topics that use the SOFT-IoT as an environment to perform and to develop studies were presented.

## References

1. Abadi, F.A., Ellul, J., Azzopardi, G.: The blockchain of things, beyond bitcoin: a systematic review. In: 2018 IEEE International Conference on 2018 IEEE Cybermatics, pp. 1666–1672. IEEE, Piscataway (2018)
2. Abdelshkour, M.: IoT, from cloud to fog computing. http://blogs.cisco.com/perspectives/iot-from-cloud-to-fog-computing (2015). Accessed 20 July 2017

3. Al-Fuqaha, A., Guizani, M., Mohammadi, M., Aledhari, M., Ayyash, M.: Internet of things: a survey on enabling technologies, protocols, and applications. IEEE Commun. Surv. Tutorials **17**(4), 2347–2376 (2015). https://doi.org/10.1109/COMST.2015.2444095

4. Andrade, L., Serrano, M., Prazeres, C.: The data interplay for the Fog of Things: a transition to edge computing with IoT. In: 2018 IEEE International Conference on Communications (ICC), pp. 1–7. IEEE, Piscataway (2018). https://doi.org/10.1109/ICC.2018.8423006

5. Bassi, A., Bauer, M., Fiedler, M., Kramp, T., van Kranenburg, R., Lange, S., Meissner, S. (eds.): Enabling Things to Talk: Designing IoT Solutions with the IoT Architectural Reference Model, 1st edn. Springer, Berlin (2013)

6. Batista, E., Andrade, L., Dias, R., Andrade, A., Figueiredo, G., Prazeres, C.: Characterization and modeling of IoT data traffic in the Fog of Things paradigm. In: 2018 IEEE 17th International Symposium on Network Computing and Applications (NCA), pp. 1–8 (2018). https://doi.org/10.1109/NCA.2018.8548340

7. Bonomi, F., Milito, R., Zhu, J., Addepalli, S.: Fog computing and its role in the Internet of Things. In: Proceedings of the First Edition of the MCC Workshop on Mobile Cloud Computing, MCC '12, pp. 13–16. ACM, New York (2012). https://doi.org/10.1145/2342509.2342513

8. Carrez, F., Bauer, M., Boussad, M., Bui, N., Jardak, C., De Loof, J., Magerkurth, C., Meissner, S., Nettsträter, A., Olivereau, A., et al.: Internet of Things—architecture IoT-a, deliverable d1. 5—final architectural reference model for the IoT v3.0. European Union, 7th Framework Programme (2013)

9. Chappell, D.: Enterprise Service Bus. O'Reilly Media, Inc., Sebastopol (2004)

10. de Santana, C.J.L., de Mello Alencar, B., Prazeres, C.V.S.: Microservices: a mapping study for Internet of Things solutions. In: 2018 IEEE International Symposium on Network Computing and Applications (NCA), pp. 1–4 (2018)

11. de Santana, C.J.L., de Mello Alencar, B., Prazeres, C.V.S.: Reactive microservices for the Internet of Things: a case study in fog computing. In: Proceedings of the 34th ACM/SIGAPP Symposium on Applied Computing, SAC '19, pp. 1243–1251. ACM, New York (2019). https://doi.org/10.1145/3297280.3297402

12. Escoffier, C.: Building Reactive Microservices in Java. O'Reilly, Sebastopol (2017)

13. Fowler, M., Lewis, J.: Microservices, 2014. http://martinfowler.com/articles/microservices.html (2014)

14. Hassija, V., Chamola, V., Saxena, V., Jain, D., Goyal, P., Sikdar, B.: A survey on IoT security: application areas, security threats, and solution architectures. IEEE Access **7**, 82721–82743 (2019)

15. Khan, R., Khan, S.U., Zaheer, R., Khan, S.: Future internet: the internet of things architecture, possible applications and key challenges. In: 2012 10th International Conference on Frontiers of Information Technology, pp. 257–260 (2012). https://doi.org/10.1109/FIT.2012.53

16. Kumar, S., Sahoo, S., Mahapatra, A., Swain, A.K., Mahapatra, K.: Security enhancements to system on chip devices for IoT perception layer. In: 2017 IEEE International Symposium on Nanoelectronic and Information Systems (iNIS), pp. 151–156. IEEE, Piscataway (2017)

17. Leiba, B.: Oauth web authorization protocol. IEEE Internet Comput. **16**(1), 74–77 (2012)

18. Lin, S., Crawford, M., Mellor, S.: The industrial Internet of Things-volume G1: reference architecture. Industrial internet consortium. IIC:PUBG1

19. Newman, S.: Building Microservices: Designing Fine-Grained Systems. O'Reilly Media, Inc., Sebastopol (2015)

20. Pinto, G.P., Prazeres, C.V.S.: Web of things data visualization: from devices to web via fog and cloud computing. In: IEEE International Conference on Enabling Technologies: Infrastructure for Collaborative Enterprises (WETICE), pp. 1–6. IEEE, Piscataway (2019)

21. Prazeres, C., Serrano, M.: SOFT-IoT: self-organizing FOG of Things. In: 2016 30th International Conference on Advanced Information Networking and Applications Workshops, pp. 803–808 (2016). https://doi.org/10.1109/WAINA.2016.153

22. Prazeres, C., Barbosa, J., Andrade, L., Serrano, M.: Design and implementation of a message-service oriented middleware for Fog of Things platforms. In: Proceedings of the Symposium on Applied Computing, SAC '17, pp. 1814–1819. ACM, New York, (2017). https://doi.org/10.1145/3019612.3019820

23. Puschmann, D., Barnaghi, P., Tafazolli, R.: Adaptive clustering for dynamic IoT data streams. IEEE Internet of Things J. **4**(1), 64–74 (2017)

24. Sciancalepore, S., Piro, G., Caldarola, D., Boggia, G., Bianchi, G.: Oauth-IoT: an access control framework for the Internet of Things based on open standards. In: 2017 IEEE Symposium on Computers and Communications (ISCC), pp. 676–681. IEEE, Piscataway (2017)

25. Soldatos, J.: Building Blocks for IoT Analytics: River Publishers Series in Signal, Image and Speech Processing. River Publishers, Gistrup (2016). https://books.google.com.br/books?id=svQRMQAACAAJ

26. Sousa, N.R., Prazeres, C.V.S.: M2-fot: a proposal for monitoring and management of Fog of Things platforms. In: 2018 IEEE Symposium on Computers and Communications (ISCC), pp. 1–6. IEEE, Piscataway (2018)

27. Zhu, X., Badr, Y.: A survey on blockchain-based identity management systems for the Internet of Things. In: 2018 IEEE International Conference on 2018 IEEE Cybermatics, pp. 1568–1573. IEEE, Piscataway (2018)

**Leandro Andrade**, Msc., is a Ph.D. candidate at Federal University of Bahia (UFBA) and received MS (2014) and BS (2012) in Computer Science at UFBA. He is researcher of the Web, Internet and Intelligent Systems Research Group (WISER) where he works in projects related to Internet of Things, Fog Computing, and Big Data. In 2017, Andrade has done a Ph.D. internship at Insight Centre for Data Analytics (former DERI) at the National University of Ireland, Galway (NUIG). Leandro is a member of the Brazilian Computer Society (SBC) and IEEE Communications Society, and he has publications in international and national conferences. He is a substitute lecturer at the Department of Computer Science in UFBA and his research interests are Web Semantic, Web Services, Internet/Web of Things, Fog Computing, Machine Learning, Education, and Free Software.

**Cleber Lira**, Msc., is a Ph.D. candidate at Federal University of Bahia (UFBA) and received MS (2015) in Computer Systems at UNIFACS. He is a researcher of the Web, Internet and Intelligent Systems Research Group (WISER) and Nucleus of Mathematics in Computational Environment (NUMAC), where he works in projects related to Microservices, Internet of Things, Semantic Web Services, and Education. Santana is a member of IEEE Communications Society and he has publications in international and national conference. Since 2013, he has been a professor of the Federal Institute of Bahia (IFBA) and his research interests are Web Semantic, Web Services, Internet of Things, Fog Computing, Artificial intelligence, and Education.

**Brenno de Mello** is a MSc. candidate at Federal University of Bahia (UFBA) and received a degree in Systems Analysis and Development (2016) from the Federal Institute of Bahia (IFBA). He has experience in the area of Computer Science, with emphasis on Information Systems and Software Engineer. Currently, Mello is participant in the Web, Internet and Intelligent Systems Research Group (WISER) and his research interests are in Internet of Things, Data Stream Mining, Fog Computing, and Smart Water.

**Andressa Andrade** received BS (2018) in Computer Engineering from Federal University of Bahia (UFBA). She has acted as a monitor in the subject of Robotics Intelligent at UFBA and currently works with database management. Since 2015, she has been a member of the Web, Internet and Intelligent Systems Research Group (WISER). Her research interests are in the Perception Layer technologies, working mainly on the development of physical devices based on IoT architecture.

**Antonio Coutinho**, MSc., is a Ph.D. candidate at UFBA and received a MS (2000) and BS (1998) in Computer Science from Federal University of Campina Grande (UFCG). Since 2004, he has been assistant professor of the Department of Technology (DTEC) at the State University of Feira de Santana (UEFS). Since 2016, he has been a member of the WISER and GAUDI research groups at UFBA. His research interests are in Fog Computing, working mainly on its integration with distributed ledger technologies. Particularly in the SBRC 2016, he authored and taught the minicourse "Fog Computing: Concepts, Applications and Challenges". At SBRC 2018, he authored and taught the minicourse "Blockchain and the Revolution of Consensus on Demand".

**Cássio Prazeres**, DSc., has been an assistant professor at Federal University of Bahia (UFBA) since 2010, where he leads research activities and projects in the Web/Internet area, teaches undergraduate and postgraduate courses, and is advisor for Ph.D., MSc, and BSc students. Also at UFBA, Prazeres is a co-founder and leader of Web, Internet and Intelligent Systems Research Group (WISER). He received a Ph.D. (2009) in Computer Science from University of Sao Paulo (USP). He has several publications in international conferences and journals. Prazeres is member of: Brazilian Computer Society (SBC); IEEE Communications Society; IEEE Computer Society Technical Committee on Services Computing; IEEE Smart Cities Technical Community; IEEE Internet of Things Technical Community; ACM SIGWEB (Special Interest Group on Hypertext the Web); W3C Web of Things Community Group. He is interested in research involving topics of Internet of Things, Web of Things, Web Services, Semantic Web, Microservices, Fog Computing, Fog of Things, Web of Data, and Linked Data. Prazeres has coordinated projects in the Internet/Web of Things themes in the last years and has participated in other related projects such as Digital TV, crowdsourcing, and e-learning. Recently, Dr. Prazeres had a sabbatical year as a Postdoctoral Researcher at Insight Centre for Data Analytics (former DERI) at the National University of Ireland, Galway (NUIG).

# Chapter 3
# Using Mobile Cloud Computing for Developing Context-Aware Multimedia Applications

**Fernando Trinta, Paulo A. L. Rego, Francisco Gomes, Lincoln Rocha, Windson Viana, and José Neuman de Souza**

## 3.1 Contextualization

Mobile devices such as smartphones and tablets have become important tools for daily activities in modern society. These devices have improved their processing power due to faster processors, increased storage resources, and better network interfaces. Mobile devices have also been gradually equipped with a plethora of sensors that gather data from the user's environment (e.g., location and temperature). One challenge for mobile and distributed computing is to explore the changing environment where mobile devices are inserted with a new kind of mobile application that take benefits from features of their dynamic environment. These new types of systems are called context-aware applications.

Nowadays, context management and inferences are becoming complex processes, as the amount of data increases and new algorithms are being proposed [31]. In this scenario, cloud services can offer an interesting option by taking on more intensive context management tasks and performing these tasks only once for multiple users. However, since most contextual information is sensed and captured by mobile devices themselves, it is not always clear whether it is wise to send all the sensor data to the cloud for a remote processing or perform the whole processing of contextual data locally by the mobile device [32]. These trade-offs depend on factors such as the amount of data being transferred and the type of processing that is required. According to [56], the Mobile Cloud Computing paradigm, from a context-sensitive perspective, can be seen as a promising field of research that seeks to find effective ways of doing service in Cloud-aware applications and clients.

F. Trinta (✉) · P. A. L. Rego · F. Gomes · L. Rocha · W. Viana · J. N. de Souza
Federal University of Ceará (UFC), Fortaleza, Brazil
e-mail: fernando.trinta@dc.ufc.br; pauloalr@ufc.br; franciscoanderson@great.ufc.br;
lincoln@dc.ufc.br; windson@virtual.ufc.br; neuman@ufc.br

Offloading is the main research topic in MCC [28] and represents the idea of moving data and computation from mobile devices with scarce resources to more powerful machines [63]. There are several opportunities where computation and data offloading can bring improvements to context-aware mobile applications as well as multimedia applications. Some scenarios include: (1) devices with low processing power can use the cloud to act on their behalf (e.g., rendering images or videos) [15], (2) it would be possible to leverage cloud resources to save energy by delegating tasks away from mobile devices [6], and (3) to save data storage from mobile devices.

This chapter presents different approaches, concepts, and challenges about the integration between Mobile Cloud Computing (MCC) and context-aware computing. We will introduce a framework developed by the GREat research group,[1] called CAOS—Context-Aware and Offloading System [33], which is a software platform for the development of context-aware mobile applications based on the Android platform. CAOS supports both data and computing offloading (i.e., it enables the migration of computing and contextual data from mobile devices to cloud platforms in a transparent and an automatic way).

The integration of cloud services is an increasing trend in several areas. This chapter aims to present how this integration for the domain of context-aware applications can be done, focusing mainly on multimedia applications.

## 3.2  Theoretical Background

### 3.2.1  Context-Aware Computing

Mobile devices, such as smartwatches, smartphones, tablets, and ultrabooks, have become part of our everyday lives. They allow users to access a vast range of applications on the go, from personal agendas to existing social networks, from standalone applications running on the device to distributed applications interacting with the environment [35]. An important benefit of using an application on a mobile device is the possibility to use it anywhere and anytime. In fact, it can be seen as a step toward to achieve the Mark Weiser's Ubiquitous Computing [73] vision, embedding the computation in the user's devices and turning the user-interaction more soft and natural.

To achieve the calm interaction between users and computers is a complex task. Applications running on mobile devices have to interact with a dynamic environment, where available users, devices, and resources change over time. Therefore, the software running on these devices, interacting with users and the environment, must be designed from scratch taking into account these changes

---

[1]GREat website: http://www.great.ufc.br.

and adapting itself in order to achieve the desired behavior. The ability to perceive changes in the environment and adapt its behavior to meet these changes is called context-awareness. [59].

A context-aware system guides its behavior according to a context of use. Most of the time, the term "context awareness" is associated with a process of system adaptation, which changes its behavior, interfaces, configuration, and data visualization according to the state of the physical environment and the users' needs. Context-aware systems exploit this information aiming at improving their use and performance [2, 5]. However, a context-aware system can use context information for other purposes beyond adaptation, such as multimedia recommendation [72], multimedia annotation [21], service composition [69], and device discovery [7].

We find on the scientific literature many notions of context thanks to this diversity of uses of contextual information. The most accepted definition of context is those given by Dey [22]:

> Context is any information that can be used to characterize the situation of an entity. An entity is a person, place, or object that is considered relevant to the interaction between a user and an application, including the user and applications themselves [22].

> A system is context-aware if it uses context to provide relevant information and/or services to the user, where relevancy depends on the user's task [22].

Dey's definition is focused on contextual data that affects the computer–user interaction. Its innovation is the inclusion of the user (preferences, situation) and the system's states in the context. Nevertheless, this definition remains very general. It leaves to the developers the obligation to define which elements will compose the context and how they will be gathered. Unlike Dey, Schilit et al. [2] propose a notion of context whose elements are well defined: user's location, the physical environment, the identity of the people present in the neighborhood, and time. Hong et al. divide context into primary, integrated, and final dimensions. The preliminary context considers raw data (e.g., sensor data) [2]. The integrated context contains accumulated, aggregated, and inferred information. The final context is the context representation that the context-aware application manipulates. Similar to these discussions other several approaches propose context aspects, diverse taxonomies, categorizations, and design frameworks to capture context factors [2, 5]. In this document, we adopt the context definition given by Viana et al. [71].

Viana et al. [71] extends Dey's definition taking into account the dynamic nature of the context structure and its acquisition. In that sense, not only the values of the context elements evolve over time, but also the number of context elements changes. According to Viana et al. [71], the elements composing the context depend on the system's interest and the chance to observe them. So, once the system execution evolves, the set of observed context elements also evolve. In a nutshell, the context can be determined by the intersection of two sets of information in an instant $t$. The first one is called Zone of Interest (ZoI), comprising the set of contextual elements relevant to the system. The second set is called Zone of Observation (ZoO) and it describes the set of contextual elements that can be collected by the

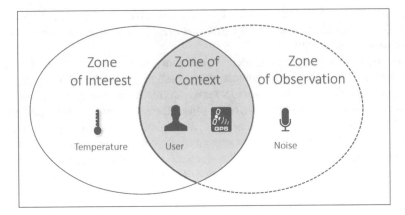

**Fig. 3.1** Context definition proposed by Viana et al. [71]

system. Figure 3.1 shows a Venn diagram with these two sets of information. Their intersection is the Zone of Context (ZoC) that is composed of any information that can be described and observed. All three zones may change over time. For instance, ZoO may change when a sensor becomes unavailable; the ZoI may change when the system changes its interests, not requiring specific contextual information any longer. At last, the ZoC changes when changes on ZoI and ZoO affect their intersection.

In short, context-awareness is the ability of the computer system to discover and react to its context changes. Mobile applications can benefit from context-awareness to provide personalized services to users and adapt their structure and behavior accordingly in order to save or optimize the mobile device resources usage. The mobile devices constrains (e.g., battery power, bandwidth, and storage capacity) and issues related to the context management (e.g., capture, process, and delivery), security, privacy, and trust turn the design and development of context-aware mobile applications into a challenging task.

A considerable research effort has been done to provide solutions to support the development of context-aware systems. In particular, context management infrastructures used to support context-aware applications have received significant attention in recent years [2, 5, 8, 58]. These infrastructures are typically implemented as a middleware platform or a horizontal framework, providing support to capture, aggregate, store, infer, and delivery context information. Usually, such infrastructure follows a thin client/server architecture style, where the application running on the mobile device (client) performs no or few tasks related to the context management and all or most of the context management processing are performed on the server side. As a drawback, these infrastructures are not adaptable, in a sense they are not able to adapt its own context management mechanism [18, 52].

### 3.2.1.1 Solutions

The solutions found in the literature review were classified according to the following taxonomy divided into seven aspects: (1) **Research Subject**—this aspect concerns to the kind of software infrastructure is provided to support development of context-aware application (e.g., framework and middleware); (2) **Target-Platform**—represents the mobile platform and development technology on which the solution was evaluated/implemented (e.g., Java, Android, Titanium, RESTful); (3) **Interaction Paradigm**—this aspect captures the kind of interaction paradigm used between applications and the context management infrastructure (e.g., tuple-space, publish/subscribe, and request/response); (4) **Context Type**—this aspect comprises the type of context each solution supports, following the Yurur et al. [77] classification: device context (e.g., available network interfaces, battery load, CPU and memory usage); physical context (e.g., temperature, noise level, light intensity, and traffic conditions) user context (e.g., personal profiles, location and people surrounding them, social situation); and temporal context (e.g., time, day, week, month, season, and year); (5) **Dependency**—this aspect indicates if the solution has any software dependence, such as an external framework or library; (6) **Modularity**—this aspect indicates that context management is handled independently of the application's business logic, ie, as a crosscutting-concern; and (7) **Cloud Interaction**—this aspect concerns to the usage of Cloud Computing concepts to manage context information. Table 3.1 summarized the review and classification according to the proposed taxonomy.

All papers report solutions that were implemented as a framework (S02, S04, S05, S07, S10, and S12–S15) or as middleware platform (S01, S03, S08, S09, and S11) to manage context information. Only one solution (S06) combines both framework and middleware strategies. Most of them are implemented on top of Android platform (S01–S05, S08, S12–S15). The other three solutions focus on RESTful services (S07 and S09) and cross-platform technology (S10). These solutions implement different coordination models to perform interaction between context management infrastructure and the mobile applications. Most of them support both synchronous request-response interaction (S01, S02, S03, S07–S011) and asynchronous publish-subscribe interaction (S02–S07, S10, S11, S13–S15). Only three solutions provide support for tuple-space interaction model (S06, S08, and S12). All these solutions support different context data, which vary from raw sensor data to personal user information extracted from social networks. Most solutions do not have third-parties dependencies, except S06, S08, S11, and S13 solutions. These four solutions depend on specific implementations of OSGi specification.[2] Once most of the solutions are implemented as a framework or a middleware platform, the context management concerns are well modularized. Finally, regarding the cloud integration aspect, only a few solutions (S10, S12, and S15) use cloud services to manage context information, but none of them mention to have support for offloading techniques.

---

[2]https://www.osgi.org/developer/specifications/.

**Table 3.1** The context-awareness solutions survey summary

| ID | Paper | Research subject | Target-platform | Interaction paradigm | Context type | Dependency | Modularity | Cloud interaction |
|---|---|---|---|---|---|---|---|---|
| S01 | [53] | Middleware | Android | Request/response | Device, physical, user, and temporal context | – | Yes | No |
| S02 | [19] | Framework | Android Java SE | Request/response Publish/subscribe | Device, physical user, and temporal context | – | Yes | No |
| S03 | [20] | Middleware | Android Java SE | Request/response Publish/subscribe | Device, physical user, and temporal context | – | Yes | No |
| S04 | [74] | Framework | Android | Publish/subscribe | Device context | – | Yes | No |
| S05 | [30] | Framework | Android | Publish/subscribe | Device, physical, user, and temporal context | – | Yes | No |
| S06 | [52] | Framework Middleware | Android | Publish/subscribe Tuple-space | Device, physical user, and temporal context | OSGi | Yes | No |
| S07 | [12] | Framework | RESTful | Request/response Publish/subscribe | Physical context | – | Yes | No |
| S08 | [61] | Middleware | Android | Request/response Tuple-space | Device context Physical context | OSGi JSON | Yes | No |
| S09 | [24] | Middleware | Java ME RESTful | Request/response | Physical context | – | Yes | No |
| S10 | [25] | Framework | Titanium | Request/response Publish/subscribe | Device, physical, user, and temporal context | – | Yes | Yes |
| S11 | [17] | Middleware | RESTful | Request/response Publish/subscribe | Device, physical, and user context | OSGi | Yes | No |
| S12 | [9] | Framework | Android | Tuple-space | Physical context | – | Yes | Yes |
| S13 | [10] | Framework | Android | Publish/subscribe | Device, physical, user, and temporal context | OSGi | Yes | No |
| S14 | [46] | Framework | Android | Publish/subscribe | Physical context | – | Yes | No |
| S15 | [55] | Framework | Android | Publish/subscribe | Device, physical, user, and temporal context | – | Yes | Yes |

### 3.2.1.2   LoCCAM

The LoCCAM (Loosely Coupled Context Acquisition Middleware) [52] is a context management infrastructure that adopts the mobile device as the center point of context acquisition and decision. LoCCAM provides a transparent and self-adaptive context data acquisition approach, gathering context information both locally and remotely from the device. It also uses a novel mechanism to support adaptation in the way context information is collected and inferred, following the Viana et al.'s definition [71] (see Sect. 3.2.1). An overview of LoCCAM's software architecture is given in Fig. 3.2. Basically, LoCCAM can be divided into two main parts:

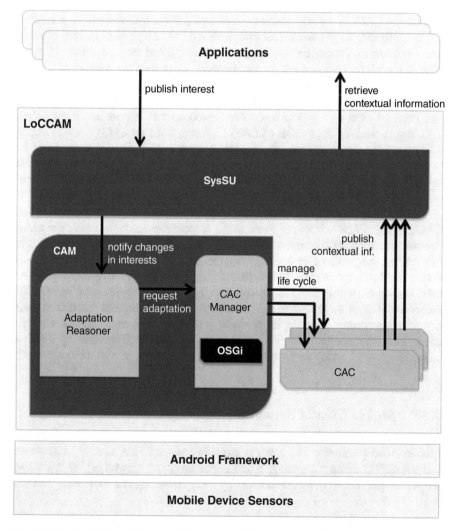

**Fig. 3.2** The LoCCAM architecture [26]

(1) the SysSU (System Support for Ubiquity) module and (2) the CAM (Context Acquisition Manager) framework.

The SysSU [47] module provides a coordination mechanism based on tuple spaces and event-based notifications. Such mechanism enhances the coupling between applications and the context acquisition layer. This acquisition layer is based on software-based sensors called CAC (Context Acquisition Component) and can be classified into physical or logical ones. The physical CACs are those that only encapsulate the access to mobile device sensor information (e.g., accelerometer, temperature, and luminosity). On the other hand, the logical CACs are those that can use more than one mobile device sensor and information from other sources (e.g., social networks and weather service on the Internet) to provide high-level context information. Furthermore, LoCCAM offers a common vocabulary that allows CACs and applications to exchange context information. Applications subscribe SysSU for the contextual information access by publishing their interests using its common vocabulary. Then, LoCCAM tries to find the more suitable CAC to provide such information. Such communication is based on the concept of Context Keys. They serve as a shared vocabulary to represent each type of contextual information that can be accessed. Each Context Key provides a unique name that must be used by CAC to determine the contextual information it publishes. This key is used by applications to make subscriptions on SysSU. For example, a Context Key that represents the ambient temperature in Celsius scale could be "context.ambient.temperature.celsius". To improve the context data selection, applications can use the concept of a filter, which defines a set of fine-grained selection criteria to precisely select the desired context information.

The CAM framework is divided into two modules: Adaptation Reasoner and CAC Manager. The Adaptation Reasoner is responsible for maintaining the applications subscription list of interest and keep it updated. When any change occurs in this list, the Adaptation Reasoner builds a reconfiguration plan to adapt the context acquisition layer and sends it to the CAC Manager responsible for performing it. The CAC Manager controls the CAC's lifecycle using a specific implementation of OSGi framework.[3] The CAC Manager can install, uninstall, activate, and deactivate CACs at runtime, according to the application's interest regarding a contextual information access and the reconfiguration plan. A CAC is only activated when an application subscribes SysSU asking for specific contextual information provided by such CAC.

### 3.2.2  Mobile Cloud Computing

Mobile cloud computing is a new paradigm that incorporates three heterogeneous technologies (mobile computing, cloud computing, and networking) and aims to reduce the limitations of mobile devices by taking advantage of ubiquitous wireless

---

[3] Apache Felix distribution—http://felix.apache.org/.

access to local and public cloud resources. Such resources are used to augment mobile devices computing capabilities, conserve local resources, extend storage capacity, and enrich the computing experience of mobile users.

Several authors have also defined mobile cloud computing:

> Mobile cloud computing is an integration of cloud computing technology with mobile devices to make mobile devices resource-full in terms of computational power, memory, storage, energy, and context awareness. Mobile cloud computing is the outcome of interdisciplinary approaches comprising mobile computing and cloud computing [38].

> Mobile cloud computing is a rich mobile computing technology that leverages unified elastic resources of varied clouds and network technologies toward unrestricted functionality, storage, and mobility to serve a multitude of mobile devices anywhere, anytime through the channel of Ethernet or Internet regardless of heterogeneous environments and platforms based on the pay-as-you-use principle [65].

According to these definitions, the mobile cloud computing model is composed of mobile devices, wireless networks, and remote servers, where mobile devices use wireless technologies to leverage remote servers to execute their compute-intensive tasks or storage data.

Computation offloading is a popular technique to increase performance and reduce the energy consumption of mobile devices by migrating processing or data from mobile devices to other infrastructure, with greater computing power and storage. The concept of offloading, also referred as cyber foraging, appeared in 2001 [66] and was improved in 2002 [4], in order to allow mobile devices to use available computing resources opportunistically.

Migrating computation to another machine is not a new idea. The traditional client–server model is also widely used for this purpose. In fact, the ideas behind the concept of computation offloading date back to the era of dumb terminals that used mainframes for processing. With the adoption of personal computers (e.g., desktops and notebooks), the need to migrate computation has decreased. Nevertheless, with the advent of portable devices, a new need for remote computing power has emerged [23].

According to [70], offloading can be executed on a remote virtual machine-based environment (e.g., public clouds) or on any machine that is in the same WLAN in which mobile devices are connected to. In the latter case, the remote execution environment is known as cloudlet [67], and its primary goal is to deliver a better quality of service since Wi-Fi networks are less congested (i.e., they have higher speeds and lower latency) than mobile networks.

It is important to highlight that offloading is different from the traditional client–server model, in which a thin client *always* migrates computation to a remote server. Depending on the availability and the condition of the network, which is highly influenced by users' mobility, offloading may not be possible or advantageous. Therefore, it is important to state that, in mobile cloud computing, the concept of computation offloading is usually implemented by a special program structure, or a design pattern, that enables a piece of code to execute locally on the mobile device or remotely, without impacting on the correctness of the application [78].

In the next subsections we present a further discussion about the types of mobile applications and explore the concept of offloading, by addressing the questions *How?*, *When?*, *Where?*, and *Why?* to perform computation offloading.

### 3.2.2.1 Types of Mobile Applications

According to [41], applications for mobile devices can be classified as offline, online, and hybrid. Offline applications, which are also called native applications, act as fat clients that process the presentation and business logic layer locally on mobile devices, usually with data downloaded from remote servers. Also, they may periodically synchronize data with a remote server, but most resources are available locally, rather than distributed over the network.

Some advantages of native applications are: good integration with features of the device, optimized performance for specific hardware and multitasking, always available capabilities, even without Internet access. On the other hand, the main disadvantages are: they are not portable to other platforms and dependent exclusively on storage and processing power of the device, which may not be enough to execute certain types of computation.

Online applications assume that the connection between mobile devices and remote servers is available most of the time. They are usually based on Web technologies and present a few advantages when compared to offline applications, such as the fact that they are multiplatform and are accessible from anywhere. Nevertheless, they also present some disadvantages: the typical Internet latency can be a problem for some types of applications (e.g., real-time applications), difficulty in dealing with scenarios that require keeping the communication session opened for extended periods of time, and no access to device's sensors such as camera or GPS.

Hybrid applications are targets of mobile cloud computing and offloading researchers. They can execute locally (as native applications) when there is no connection to remote servers. However, when there is connectivity between mobile devices and remote servers, they can migrate some of the computation to be performed out of the mobile device or access web services (as online applications). The idea is to combine the advantages of online and offline applications.

In the rest of this chapter, we consider only hybrid applications, which are the ones that can benefit from offloading techniques.

### 3.2.2.2  Where to Perform Offloading?

Mobile devices use remote resources[4] to improve application performance by leveraging offloading techniques. These remote resources are public cloud, cloudlets, or another mobile device.

### Public Cloud

The execution of services in the public cloud is common among mobile application developers since they can leverage features such as elasticity and connectivity to social networks to improve services. Applications such as Gmail and Google Docs are examples of online applications that require smartphones to be connected to the Internet all the time to be able to access data.

In order to connect to the public cloud, mobile devices can use mobile networks (e.g., 2G, 3G, and 4G) or a Wi-Fi hotspot. Figure 3.3 illustrates a mobile device accessing an application that relies on Internet connection.

### Cloudlet

The idea of using nearby servers to reduce the connection latency and improve users' quality of experience is being used since the emergence of the term cyber foraging, introduced by [66]. On that time, the authors used servers in the vicinity to handle the limited capabilities of mobile devices.

The concept of cloudlet is newer and was proposed in [67] also to use resources of servers that are close to mobile devices. The difference is that the authors have used virtual machines, in a trusted environment, as remote servers. Today, several studies have used the term offloading or cyber foraging to indicate that there is a migration of data and/or computation of mobile devices to another location; as well as the terms cloudlet and surrogate that have been used indiscriminately to indicate a computer or cluster of computers directly connected to the same WLAN of mobile devices. Figure 3.4 illustrates the concept of cloudlets by showing mobile devices and remote servers connected to the same wireless network.

The vision of [67] is that cloudlets would be conventional equipment deployed such as access points, which would be located in public areas (e.g., cafes, pubs,

**Fig. 3.3** Public cloud as remote execution environment

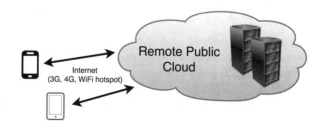

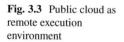

---

[4]In this chapter, when we use terms such as remote servers, remote resources, or remote execution environments, we refer to any real or virtual remote equipment where the computation of mobile devices can be migrated to.

**Fig. 3.4** Cloudlet as remote
execution environment

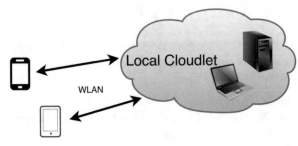

**Fig. 3.5** Cluster of mobile
devices as remote execution
environment

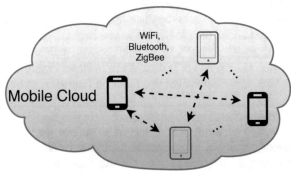

and restaurants) so that mobile devices could connect via Wi-Fi networks and
perform offloading without facing high latency and the typical variation of Internet
bandwidth.

**Other Mobile Device**

There is another approach in the literature, commonly referred as "mobile cloud,"
that considers using other mobile devices as the source of resources, especially to
perform a computation. Figure 3.5 illustrates this approach, in which mobile devices
are usually connected using a peer-to-peer network and create a cluster (or cloud)
of devices.

The idea behind this solution is to enable people, that are in the same place and
share the same interests, to create a cloud of mobile devices and share their resources
aiming to compute tasks more quickly or reduce energy consumption.

**Hybrid Environment**

A hybrid environment is composed of two or more of the environments mentioned
above. In Fig. 3.6, we can see an example of this type of environment, where a
mobile device is part of a "mobile cloud" and can perform offloading by leveraging
cloudlets and public cloud as remote execution environments.

**Fig. 3.6** Hybrid remote execution environment composed of cloudlets, public cloud, and a cluster of mobile devices

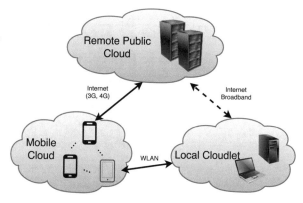

### 3.2.2.3   Why to Perform Offloading?

Given the limited resources of mobile devices, researchers have mainly used computation offloading to enhance applications' performance, save battery power, and execute applications that are unable to run due to insufficient resources. Therefore, the main reasons for performing offloading are as follows:

- **Improve Performance:** when performance improvement (i.e., reduce the execution time) is the main goal;
- **Save Energy:** when energy efficiency (i.e., reduce energy consumption) is the main goal;
- **Other:** when energy and performance are not the main reasons for performing offloading. Instead, the main reason may be to improve collaboration, extend storage capacity, or reduce monetary costs.

### 3.2.2.4   When to Perform Offloading?

The reasons for performing offloading presented in the previous section are directly related to the decision of when to offload.

Kumar et al. [45] present an analytical model to answer the question "When the offloading technique improves the performance of mobile devices?". The model compares the time to process an application task on a mobile device ($\frac{W}{P_m}$) and the time to transfer the data and perform the computation out of the device ($\frac{D_u}{T_u} + \frac{W}{P_c} + \frac{D_d}{T_d}$), either on a public cloud instance or on a cloudlet. The model considers the following parameters: $W$ is the total computation to be performed, which may be expressed in MI (million instructions); $P_m$ and $P_c$ are, respectively, the processing power of the mobile device and the cloud (or cloudlet), which may be expressed in MIPS (million instructions per second); $D_u$ is the amount of data sent from the device to the cloud (bytes), while $D_d$ is the amount of data received by the device (bytes); and $T_u$ and $T_d$ are the upload and download rate (bytes/second), respectively.

**Fig. 3.7** Offloading decision
trade-off adapted from [44]

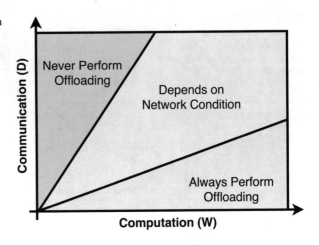

$$\frac{W}{P_m} > \frac{D_u}{T_u} + \frac{W}{P_c} + \frac{D_d}{T_d} \tag{3.1}$$

Analyzing the model presented in (3.1), we can see that, to improve performance, the computation should be heavy (high value to $W$) and the communication between mobile device and the cloud should be brief (low value to $\frac{D_u}{T_u} + \frac{D_d}{T_d}$), either by transferring few data or by having a high throughput.

Kumar et al. [45] highlight that increasing the difference between the processing power of mobile devices and clouds does not bring great impact to the decision. This fact can be observed in (3.2), when we consider a cloud $K$ times faster than a smartphone ($P_c = K \cdot P_m$). Clearly, for large values of $K$, Eq. (3.1) can be simplified to $\frac{W}{P_m} > \frac{D_u}{T_u} + \frac{D_d}{T_d}$, which means that the time required to transfer the data between mobile device and cloud has a key role in deciding when to perform offloading. Figure 3.7 depicts the trade-off between the amount of communication and computation for deciding whether or not to perform offloading.

$$\frac{W}{P_m} - \frac{W}{K \cdot P_m} > \frac{D_u}{T_u} + \frac{D_d}{T_d} \Rightarrow \frac{W}{P_m} \cdot \left(\frac{K-1}{K}\right) > \frac{D_u}{T_u} + \frac{D_d}{T_d}$$
$$\Rightarrow \frac{W}{P_m} > \frac{D_u}{T_u} + \frac{D_d}{T_d} \tag{3.2}$$

Other researchers focus on different objectives such as throughput maximization [75], energy saving [39], and cost reduction [40].

Regarding energy savings, [44] list the following four basic approaches to save energy and extend the battery lifetime of mobile devices:

1. **Adopt a new generation of semiconductor technology.** Unfortunately, as transistors become smaller, more transistors are needed to provide more func-

tionalities and better performance; as a result, the power consumption actually increases;

2. **Avoid wasting energy.** Whole systems or individual components may enter standby or sleep modes to save power;
3. **Execute programs slowly.** When a processor's clock speed doubles, the power consumption nearly octuples. If the clock speed is reduced by half, the execution time doubles, but only one-quarter of the energy is consumed. Therefore, executing applications more slowly is a good option to save energy. That is indeed done in some smartphone with DVFS to put devices in energy-saving mode. However, it is important to assess the trade-off between performance and energy saving.
4. **Eliminate computation altogether.** A mobile device does not perform computations; instead, the computation is performed somewhere else, thereby extending the battery lifetime of mobile devices.

The last approach can be realized by using offloading techniques to migrate computations from mobile devices to remote servers. We refer to [51] for an energy savings analytical model for answering the question "When the offloading technique saves energy of mobile devices?".

Regardless of the reasons that motivate the use of offloading mechanisms, the solutions also differ regarding the **Offloading Decision**, which is related to how an offloading solution decides when to perform offloading. In short, the offloading is called:

1. **Static:** when the developer or system defines prior to execution (at design or installation time) what parts of the application should be offloaded and to where;
2. **Dynamic:** when the framework/system decides at runtime which parts of the application should be offloaded and where to offload, based on metrics related to the current condition of the network, mobile devices, and remote server.

### 3.2.2.5  What to Offload?

When the application is not available on a remote server, there is a need to migrate parts of (or the whole) application to the server along to the computation request and input data. In order to separate the intensive mobile application components that operate independently in the distributed environment, a partitioning procedure can be used to partition the application at different levels of granularity [48].

Partitioning of an application can be done automatically by the offloading system, or it can be provided by developers using a code markup (e.g., annotations on Java programming language). In the latter case, developers add some kind of syntactic metadata to the application source code to identify the components that are candidates to be offloaded. This markup process is usually done by applications' developers at the design phase and involves examining the complexity and dependency of methods.

Several strategies to perform offloading were proposed in the literature, and they differ in relation to which parts of the application are sent to be executed out of mobile devices. Thus, the parts of applications that are most commonly offloaded are as follows:

- **Methods:** when methods are used to partition the application (e.g., remote procedure calls);
- **Components/Modules:** when entire modules or components of an application are executed on another resource execution environment. It involves using specific frameworks for designing and developing modular applications (e.g., OSGi) or just a group of classes that may or may not be coupled;
- **Threads:** when threads of an application are migrated between mobile devices and remote execution environments. It usually involves performing changes on the Android virtual machine (DalvikVM);
- **Whole Application:** when virtualization techniques are used to run clones of mobile devices and the entire state of the application process is migrated and executed out of mobile devices (e.g., in a virtualized clone device). In this case, a synchronization module is usually required for keeping the applications running on mobile device and clone updated, by replicating all changes.

It is common for mobile applications to interact with sensors embedded in mobile devices (e.g., GPS and camera), thus, offloading the whole application may be impractical. That is why [16] defend that a fine-grain strategy leads to large energy savings as only the parts that benefit from remote executions are offloaded.

### 3.2.2.6   How to Perform Offloading?

There is no unique answer to the question "How to perform offloading?". In fact, several offloading frameworks/systems/middleware have been proposed to address such question, and they usually differ regarding *What?*, *Where?*, *When?*, and *Why?* to perform offloading.

Existing offloading solutions have applied various strategies and mechanisms to handle steps of the offloading process, such as cloudlet discovery, resources profiling, application partitioning, and offloading decision [68]. Since the strategies used are quite varied, we have performed a literature review that helped us to identify the common approaches used for performing offloading and also have allowed us to create a taxonomy to assist in the classification of related works.

The categories of the taxonomy related to the question "How to perform offloading?" are discussed below:

Method Annotation:   when an offloading solution supports granularity of methods and some type of syntax for marking methods is used to identify the methods prone to be offloaded:

1. **Yes:** when syntactic metadata is added to the application source code. The annotation is usually done by developers at design phase, and involves examining the complexity and dependency of methods;

2. **No:** when there is no annotation or when the framework uses a profiler component to collect information and annotate the relevant methods in an automatic fashion.

Decision Module Location: the module responsible for decision-making usually executes compute-intensive operations to decide when and where to perform offloading, which inevitably consumes resources of the mobile device when the module is executed locally. Despite the computation cost reduction when executing the decision module out of a mobile device, this solution imposes more communication costs, which is a clear trade-off that must be considered.

1. **Mobile Device:** when compute-intensive operations of the decision module are executed on mobile devices;
2. **Remote Execution Environment:** when compute-intensive operations of the decision module are executed out of mobile devices.

Decision Module Features: regards approaches and techniques used by a decision module.

1. **Online Profiling:** when the decision module uses measurements (collected at runtime) of different metrics of the environment, network, and application to improve the offloading decision;
2. **Historical Data:** when the solution collects and uses historical data to improve the decision module.

Metrics Used for Decision: regards the metrics considered by a decision module for deciding when and where to offload.

1. **Based on hardware:** when the solution uses metrics related to the hardware of mobile devices and remote servers (e.g., memory, CPU, battery);
2. **Based on software:** when the solution uses metrics related to the software of mobile devices and remote servers (e.g., size of data that will be transferred, execution time, code size or complexity, interdependence between modules or components);
3. **Based on network:** when the solution uses metrics related to network conditions (e.g., connection type, latency, jitter, packet loss, Wi-Fi signal strength, throughput).

Supported Platform/Programming Language: regards mobile platforms and programming languages supported by a solution.

1. **Android**;
2. **Windows Phone**;
3. **iOS**.

Discovery Mechanism:   considers whether a solution uses any mechanism for discovering remote execution environments (usually cloudlets or other mobile devices).

1. **Yes:** when a solution automates the remote execution environment discovery;
2. **No:** when the address of a remote execution environment is somehow provided in advance by developers or when a DNS-based service discovery is used.

### 3.2.2.7   Taxonomy

During the literature review that we have performed, we identified several approaches used in offloading solutions. Then we categorized such approaches in groups based on the questions *What?*, *Why?*, *When?*, *Where?*, and *How?* to perform offloading. Inspired by those questions and also in [68] and [48] taxonomies, we propose a taxonomy for offloading solutions.

Figure 3.8 depicts the proposed taxonomy, which is based on the aforementioned questions about offloading. Therefore, *What?* is related to the offloading

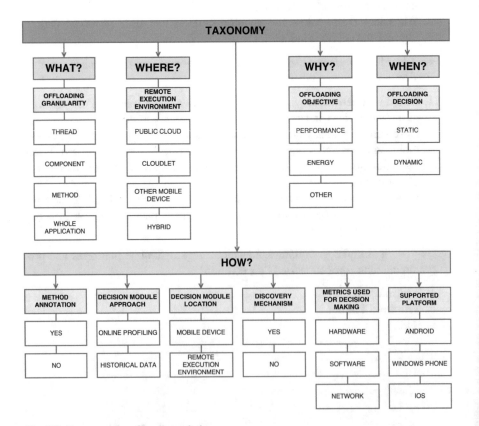

**Fig. 3.8** Taxonomy for offloading solutions

granularity discussed in Sect. 3.2.2.5, *Why?* is related to the offloading objective discussed in Sect. 3.2.2.3, *When?* is related to the offloading decision discussed in Sect. 3.2.2.4, while *Where?* is related to the remote execution environments discussed in Sect. 3.2.2.2 and *How?* is related to all categories discussed in Sect. 3.2.2.6.

### 3.2.2.8 Solutions

Several solutions have been developed in response to the challenges offered by MCC. In this section, we present some of these solutions, and we use the proposed taxonomy to classify them.

Regarding the offloading granularity, solutions like eXCloud [50] and MECCA [36] perform offloading of the whole application by leveraging virtualization techniques to run a clone of the mobile device. eXCloud uses a compact version of the Java virtual machine, called JamVM, and migrates the state of the application by transferring the Java virtual machine stack from the mobile device to its clone, which is running on the cloud. MECCA supports the Android platform and migrates an entire application process to a clone and allows the user to access the screen of the device using VNC (Virtual Network Computing).

Other solutions like $\mu$Cloud [54] and MACS [42] perform offloading of modules/components of the application. Such solutions usually require the use of specific frameworks for designing and developing modular applications (e.g., OSGi and Android Services). For instance, to use MACS, developers have to design their applications using standard Android services, where the compute-intensive components must be implemented as services. Since Android services use inter-process communication channels to perform remote procedure call, MACS intercepts the requests sent to the services and decide whether the request must be executed on local or cloud services.

CloneCloud [13] and COMET [34] are examples of frameworks that perform offloading of threads, which usually involves modifying the Android virtual machine to allow the seamless transfer of application's threads. Both solutions require a modified version of the Android operation system and also a clone of the mobile device running on the cloud.

The works that implement offloading of methods usually leverage techniques like Java Annotations to allow developers to identify the methods that are candidates to be offloaded. MAUI [16] is a framework developed in .NET for Windows Phone 6.5 that uses remote procedure calls to execute methods outside of mobile devices. MAUI uses an approach based on a proxy to intercept methods and redirect them to a server running on the cloud. On the other hand, Scavenger [43] is a framework developed in Python that uses annotation of methods (using the concept of Python Decorators), and its decision module uses online profiling and historical data analysis to decide whether a method must be executed on mobile device or cloud.

The solutions AIOLOS [70], ThinkAir [40], and ARC [29] use methods as offloading units, and they were developed for the Android platform. AIOLOS relies on code refactoring to generate OSGi components for a mobile application at building time. Despite executing OSGi components on the cloud, the decision of when to offload is based on methods provided by the components. On the other hand, ThinkAir relies on Java annotations to identify the methods that can be offloaded and allow such methods to be executed in parallel on multiple servers, while ARC is a framework where a method can be opportunistically offloaded to any available device that can be accessed through the wireless LAN (i.e., other mobile device or a dedicated server, such as in the cloudlet concept). MpOS [15, 63] is a framework that also uses methods as offloading units, but it can be used to develop Android and Windows Phone applications. The framework was developed in our research group and is discussed in more detail in the next section.

Regarding the remote execution environment, most works perform offloading to cloudlets or cloud environments (e.g., eXCloud, MpOS, ThinkAir, $\mu$Cloud, CloneCloud, AIOLOS, MAUI, Scavenger). ARC and DroidCloudlet [27] are some of the solutions that use mobile devices as remote execution environments. In DroidCloudlet, the authors propose the creation of a mobile cloud of Android devices that can be used to improve performance and save energy of a device by offloading methods to other devices.

Regarding the offloading decision, $\mu$Cloud uses static decision, while the other mentioned solutions support dynamic decision. Besides that, the solutions have different offloading objectives. While MpOS, COMET, and eXCloud only focus on improving the performance of mobile applications; and Scavenger and $\mu$Cloud only care about saving energy, ThinkAir, CloneCloud, DroidCloudlet, and AIOLOS consider both objectives (e.g., by solving multi-objective optimization problems).

### 3.2.2.9   MpOS

MpOS (Multiplatform Offloading System) is a framework for developing mobile applications that support offloading of methods for Android and Windows Phone platforms. MpOS was developed to address the lack of an offloading solution for multiple platforms, and its main goal is to improve performance.

To use MpOS, developers must mark the methods that can be executed out of the mobile device, and they can choose whether the offloading decision will be static or dynamic. If the dynamic offloading is defined, the Offloading System (illustrated in Fig. 3.9) checks if it is worthwhile to perform the offloading operation before sending the method to the remote server. Otherwise, when the static offloading is defined, MpOS verifies only if the remote server is available before performing offloading. In order to decide when to offloading, the decision module uses metrics (e.g., latency, download, and upload rate) that are online collected by the Network Profiler module.

MpOS has a Discovery Service that uses a multicast-based discovery mechanism to identify nearby servers (cloudlets) and applications already running on the remote

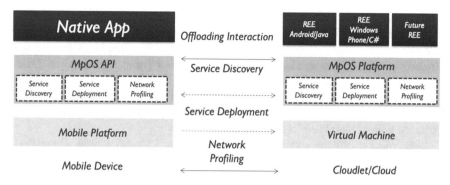

**Fig. 3.9** Overview of MpOS main components. Based on [63]

server. If the application is not running on the server, MpOS automatically sends the application and all dependencies to the remote server by means of the Deployment Service. All deployed applications are handled by the Remote Execution Environment (REE) module, which instantiates the applications in different endpoints. In order to support multiple platforms, MpOS provides Android and Windows Phone REEs, which run Java and C# code, respectively. Once an application is instantiated on the REE, the mobile device can directly access the application's endpoint and perform offloading. More details about MpOS can be found in [15] and [63].

### 3.2.3   Context-Aware and MCC Integration

The advances in mobile computing have made the use of contextual information increasingly present in today's mobile applications. The adaptation of the applications according to contextual situations will improve the users' quality of experience while running the most diverse applications. However, as mentioned earlier in this document, the inference process of the user's contextual situation requires processing and data resources that may sometimes be unsuitable for processing locally on mobile devices.

This issue also occurs when the multimedia data is required to infer users' contextual situation. The use of complex data such as video, audio, or images for determining the current context is pointed out as a future trend for mobile applications, but also brings processing requirements that become a problem for mobile computing environments with uncontrolled characteristics due to resource scarcity, low storage capabilities, intermittent connectivity, and power constraints.

In this sense, computing and data offloading fits like a glove to allow the integration of more advanced techniques for contextual inference (such as the use of machine learning algorithms, among others), while also allowing performance gains and energy savings for mobile devices.

It is important to notice that many research projects and reports that address the integration between Context-aware Mobile Computing and Mobile Cloud Computing use "context" as the situation in which a mobile application is running (network condition, remaining battery, and/or size of parameters data) to decide whether is worthy to migrate data or processing to the cloud. This document presents a different point of view. We focus on how the management of contextual information may be enhanced (for instance, better or faster inference procedures) with the help of cloud services.

According to [56], the use of cloud services by context-aware mobile applications is a future trend with no turning back, even with the lack of reports about how this integration should be made. Once adaptation processes are becoming more and more complex, context analysis requires appropriate and robust services.

According to a brief literature review, a few solutions seek to integrate the management of contextual information with concepts of Mobile Cloud Computing, or even just cloud computing.

One of these is the CARMiCLOC [1], a reflexive middleware architecture based on autonomic computing, which uses cloud services to provide scalability, self-adaptability, integration, and interoperability of context-aware applications. CARMiCLOC uses reflection to inspect its state and ensures a dynamic behavior of its operation. However, the use of cloud resources is restricted only to the storage of the contextual data obtained by sensors. Despite its merit, the cloud potential is underutilized in the proposal, because cloud resources are not used for data processing remotely in the Cloud.

O'Sullivan and Grigoras [57] presents CAMCS (Context Aware Mobile Cloud Services), a mobile cloud middleware solution that has been designed to deliver cloud-based services to mobile users while respecting the goal of providing an integrated user experience of mobile cloud applications and services. CAMCS supports the application partitioning, where some functionalities run on cloud services. Integration with contextual management services uses a component called Context Processor. This component can promote the customization of actions to be taken by the applications, which is performed by other component called Cloud Personal Assistant (CPA). CPA can perform task processing in the cloud on behalf of the user, asynchronously. CAMCS allows the use of historical data and ontologies, which are still prohibitive on mobile devices, due to their intensive processing.

### 3.2.3.1 Motivating Scenarios

In order to present some examples where context-aware mobile computing and MCC may improve the user experience, this subsection presents some possible scenarios for such integration.

**Crowdsensing** Mobile crowdsensing refers to an approach where a large group of people uses mobile devices capable of sensing and computing (such as smartphones, tablet computers, wearables) to collectively share data and extract information to measure, map, analyze, estimate, or infer (predict) processes of common interest [49]. This situation may enable to detect some contextual situations based on shared data from multiple users. MCC can improve this aggregation and processing of contextual situations based on hierarchies, for example, by aggregating contextual data from users connected to the same cloudlet, and infer some contextual situations in a collaborative way [31, 76].

**Healthcare and Well-Being** With the advancements and increasing deployment of microsensors and low-power wireless communication technologies, the studies conducted on healthcare domain have grown, particularly the studies regarding the recognition of human activities. In this case, information corresponding to human postures (e.g., lying, sitting, standing, etc.) and movements (e.g., walking, running, etc.) can be inferred in order to provide useful feedbacks to the caregiver about a patient's behavior analysis [77]. Recognizing such activities depends on monitoring and analyzing contextual data such as vital sign (e.g., heart rate, pressure level, and respiration rate), which might be aggregated by mobile devices. MCC can improve the execution and save energy of mobile devices when offloading the compute-intensive operations required to recognize complex events.

**Augmented Reality** A typical mobile augmented reality system comprises mobile computing platforms, software frameworks, detection and tracking support, display, wireless communication, and data management [11]. Contextual data is important for providing information about the user's environment, which might be used to present personalized content and improve user's experience. The problem is that vision-based applications are almost impossible to run on wearables and very difficult on smartphones since they require capable GPUs [60]. MCC can, therefore, be used to offload the execution of heavy computations to a powerful remote device.

## 3.3 Context-Aware and Offloading System (CAOS)

In order to conceive CAOS, we surveyed frameworks and middleware that support both context-aware and offloading features. This survey provides us an insight of good design decisions that were used to build CAOS. According to these design principles, we designed a software architecture that supports both method and data offloading into cloud infrastructures. We implemented a prototype of CAOS, and we conducted experiments to evaluate its impact on performance and energy consumption of Android applications [33].

Before showing how to use CAOS to develop context-aware Android applications, the next section introduces CAOS architecture and main components.

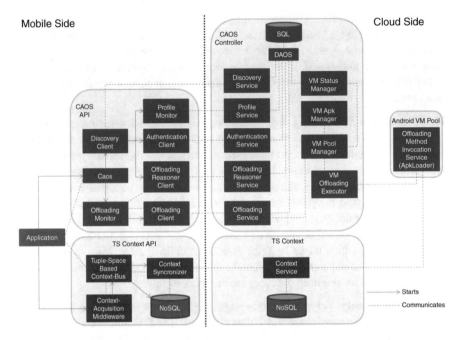

**Fig. 3.10** Overview of CAOS main components. Based on [33]

## 3.3.1 Architecture and Components

CAOS rests on a traditional client/server architecture, where mobile devices act as clients for services running on the top of cloud/cloudlets infrastructures. Figure 3.10 shows the CAOS architecture where its main components are divided into two groups: mobile side and cloud side components.

### 3.3.1.1 The Mobile Side

CAOS mobile side is composed by 10 (ten) components: CAOS (which is responsible for synchronizing the startup of other components of the mobile side), *Offloading Monitor*, *Offloading Client*, *Discovery Client*, *Authentication Client*, *Profile Monitor*, *Offloading Reasoner Client*, *Context-Acquisition Middleware*, *Tuple-Space Based Context-Bus*, and *Context Synchronizer*. Each one of these components is detailed as follows.

The *Discovery Client* component uses a mechanism based on UDP/Multicast communication to discover CAOS Controllers running in the user's local network (i.e., cloudlets). Once the *Discovery Client* detects a CAOS Controller, the *Authentication Client* authenticates the mobile application and sends device data to the cloud side to keep the list of devices attached to a specific CAOS Controller.

In CAOS, application's methods can be marked by developers with a Java annotation @*Offloadable*, which denotes that those methods can be executed out of the mobile device. The *Offloading Monitor* is the components responsible for monitoring the application execution and intercepting the execution flow whenever an annotated method is called. After intercepting the method call, the *Offloading Monitor* asks the *Offloading Reasoner Client* module whether it is possible to start the offloading process or not.

The *Offloading Reasoner Client* assists the offloading decision using a decision data structure that is asynchronously received from the *Offloading Reasoner Service*. In CAOS, the decision whether is worthy or not to offload a method is performed in two steps: one at the cloud side and another on the mobile side. The cloud side keeps receiving profiling data from each mobile device connected to its infrastructure and creates a two-class decision tree [62] with the parameters that should be considered to decide if it is worth to offload a method, such as latency, parameters types, and so on. Once the decision tree is created or updated, it is sent to the mobile device, so the *Offloading Reasoner Client* only has to enforce the decision based on current values of the monitored data and the decision tree structure.

Figure 3.11 presents an example of offloading decision tree for a dummy application. In this example, if the upload rate is equal to 200 KB/s and RTT is equal to 100 ms, the method Bar must be executed locally. Moreover, in all cases the method Foo must be executed on the remote server.

By using the received data structure, the *Offloading Monitor* can decide locally when it is worth performing offloading. If the answer is negative, the method execution flow is resumed, and its execution is performed locally. Otherwise, when the answer is positive, the *Offloading Monitor* requests the *Offloading Client* to start

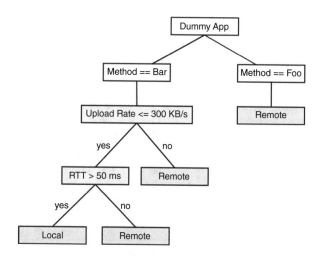

**Fig. 3.11** Example of offloading decision tree. Based on [64]

the method offloading process, which in turn transfers the method and its parameters to the *Offloading Service* in the cloud side.

The *Profile Monitor* component is responsible for monitoring the mobile device environment (e.g., network bandwidth and latency, power and memory status) and sends such information periodically to the *Profile Services*, which will be used in the *Offloading Reasoner Service* (cloud side), that generates the offloading decision tree based on the mobile device information and then sends it back to the *Offloading Reasoner Client*.

The *Context-Acquisition Middleware* component is a new version of the former CAM component in the LoCCAM framework, which has been adapted for this project. The original component has been extended to provide a better integration with cloud/cloudlets. A new optimized manager was built from the scratch to control CAC's lifecycle, removing OSGi dependency.

This component manages the software-based sensors lifecycle (i.e., search, deploy, start and stop) that encapsulates how context information is acquired. These sensors are called *Context Acquisition Component—CAC* and can be classified into physical or logical ones. The physical CACs are those that only encapsulate the access to mobile device sensor information (e.g., accelerometer, temperature, and luminosity). On the other hand, the logical CACs are those that can use more than one mobile device sensor and information from other sources (e.g., social networks and weather service on the Internet) to provide high-level context information. This middleware also provides an API to build new CACs and incorporate them into new and existing applications.

All context information acquired by CACs is stored in the *Tuple-Space Based Context-Bus module*, which is a new version of the former SysSU module. The *Tuple-Space Based Context-Bus* stores the context information in a tuple-based format and delivers such information to applications using event notification via a contextual event-bus. This new version has a new feature, the Tuple-Space Based Context-Bus that stores more than one tuple for a particular sensor, creating a list of samples. The initial version of SysSU stored only the last collected sample, overlapping the previous one. This feature may improve inferences using a larger amount of contextual data.

All context information of each mobile device connected to a CAOS Controller is sent to the Context Service (cloud side) to keep a database of contextual information history. The idea is to explore the global context (i.e., the context of all mobile devices) to provide more accurate and rich context information. The *Context Synchronizer* exchanges contextual data between the mobile and the cloud sides. This data migration is important because, in CAOS, filters can be performed in both local context information repository (*Tuple-Space Based Context-Bus*) and global context repository (*Context Service*). If an application has an @*Offloadable* marked method that accesses context information using the filter concept, it can benefit itself from the offloading process to access the global context repository. This can be done using two filters: one to be executed locally (on the mobile device) and another that runs in the global context repository when the method is offloaded to the cloud. The decision of which filter will be executed is performed automatically by CAOS.

### 3.3.1.2  The Cloud Side

The CAOS cloud side is composed by 11 (eleven) components: *Discovery Service, Profile Services, Authentication Service, Offloading Reasoner Service, Offloading Service, VM Pool Manager, VM Apk Manager, VM Status Manager, VM Offloading Executor, Context Service,* and *Offloading Method Invocation Service.*

The *Discovery Service* provides correct endpoints information so that clients can access CAOS services. The *Authentication Service* is responsible for saving device information and controlling which devices are currently connected to the CAOS Controller. The *Profile Services* is a set of services which receives device monitored data related to the network quality and local execution time of offloadable methods, in order to keep historical records of executed methods. These records will be used during the offloading decision tree creation process.

The *Offloading Reasoner Service* is responsible for processing the mobile device profile data and creating the decision tree that will be used by the *Offloading Reasoner Client* component (on the mobile side) to decide about the offloading process execution. The *Offloading Service* receives offloading requests directly from *Offloading Client* and redirects them to the *VM Pool Manager*. When the offloading process finishes, the *Offloading Service* returns the result to the *Offloading Client* and persists offloading information.

In CAOS, offloaded methods are executed on Android Virtual Machines running on traditional x86 machines. The *VM Pool Manager* component is responsible for providing an environment that redirects offloading requests to a proper Android Virtual Machine where the offloading execution happens. In order to run a method from a specific application, CAOS requires that the corresponding deployment packages (a.k.a. APK) of CAOS compliant applications must be stored in a special folder on the CAOS platform. The *VM Apk manager* pushes all APK files to all reachable Android Virtual Machines listed in this special folder. The *VM Status Manager* is responsible for monitoring and maintain information (e.g., the current number of offloading executions) about each virtual machine managed by the VM Pool Manager in a repository. The *VM Offloading Executor* component is responsible for requesting the offloading execution in an Android Virtual Machines calling the *Offloading Method Invocation Service*, which runs on the virtual machine and performs the offloading method execution.

The *Context Service* acts like a global context repository, and stores all context information data sent from all mobile devices connected to the CAOS Services. It maintains this context information in a NoSQL database and provides a proper interface that can be used by logical CACs to access this information to generate high-level context information for an application running on the mobile device.

Related to our architecture, it is possible to store the private contextual data in special cloudlet, called *Gateway*. In short, a Gateway is a cloudlet with privacy policies where its data are chosen by each user to be sent to Cloud or not. This approach filters all information that the user does not want to share with other users, but wants to use for personal purposes. This information is stored in a gateway, but not sent to the cloud.

### 3.3.1.3   Implementation Details

The technologies employed in the CAOS reference implementation are described in the following. In the mobile side, the CAOS modules were implemented using the Android SDK on Android Studio IDE. The Couchbase (a NoSQL database) was adopted to maintain a local cache of context information history to be offload to a remote side following the CAOS context data offloading strategy. The Bouncy Castle encryption API was chosen to improve the CAOS wireless communication security. The JCoAP (Java Constrained Application Protocol) was adopted as a protocol to achieve the standardization level requested by the project sponsor.

In the cloud/cloudlet side, the CAOS Controller modules were implemented using Java SE/EE and deployed on Apache Tomcat web container. All server side services were implemented as RESTful Web services using the Jersey framework. All data in CAOS Controller are stored in a PostgreSQL database using the Hibernate framework. The Context Service stores the context tuples on a MongoDB (a NoSQL database). The VirtualBox hypervisor technology was employed in the Android environment virtualization in the server side using an ISO Android x86 version (4.4.2) KitKat.

## 3.3.2   CAOS Experiments—MyPhotos App

This section presents a context-aware multimedia Android application with offloading capability developed using CAOS, called MyPhotos, whose main screen is presented in Fig. 3.12.

Such application allows users to apply filters to their photos and share them on social networks along with hashtags, to make it easier to search for them. Also, photos can be tagged with contextual information, such as location, date, and time at which they were captured. MyPhotos uses CAOS to offload methods related to image filters execution and contextual data into CAOS servers. The CAOS server enables MyPhotos to recommend hashtags for photos with similar context, by leveraging contextual data offloaded by other users. MyPhotos has different image filters that can be applied to a photo, such as RedTone and Cartoonized. The former applies a red tone filter, and the latter is more compute intensive and produces a cartoonized version of the image, where the new photo looks like a pencil sketch. MyPhotos's main screen also shows the time elapsed for the last filter execution.

Besides the use of images filters, MyPhotos also allow users to tag their photos using *hashtags*, and share them together with contextual information. For instance, Fig. 3.13a shows the version of the Maracanã Stadium image after applying the Cartoonized filter.

In Fig. 3.13b, the settings available for the use of *hashtags* are presented. Two parameters are required: the location range (in meters) and the time interval (in

**Fig. 3.12** MyPhotos main screen

**Fig. 3.13** MyPhotos screenshots

seconds). Thus, the user defines how far and how late these data are according to his/her geographical position and time. The "Recommended" button retrieves *hashtags* used previously on images with the same context of the current photo. The "Send" button publishes the image. As MyPhotos was first executed with the device disconnected from the network, it forces the image filter and tags recommendation to run locally. Figure 3.13a shows that it takes more than 56 s to apply the Cartoonized Filter. Figure 3.13b shows that when the mobile device is not connected to the CAOS server, it only retrieves *hashtags* stored in the local Tuple-Space Based Context-Bus. Since the user labeled the photo with two *hashtags*, #olympicstadium and #openinggames2016, these two tags are also the only *hashtags* that could be recommended to the user. Figure 3.13c, the device is connected to the CAOS server, and when the *hashtags* recommendation is requested, the application retrieves up to the five most popular *hashtags* with a context similar to the current user.

It is important to mention that in order to run CAOS on the mobile side, a configuration service must be installed. This application acts as a service, in which contextual data synchronization policies are configured as well as the privacy settings of such data. Figure 3.14 shows screenshots of the CAOS app. The user can start to offload contextual data at any time by pressing the start button (Fig. 3.14a). The Settings Tab (Fig. 3.14b) allows users to configure synchronization policies and its contextual data privacy. For instance, according to Fig. 3.14b, the synchronization policy is set to Wi-Fi, which means that contextual data will be offloaded only when the user is connected to an 802.11 network. Concerning privacy, a list of available CACs is presented, and the user may mark the information that he/she wants to offload. In Fig. 3.14c, we can see that the location information (context.device.location) is not configured to be shared with other users and with the platform.

**Fig. 3.14** Screenshots of the CAOS application running on mobile device

## 3.4   Trends and Research Challenges

Although the combination of context-aware Computing and MCC has great potential for future mobile applications, it is also important to understand that there are issues that raise new challenges to enable such integration. Some of these issues are mentioned in this section.

### 3.4.1   Costs for Raw Data Transfer to Compute the Context Inference on Cloud Services

For some scenarios, the amount of data required to process a contextual situation may be a barrier for the use of MCC. Sometimes, multiple sources of information are needed to derive a Context information, i.e., a multi-sensory process. This is a common scenario for data-intensive applications, in which some cases of context sensing may fit. Naqvi et al. [56] cites that step counting or falling detection algorithms from sensor samples such as accelerometer and gyroscope may require a reasonable amount of data to produce good results. However, transferring a huge amount of data very frequently may bring side effects related to energy consumption or charging fees while using mobile operator network.

### 3.4.2   High Latency Between Mobile Devices and Cloud Resources

According to [56], certain applications such as live gaming, augmented reality do not perform efficiently on most mobile devices nowadays. Although the use of cloud resources can improve the processing of these applications, they are also sensitive to latency in communication between mobile devices and the cloud. Some context-aware mobile applications may suffer from the delay in processing contextual information, make it even unpractical. As pointed out in [37], "by the time the data makes its way to the cloud system for analysis, the opportunity to act on it might be gone." Studies conducted by our research group show how current mobile infrastructures in Brazil do not guarantee adequate QoS to transfer processing between mobile devices and the cloud [14]. This is mainly due to the distance between mobile devices and the centralized resources in cloud provider data centers. In these situations, cloud-based approaches or fog computing appear as strong candidates for meeting low latency requirements, since they typically involve one-hop communication. However, the large-scale dissemination of cloudlets or similar infrastructures is still in its infancy. There is also the fact that there are no formed business models that indicate how to encourage the popularization of these devices.

### 3.4.3   Security and Privacy

Cloud computing is often criticized for its centralized model of information storage on third-party machines. When thinking about the integration of context-aware computing with mobile cloud computing, this problem also rises, since the inference of contextual situations typically makes use of sensitive information from users (such as their location), which for many people, it can be seen as a breach of privacy. Traditional techniques such as information cryptography or data anonymization may be employed, but they also impose additional processing, and consequently delays and additional power consumption.

### 3.4.4   Power Consumption

Extending the device autonomy time is one of the biggest (if not the biggest) concerns for mobile application applications. While there has been a significant increase in the processing capacity of mobile devices each year, the same advancement is not seen in relation to the device's batteries. As a result, there are still barriers to processing or even intense data exchange, since radio transmission is one of the biggest villains for the power consumption of a mobile device. With this, the decision to process the contextual situation locally or remotely becomes even more difficult, making it a trade-off between performance and energy savings. It is also possible that according to the decision, the inference of the contextual situation can be carried out in different ways, according to the context of the device. If the current situation allows to offload the inference of context to the cloud, more complex processing with more accurate results may be performed, based on larger datasets. If it is not possible, a simpler treatment can be offered, but decreasing the quality of the result of the inference. Finally, some scenarios can lead to situations where context management tasks can be divided between mobile device and cloud. This decision balances a choice between improving the accuracy of contextual inference and preserving device features.

### 3.4.5   Large-Scale Availability of MCC Infrastructures

Despite the benefits that infrastructures such as cloudlets offer, having such services spread across multiple locations globally requires considerable investment, which is prohibitive for application providers. There is currently no commercial deployments that use MCC technology [3], probably due to the lack of appropriate business models. Even if we think of specialized companies that support MCC, or even users who want to offer resources spontaneously, aspects such as security and privacy can be obstacles to popularizing these initiatives.

### 3.4.6 Missing Killer Applications

Experiments reports with MCC include topics such as image processing, recommendation systems, face recognition, and language translation. However, according to [3], the popularization of the use of MCC faces two main problems. First, more advanced deep learning techniques typically used in these applications require large data sets, which impacts on the overall response time on these applications. Second, advances in the processing capability of mobile devices suppress the need of offloading tasks out of the mobile device. While this statement is true, our particular view is that only a category of mobile devices (high-end devices) meets processing capabilities for these applications. Balan and Flinn [3] claims that real-time video processing applications have a good potential to become a killer application in MCC field, since processing video streams does not require a huge amount of data, but demands an intensive processing to obtain data from a scene (such as subtitles on certain locations).

## 3.5 Conclusion

Contextual-Aware features are increasingly present in current mobile applications. Even with advances made over the past few years in mobile devices' capabilities, scenarios envisioned for context-aware mobile applications indicate the use of large datasets and machine learning techniques that will require resources not found (at least on most) in current mobile devices. This chapter focuses on this problem, by presenting how Mobile Cloud Computing (MCC), especially offloading techniques, may improve the support for future context-aware mobile applications.

The use of "context" is already widely used in MCC integration. However, previous research works found on a literature review use this term as the situation for decision-making if data or tasks offloading between mobile devices and cloud infrastructures are worthy or not, regarding performance or energy savings. In this chapter, our approach focuses on how context management services can be improved with MCC concepts. This view is presented in a practical way through the framework CAOS, an Android-based platform that supports both data and computing offloading. A case study illustrating how CAOS can be used to implement a context-aware multimedia application is described. To the best of our knowledge, this is one of the few initiatives where context management integration with cloud services is supported.

As future work, we plan to keep evolving our framework. We currently study a complete refactoring of CAOS architecture, where its services will be designed using Microservices approach. We aim at improving CAOS' scalability and flexibility by modeling its services as independent units.

# References

1. Aguilar, J., Jerez, M., Exposito, E., Villemur, T.: CARMiCLOC: context awareness middleware in cloud computing. In: 2015 Latin American Computing Conference (CLEI), pp. 1–10 (2015). https://doi.org/10.1109/CLEI.2015.7360013
2. Alegre, U., Augusto, J.C., Clark, T.: Engineering context-aware systems and applications: a survey. J. Syst. Softw. **117**, 55–83 (2016)
3. Balan, R.K., Flinn, J.: Cyber foraging: fifteen years later. IEEE Pervasive Comput. **16**(3), 24–30 (2017). https://doi.org/10.1109/MPRV.2017.2940972
4. Balan, R., Flinn, J., Satyanarayanan, M., Sinnamohideen, S., Yang, H.I.: The case for cyber foraging. In: Proceedings of the 10th Workshop on ACM SIGOPS European Workshop, EW 10, pp. 87–92. ACM, New York (2002). https://doi.org/10.1145/1133373.1133390
5. Baldauf, M., Dustdar, S., Rosenberg, F.: A survey on context-aware systems. Int. J. Ad Hoc Ubiquitous Comput. **2**(4), 263–277 (2007)
6. Barbera, M.V., Kosta, S., Mei, A., Stefa, J.: To offload or not to offload? The bandwidth and energy costs of mobile cloud computing. In: Proceedings of IEEE INFOCOM, vol. 2013 (2013)
7. Barreto, F.M., de S. Duarte, P.A., Maia, M.E.F., de Castro Andrade, R.M., Viana, W.: CoAP-CTX: a context-aware CoAP extension for smart objects discovery in Internet of Things. In: Reisman, S., Ahamed, S.I., Demartini, C., Conte, T.M., Liu, L., Claycomb, W.R., Nakamura, M., Tovar, E., Cimato, S., Lung, C., Takakura, H., Yang, J., Akiyama, T., Zhang, Z., Hasan, K. (eds.) 41st IEEE Annual Computer Software and Applications Conference, COMPSAC 2017, Turin, July 4–8, 2017, vol. 1, pp. 575–584. IEEE Computer Society, Washington (2017). https://doi.org/10.1109/COMPSAC.2017.87
8. Bettini, C., Brdiczka, O., Henricksen, K., Indulska, J., Nicklas, D., Ranganathan, A., Riboni, D.: A survey of context modelling and reasoning techniques. Pervasive Mob. Comput. **6**(2), 161–180 (2010)
9. Buthpitiya, S., Luqman, F., Griss, M., Xing, B., Dey, A.: Hermes – a context-aware application development framework and toolkit for the mobile environment. In: 2012 26th International Conference on Advanced Information Networking and Applications Workshops (WAINA), pp. 663–670 (2012)
10. Carlson, D., Schrader, A.: Dynamix: an open plug-and-play context framework for android. In: 2012 3rd International Conference on the Internet of Things (IOT), pp. 151–158 (2012)
11. Chatzopoulos, D., Bermejo, C., Huang, Z., Hui, P.: Mobile augmented reality survey: from where we are to where we go. IEEE Access **5**, 6917–6950 (2017). https://doi.org/10.1109/ACCESS.2017.2698164
12. Chihani, B., Bertin, E., Crespi, N.: Decoupling context management and application logic: a new framework. In: 2013 IEEE 14th International Symposium and Workshops on a World of Wireless, Mobile and Multimedia Networks (WoWMoM), pp. 1–6 (2013)
13. Chun, B.G., Ihm, S., Maniatis, P., Naik, M., Patti, A.: CloneCloud: elastic execution between mobile device and cloud. In: Proceedings of the Sixth Conference on Computer Systems, EuroSys '11, pp. 301–314. ACM, New York (2011)
14. Costa, P.B., Rego, P.A.L., Coutinho, E.F., Trinta, F.A.M., d. Souza, J.N.: An analysis of the impact of the quality of mobile networks on the use of cloudlets. In: 2014 Brazilian Symposium on Computer Networks and Distributed Systems, pp. 113–121 (2014). https://doi.org/10.1109/SBRC.2014.14
15. Costa, P.B., Rego, P.A.L., Rocha, L.S., Trinta, F.A.M., de Souza, J.N.: MpOS: a multiplatform offloading system. In: Proceedings of the 30th Annual ACM Symposium on Applied Computing, SAC '15, p. 577–584. ACM, New York (2015). https://doi.org/10.1145/2695664.2695945
16. Cuervo, E., Balasubramanian, A., Cho, D.K., Wolman, A., Saroiu, S., Chandra, R., Bahl, P.: Maui: making smartphones last longer with code offload. In: Proceedings ACM MobiSys 2010, pp. 49–62. ACM, New York (2010)
17. Curiel, P., Lago, A.: Context management infrastructure for intelligent-mobile-services execution environments. In: 2012 7th Iberian Conference on Information Systems and Technologies (CISTI), pp. 1–6 (2012)

18. Da, K., Dalmau, M., Roose, P.: A survey of adaptation systems. Int. J. Internet Distrib. Comput. Sys. **2**(1), 1–18 (2011)
19. Da, K., Dalmau, M., Roose, P.: Kalimucho: middleware for mobile applications. In: Proceedings of the 29th Annual ACM Symposium on Applied Computing, SAC '14, pp. 413–419. ACM, New York (2014)
20. Da, K., Roose, P., Dalmau, M., Nevado, J., Karchoud, R.: Kali2Much: a context middleware for autonomic adaptation-driven platform. In: Proceedings of the 1st ACM Workshop on Middleware for Context-Aware Applications in the IoT, M4IOT '14, pp. 25–30. ACM, New York (2014)
21. de Andrade, D.O.S., Silva, L.F.M., de Figueirêdo, H.F., Viana, W., Trinta, F., de Souza Baptista, C.: Photo annotation: a survey. Multimed. Tools Appl. **77**(1), 423–457 (2018). https://doi.org/10.1007/s11042-016-4281-6
22. Dey, A.K.: Understanding and using context. Pers. Ubiquit. Comput. **5**(1), 4–7 (2001)
23. Hoang, D.T., Lee, C., Niyato, D., Wang, P.: A survey of mobile cloud computing: architecture, applications, and approaches. Wirel. Commun. Mob. Comput. **13**(18), 1587–1611 (2013). http://dblp.uni-trier.de/db/journals/wicomm/wicomm13.html#HoangLNW13
24. Dogdu, E., Soyer, O.: MoReCon: a mobile restful context-aware middleware. In: Proceedings of the 51st ACM Southeast Conference, ACMSE '13, pp. 37:1–37:6. ACM, New York (2013)
25. Doukas, C., Antonelli, F.: Compose: building smart amp; context-aware mobile applications utilizing IoT technologies. In: Global Information Infrastructure Symposium, 2013, pp. 1–6 (2013)
26. Duarte, P.A., Silva, L.F.M., Gomes, F.A., Viana, W., Trinta, F.M.: Dynamic deployment for context-aware multimedia environments. In: Proceedings of the 21st Brazilian Symposium on Multimedia and the Web, WebMedia '15, pp. 197–204. ACM, New York (2015). https://doi.org/10.1145/2820426.2820443
27. El-Derini, M., Aly, H., El-Barbary, A.H., El-Sayed, L.: DroidCloudlet: towards cloudlet-based computing using mobile devices. In: 2014 5th International Conference on Information and Communication Systems (ICICS), pp. 1–6 (2014)
28. Fernando, N., Loke, S.W., Rahayu, W.: Mobile cloud computing: a survey. Futur. Gener. Comput. Syst. **29**(1), 84–106 (2013). https://doi.org/10.1016/j.future.2012.05.023
29. Ferrari, A., Giordano, S., Puccinelli, D.: Reducing your local footprint with anyrun computing. Comput. Commun. **81**, 1–11 (2016). https://doi.org/10.1016/j.comcom.2016.01.006
30. Ferroni, M., Damiani, A., Nacci, A.A., Sciuto, D., Santambrogio, M.D.: cODA: an open-source framework to easily design context-aware android apps. In: Proceedings of the 2014 12th IEEE International Conference on Embedded and Ubiquitous Computing, EUC'14, pp. 33–38. IEEE Computer Society, Washington (2014)
31. Gomes, F.A., Viana, W., Rocha, L.S., Trinta, F.: A contextual data offloading service with privacy support. In: Proceedings of the 22nd Brazilian Symposium on Multimedia and the Web, pp. 23–30. ACM, New York (2016)
32. Gomes, F., Viana, W., Rocha, L., Trinta, F.: On the evaluation of a contextual sensitive data offloading service: the COP case. J. Inf. Data Manag. **8**(3), 197 (2017)
33. Gomes, F.A.A., Rego, P.A.L., Rocha, L., de Souza, J.N., Trinta, F.: CAOS: a context acquisition and offloading system. In: 2017 IEEE 41st Annual Computer Software and Applications Conference (COMPSAC) (2017)
34. Gordon, M.S., Jamshidi, D.A., Mahlke, S., Mao, Z.M., Chen, X.: COMET: code offload by migrating execution transparently. In: USENIX 2012, Proceedings ACM, pp. 93–106. USENIX Association, Berkeley (2012)
35. Herrmann, K.: Self-organized service placement in ambient intelligence environments. ACM Trans. Auton. Adapt. Syst. **5**(2), 6:1–6:39 (2010). https://doi.org/10.1145/1740600.1740602
36. Kakadia, D., Saripalli, P., Varma, V.: MECCA: mobile, efficient cloud computing workload adoption framework using scheduler customization and workload migration decisions. In: Proceedings of the First International Workshop on Mobile Cloud Computing &#38; Networking, MobileCloud '13, pp. 41–46. ACM, New York (2013)

37. Khan, R., Khan, S.U., Zaheer, R., Khan, S.: Future internet: the internet of things architecture, possible applications and key challenges. In: 2012 10th International Conference on Frontiers of Information Technology, pp. 257–260 (2012). https://doi.org/10.1109/FIT.2012.53
38. Khan, A., Othman, M., Madani, S., Khan, S.: A survey of mobile cloud computing application models. IEEE Commun. Surv. Tutorials 16(1), 393–413 (2014). https://doi.org/10.1109/SURV.2013.062613.00160
39. Kharbanda, H., Krishnan, M., Campbell, R.: Synergy: a middleware for energy conservation in mobile devices. In: 2012 IEEE International Conference on Cluster Computing (CLUSTER), pp. 54–62 (2012). https://doi.org/10.1109/CLUSTER.2012.64
40. Kosta, S., Aucinas, A., Hui, P., Mortier, R., Zhang, X.: ThinkAir: dynamic resource allocation and parallel execution in the cloud for mobile code offloading. In: 2012 Proceedings IEEE INFOCOM, pp. 945–953 (2012)
41. Kovachev, D., Cao, Y., Klamma, R.: Mobile cloud computing: a comparison of application models. CoRR abs/1107.4940 (2011). http://arxiv.org/abs/1107.4940
42. Kovachev, D., Yu, T., Klamma, R.: Adaptive computation offloading from mobile devices into the cloud. In: 2012 IEEE 10th International Symposium on Parallel and Distributed Processing with Applications (ISPA), pp. 784–791 (2012)
43. Kristensen, M.D., Bouvin, N.O.: Scheduling and development support in the scavenger cyber foraging system. Pervasive Mob. Comput. 6(6), 677–692 (2010)
44. Kumar, K., Lu, Y.H.: Cloud computing for mobile users: can offloading computation save energy? Computer 43(4), 51–56 (2010). https://doi.org/10.1109/MC.2010.98
45. Kumar, K., Liu, J., Lu, Y.H., Bhargava, B.: A survey of computation offloading for mobile systems. Mob. Netw. Appl. 18(1), 129–140 (2013). https://doi.org/10.1007/s11036-012-0368-0
46. Lee, Y., Iyengar, S.S., Min, C., Ju, Y., Kang, S., Park, T., Lee, J., Rhee, Y., Song, J.: MobiCon: a mobile context-monitoring platform. Commun. ACM 55(3), 54–65 (2012)
47. Lima, F.F.P., Rocha, L.S., Maia, P.H.M., Andrade, R.M.C.: A decoupled and interoperable architecture for coordination in ubiquitous systems. In: Proceedings of the 2011 Fifth Brazilian Symposium on Software Components, Architectures and Reuse, SBCARS'11, pp. 31–40. IEEE Computer Society, Washington (2011)
48. Liu, J., Ahmed, E., Shiraz, M., Gani, A., Buyya, R., Qureshi, A.: Application partitioning algorithms in mobile cloud computing: taxonomy, review and future directions. J. Netw. Comput. Appl. 48, 99–117 (2015)
49. Liu, J., Shen, H., Zhang, X.: A survey of mobile crowdsensing techniques: a critical component for the internet of things. In: 2016 25th International Conference on Computer Communication and Networks (ICCCN), pp. 1–6 (2016). https://doi.org/10.1109/ICCCN.2016.7568484
50. Ma, R.K.K., Lam, K.T., Wang, C.L.: eXCLoud: Transparent runtime support for scaling mobile applications in cloud. In: Proceedings of the 2011 International Conference on Cloud and Service Computing, CSC '11, pp. 103–110. IEEE Computer Society, Washington (2011)
51. Magurawalage, C.M.S., Yang, K., Hu, L., Zhang, J.: Energy-efficient and network-aware offloading algorithm for mobile cloud computing. Comput. Netw. 74(Part B), 22 – 33 (2014). https://doi.org/10.1016/j.comnet.2014.06.020. Special Issue on Mobile Computing for Content/Service-Oriented Networking Architecture
52. Maia, M.E.F., Fonteles, A., Neto, B., Gadelha, R., Viana, W., Andrade, R.M.C.: LOCCAM – loosely coupled context acquisition middleware. In: Proceedings of the 28th Annual ACM Symposium on Applied Computing, SAC '13, pp. 534–541. ACM, New York (2013)
53. Mane, Y.V., Surve, A.R.: CAPM: context aware provisioning middleware for human activity recognition. In: 2016 International Conference on Advanced Communication Control and Computing Technologies (ICACCCT), pp. 661–665 (2016). https://doi.org/10.1109/ICACCCT.2016.7831722
54. March, V., Gu, Y., Leonardi, E., Goh, G., Kirchberg, M., Lee, B.S.: $\mu$cloud: Towards a new paradigm of rich mobile applications. Procedia Comput. Sci. 5, 618 – 624 (2011). The 2nd International Conference on Ambient Systems, Networks and Technologies (ANT-2011)/The 8th International Conference on Mobile Web Information Systems (MobiWIS 2011)

55. Mitchell, M., Meyers, C., Wang, A.I., Tyson, G.: ContextProvider: context awareness for medical monitoring applications. In: Engineering in Medicine and Biology Society, EMBC, 2011 Annual International Conference of the IEEE, pp. 5244–5247 (2011)
56. Naqvi, N.Z., Preuveneers, D., Berbers, Y.: Cloud Computing: A Mobile Context-Awareness Perspective, pp. 155–175. Springer, London (2013)
57. O'Sullivan, M.J., Grigoras, D.: Context aware mobile cloud services: a user experience oriented middleware for mobile cloud computing. In: 2016 4th IEEE International Conference on Mobile Cloud Computing, Services, and Engineering (MobileCloud), pp. 67–72 (2016). https://doi.org/10.1109/MobileCloud.2016.13
58. Perera, C., Zaslavsky, A., Christen, P., Georgakopoulos, D.: Context aware computing for the internet of things: a survey. IEEE Commun. Surv. Tutorials 16(1), 414–454 (2014). https://doi.org/10.1109/SURV.2013.042313.00197
59. Preuveneers, D., Berbers, Y.: Towards context-aware and resource-driven self-adaptation for mobile handheld applications. In: Proceedings of the 2007 ACM Symposium on Applied Computing, SAC '07, pp. 1165–1170. ACM, New York (2007)
60. Pulli, K., Baksheev, A., Kornyakov, K., Eruhimov, V.: Real-time computer vision with OpenCV. Commun. ACM 55(6), 61–69 (2012). https://doi.org/10.1145/2184319.2184337
61. Punjabi, J., Parkhi, S., Taneja, G., Giri, N.: Relaxed context-aware machine learning midddleware (RCAMM) for android. In: 2013 IEEE Recent Advances in Intelligent Computational Systems (RAICS), pp. 92–97 (2013)
62. Rego, P.A.L., Cheong, E., Coutinho, E.F., Trinta, F.A., Hasan, M.Z., de Souza, J.N.: Decision tree-based approaches for handling offloading decisions and performing adaptive monitoring in MCC systems. In: 2017 5th IEEE International Conference on Mobile Cloud Computing, Services, and Engineering (MobileCloud) (2017)
63. Rego, P.A.L., Costa, P.B., Coutinho, E.F., Rocha, L.S., Trinta, F.A., de Souza, J.N.: Performing computation offloading on multiple platforms. Comput. Commun. 105, 1–13 (2017). https://doi.org/10.1016/j.comcom.2016.07.017
64. Rego, P.A., Trinta, F.A., Hasan, M.Z., de Souza, J.N.: Enhancing offloading systems with smart decisions, adaptive monitoring, and mobility support. Wirel. Commun. Mob. Comput. 2019, 18 (2019)
65. Sanaei, Z., Abolfazli, S., Gani, A., Buyya, R.: Heterogeneity in mobile cloud computing: taxonomy and open challenges. IEEE Commun. Surv. Tutorials 16(1), 369–392 (2014). https://doi.org/10.1109/SURV.2013.050113.00090
66. Satyanarayanan, M.: Pervasive computing: vision and challenges. IEEE Pers. Commun. 8(4), 10–17 (2001). https://doi.org/10.1109/98.943998
67. Satyanarayanan, M., Bahl, P., Caceres, R., Davies, N.: The case for VM-based cloudlets in mobile computing. IEEE Pervasive Comput. 8(4), 14–23 (2009). https://doi.org/10.1109/MPRV.2009.82
68. Sharifi, M., Kafaie, S., Kashefi, O.: A survey and taxonomy of cyber foraging of mobile devices. IEEE Commun. Surv. Tutorials 14(4), 1232–1243 (2012). https://doi.org/10.1109/SURV.2011.111411.00016
69. Urbieta, A., González-Beltrán, A., Mokhtar, S.B., Hossain, M.A., Capra, L.: Adaptive and context-aware service composition for IoT-based smart cities. Futur. Gener. Comput. Syst. 76, 262–274 (2017). https://doi.org/10.1016/j.future.2016.12.038
70. Verbelen, T., Simoens, P., De Turck, F., Dhoedt, B.: AIOLOS: middleware for improving mobile application performance through cyber foraging. J. Syst. Softw. 85(11), 2629–2639 (2012)
71. Viana, W., Miron, A.D., Moisuc, B., Gensel, J., Villanova-Oliver, M., Martin, H.: Towards the semantic and context-aware management of mobile multimedia. Multimed. Tools Appl. 53(2), 391–429 (2011)
72. Viana, W., Braga, R.B., Lemos, F.D.A., de Souza, J.M.O., do Carmo, R.A.F., Andrade, R.M.C., Martin, H.: Mobile photo recommendation and logbook generation using context-tagged images. IEEE Multimed. 21(1), 24–34 (2014). https://doi.org/10.1109/MMUL.2013.47
73. Weiser, M.: The computer for the 21st century. Sci. Am. 265(3), 94–104 (1991)

74. Williams, E., Gray, J.: Contextion: a framework for developing context-aware mobile applications. In: Proceedings of the 2nd International Workshop on Mobile Development Lifecycle, MobileDeLi '14, pp. 27–31. ACM, New York (2014)
75. Xia, Q., Liang, W., Xu, W.: Throughput maximization for online request admissions in mobile cloudlets. In: 2013 IEEE 38th Conference on Local Computer Networks (LCN), pp. 589–596 (2013). https://doi.org/10.1109/LCN.2013.6761295
76. Xiao, Y., Simoens, P., Pillai, P., Ha, K., Satyanarayanan, M.: Lowering the barriers to large-scale mobile crowdsensing. In: Proceedings of the 14th Workshop on Mobile Computing Systems and Applications, HotMobile '13, pp. 9:1–9:6. ACM, New York (2013). https://doi.org/10.1145/2444776.2444789
77. Yurur, O., Liu, C.H., Sheng, Z., Leung, V.C.M., Moreno, W., Leung, K.K.: Context-awareness for mobile sensing: a survey and future directions. IEEE Commun. Surv. Tutorials **18**(1), 68–93 (2016). https://doi.org/10.1109/COMST.2014.2381246
78. Zhang, Y., Huang, G., Liu, X., Zhang, W., Mei, H., Yang, S.: Refactoring android Java code for on-demand computation offloading. SIGPLAN Not. **47**(10), 233–248 (2012). https://doi.org/10.1145/2398857.2384634

**Fernando Trinta** holds a PhD degree from Federal University of Pernambuco (2007). He is an adjunct professor at Computer Science Department—Federal University of Ceará since 2011. He works mainly in Multimedia, Software Engineering and Distributed Systems. Currently, his research is focused on MCC, Context-Aware Computing and Fog Computing.

**Paulo A. L. Rego** holds a PhD in Computer Science from the Federal University of Ceará (UFC) since 2016. He is currently an adjunct professor at Computer Science Department—Federal University of Ceará, and is a member of the IEEE. He works in the area of Computer Science, with emphasis on Computer Networks and Distributed Systems. His main research interests include MCC and IoT.

**Francisco Gomes** holds a Master degree from the Federal University of Ceará. He is currently a PhD student and an assistant professor at UFC Crateús. He works in the area of Software Engineering applied to Ubiquitous Computing, Mobile Computing and MCC.

**Lincoln Rocha** holds a PhD in Computer Science from Federal University of Ceará (2013). He is currently an adjunct professor at UFC Computer Science Department since 2014. He works mainly in the area of Software Engineering. Currently, his main research interests include MCC, Context-Aware Computing, and IoT.

**Windson Viana** is Associate professor at Federal University of Ceará. He has obtained his Ph.D. degree in February 2010 from the University Joseph Fourier (Université de Grenoble) in Grenoble, France. He received his BS degree (2002) and his MS degree (2005) in Computer Science from the Federal University of Ceará, Brazil. His research interests include context-awareness, ubiquitous computing, multimedia management, and serious games.

**José Neuman de Souza** holds a PhD degree at Pierre and Marie Curie University (PARIS VI/MASI Laboratory), France, since 1994. He is currently working as a researcher full professor at the Federal University of Ceará in the Computer Science Department, and is IEEE senior member. Since 1999, he has been the Brazilian representative at the IFIP TC6. His main research interests are Cloud Computing and Network Management.

# Chapter 4
# Embedding Deep Learning Models into Hypermedia Applications

**Antonio José G. Busson, Álan Livio V. Guedes, Sérgio Colcher,
Ruy Luiz Milidiú, and Edward Hermann Haeusler**

## 4.1 Introduction

Steinmetz and Nahrstedt [15] define *hypermedia* systems as one that includes non-linear linkage of multimedia information (e.g., text, image, video), which are different from the *hypertext* systems that focus on linkage of text information. For instance, the web browsers have become the preferred development platform for experimenting with, adapting and implementing hypermedia functionalities. Such systems have been addressed in three different axes in the literature: storage, specification, and execution. In this chapter, we focus mainly on specification axis. More precisely, we aiming at providing a *specification* of those systems that support *Deep Learning* functionalities.

On the one hand, the *specification* of a hypermedia application commonly uses a domain-specific language, that is, multimedia authoring languages. These languages focus on the definition of media items as part of an application and their presentation order in time and space [2]. They commonly use a declarative approach (e.g., XML-based) to enable them separate application logic from media description. Therefore, future advances in application execution do not lead to a complete redefinition of its specification. Examples of standard declarative multimedia authoring languages

A. J. G. Busson (✉) · Á. L. V. Guedes · S. Colcher · R. L. Milidiú · E. H. Haeusler
Pontifical Catholic University of Rio de Janeiro (PUC-Rio), Rio de Janeiro, Brazil
e-mail: busson@telemidia.puc-rio.br; alan@telemidia.puc-rio.br; colcher@inf.puc-rio.br;
milidiu@inf.puc-rio.br; hermann@inf.puc-rio.br

© Springer Nature Switzerland AG 2020
V. Roesler et al. (eds.), *Special Topics in Multimedia, IoT and Web Technologies*,
https://doi.org/10.1007/978-3-030-35102-1_4

are HTML5 (HyperText Markup Language),[1] SMIL (Synchronized Multimedia Integration Language)[2], and NCL (Nested Context Language).[3]

On the other hand, *Deep Learning* tasks currently support a vastly and more accurate analysis in fields such as computer vision, speech, and natural language processing. Those tasks create models for massive quantities of data and perform a task such as learning, classification, and recognition over new related data. In hypermedia domain, particularly, some usage scenarios already used such tasks to build applications that are sensitive to its media content semantics.

The Helpicto system[4] aiming at improving communication capabilities of autistic children. To stay focused, a child with autism usually uses specific pictograms in a sequence to recognize a question. Then, the system recognizes voice commands and builds a presentation of pictogram (sequence of images) that represents a specific question. In another scenario, the Shrewsbury Museum & Art Gallery[5] developed a system that detects the visitors face and classifies their age, gender, and humor to generate a more adequate presentation. Moreover, we also cite the IBM Personalized TV system.[6] This system analyzes the TV video stream and provides additional content based on elements that are recognized in that video.

The development of applications, such as the aforementioned ones, is usually done from scratch. It may happen because the multimedia languages currently lack support for *Deep Learning* tasks inside their application specification. It happens because the models behind those languages still focus on presentations tasks such as capture, streaming, and presentation. They do not consider programmers to describe the semantic understanding of the used media and handle recognition of such understanding. In this chapter, we aim at extending multimedia languages to provide such support. More precisely, we extended the NCL (Nested Context Language) [8, 14] and its model, called NCM (Nested Context Model) [13]. In particular, we chose NCL because it follows a media-agnostic approach. More precisely, NCL has constructs to describe how the combination of individual media objects (texts, images, and videos) produces an interactive multimedia presentation, but it does not describe the objects themselves. This media agnostic is useful given the massive and multimodal type of data for machine learning tasks and facilitates the work of extending it.

Our extensions take advantage of deep learning features to enable NCL application support: (1) describe learning based on structured multimedia datasets; (2) recognize content semantics of the media elements in presentation time; (3) use the recognized semantics elements in presentation events. To achieve such goals, we propose the K-NCM (knowledge-based NCM), an extension that includes first-class

---

[1]https://www.w3.org/TR/html52//.

[2]https://www.w3.org/TR/SMIL/.

[3]http://ncl.org.br/.

[4]http://www.helpicto.com/.

[5]https://microsoft.github.io/techcasestudies/cognitive%20services/2017/0\8/04/BlackRadley.html.

[6]https://www.ibm.com/developerworks/library/cc-cognitive-media-telco-2-trs/index.html.

abstractions in the NCM, namely: (a) describe concepts based on multimedia datasets; (b) describe anchors that detect concept occurrences in multimedia content; (c) describe mechanisms for recognition events.

Some works also share our motivation and aiming at extending the NCM to support some kind of recognition during the multimedia presentation. Guedes et al. [3], for instance, studied the impact of describing recognition events in multimedia languages, but their work is restricted to recognition of multimodal interactions. Additionally, Moreno et al. [9] proposes a scheme for general recognition, but it is strong based on standards for knowledge description of Semantic Web and not focus in machine learning techniques.

The remainder of this chapter is structured as follows. In Sect. 4.2 we present an overview of the NCM. Next, in Sect. 4.3 we present an analysis of machine learning methods to identify the features for extending the NCM. Section 4.4 contains the core of the proposal, with the extensions that we propose to the NCM model. Section 4.5 shows the proposed instantiations to NCL language. The viability of applying the model is discussed in Sect. 4.6 with a usage scenario. In Sect. 4.7, we compare our approach with related work. Finally, Sect. 4.2 brings our final considerations and discusses the results and future work.

## 4.2 NCM 3.0

The NCM is based on abstraction of *Node* and *Link*. A *Node* is an entity that is composed by a collection of information units, properties, and a list of *Anchor*. A descriptor defines properties on how a node should be exhibited, such as position for graphics, frame rate for video, and volume for audio. There are two classes of *Anchor*: *ContentAnchor* and *AttributeAnchor*. A *ContentAnchor* represents a set of *Node* information units, while an *AttributeAnchor* is a reference to a property. The NCM requires that every node contains a content anchor called *LambdaAnchor*, which represents the whole content of the node.

NCM *Nodes* are specialized in two classes: *ContentNode* and *CompositeNode*. A *ContentNode*, also called media node or media object, represents the usual media objects (image, text, video, audio, etc.). A *CompositeNode* is a *node* whose content is a set of other *Nodes* (composite or content ones), besides *Anchor* list, composite nodes also have a *Port* list. A *Port* defines mappings among internal composition of nodes. Both *Anchor* and *Ports* act as references, called *Interface*, to access to content segments or attributes of a *Node*.

A *ContextNode* is a type of *CompositeNode* that contains list of *Links*. Con-textNodes are used to define a logical structure (hierarchical or not) for hypermedia documents. This structure allows the definition of several visions of a same document, in addition to improve the user orientation in document navigation. Each *Link* contained in list of *Links* defines a relationship among internal *Nodes* of the *ContextNode*. A *Link* has two additional attributes: a *Connector* and a set of *Binds*. A *Connector* defines the semantics of a relation (e.g., causal relation), while each *Bind* associates the referred Link's connector with Node's interfaces (*anchors*).

## 4.3  Deep Learning Features for Hypermedia Models

We analyze the functioning of modern machine learning methods to identify which features are essential to include in a content-ware based hypermedia model. Additionally, we also identify which features of NCM are useful to describe *datasets* for ML. The gathered features reflect both in our proposal design (presented in the next section) and implementation of hypermedia systems that execute such model. It is important to point out that, as we are particularly interested in the multimedia domain, we select only ML methods that focus on it.

In machine learning field, methods based on *Deep Learning* (e.g., CNN, RNN) become the *state-of-the-art* in several problems of the multimedia domain, especially in audio-visual tasks. Typically, the training of *Deep Learning* models is done in a supervised manner, and it is trained on *datasets* containing thousands/millions of media examples and several related concepts/classes. The NCM *CompositeNode* is useful to define compositions of multimedia data. That way, we can use composite nodes to represent whole media sets for specific concepts, as well to specify the associations between them.

During training, the *Deep Learning* models learn a hierarchy of filters which are applied to input data in order to classify/recognize the media content. In computer vision scenario, for example, given image pixels, the series of layers of the network can learn to extract visual features from it, the shallow layers can extract lower-level features (e.g., edges, corner, contours), while the deeper combine these features to produce higher-level features (e.g., textures, part of objects). These representative features can be clustered into groups, each one representing a specific concept. Additionally, we can extend the meaning of *CompositeNode* to represent the learned knowledge, where each composite node has a collection of representative features extracted from CNNs as its internal information. That way, in authoring level, for example, a *CompositeNode* that represents the "cat" concept contains a collection of cat pictures. While in the execution level, the ML-based engine understands that the "cat" concept is represented by a set of features extracted from these cat pictures.

However, different from images, videos contain not only visual information but also auditory *soundtracks*. Current video classification methods typically represent videos by features extracted from its frames and audio followed by feature aggregation over time [7]. Methods for feature extraction include audio-visual features extracted by *Deep Learning* models pre-trained on large-scale annotated datasets [4] (e.g., ImageNet,[7] COCO,[8] AudioSet[9]). We also can extend the concept based *CompositeNode* to aggregated features from different modalities of multimedia data. That way, for example, the composite node that represents the "car" concept may contain different media modalities of car, such as images, audio, and video.

---

[7]http://www.image-net.org/.

[8]http://cocodataset.org.

[9]https://research.google.com/audioset/.

*Deep Learning* models for object detection (e.g., YOLO [10], SSD [6]) analyze the whole video frames and divides it into multiple regions to predict *bounding boxes* and probabilities of object recognition for each region. The NCM *ContentAnchor* can define *bounding boxes* through *coords* attribute. Additionally, *ContentAnchors* also can define time intervals where concepts occurrences are detected through *area* attribute. However, *ContentAnchors* usually are defined in the authoring phase, as the recognition is a nondeterministic event that occurs in the execution phase, it is necessary to take advantage of NCM's virtual anchors. The virtual entities of NCM are better described in the next section, they are useful for this case, because their content may be defined in run-time.

## 4.4  K-NCM (knowledge-based NCM)

The goal of this section is to present the K-NCM (knowledge-based NCM), a model that extends NCM with ML features presented in the previous section. In Sect. 4.4.1, we present the *ConceptNode*, a new type of composite node that encapsulates media sets to represent perceptual concepts. Next, in Sect. 4.4.2, we present the *SemanticAnchor*, a type of virtual anchor that represents parts of content nodes where expected concepts occur in run-time. All the extensions are illustrated in Fig. 4.1.

### *4.4.1  Multimedia Knowledge*

Inspired on NCM, our definition of *knowledge* is based in abstraction of nodes and links. A *Multimedia Knowledge* $\theta$ is denoted as a tuple, i.e., $\theta = (C, M)$, where $C$ is a set of *ConceptNodes* and $M$ is set of *ContentNodes* (medias). A *ConceptNode* $c$ is

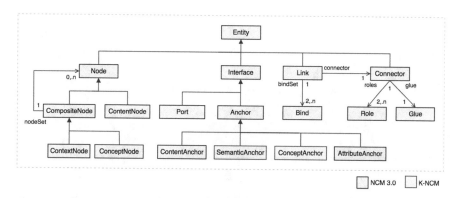

**Fig. 4.1** Entities of the NCM 3.0 (gray) and K-NCM extensions (yellow)

a 4-tupla, i.e., $c \equiv <L^c, L^m, ports, refer>$, where: $L^c \subseteq c \times C$ is a set of conceptual associations to other concept nodes; $L^m \subseteq c \times M$ is a set of media associations; *ports* are an ordered list of *NCM*'s port; And *refer* is an attribute of reference. An association is a property that allows the adaptive capability to concepts nodes interrelate itself with other concepts and media nodes. Each associated concept node is called sub-concept of $c$, and each internal media node is called an object (instantiation) of the $c$ concept.

Each association $l \equiv <c, d \times \mathbb{P}(C)> \in L^C$, where $d \in \{\Rightarrow, \vdash\}$ is an element of the set of association rules. There exist two kinds of associations, *Hierarchy* and *Mereology*. The *hierarchy* association defines a parenthood relation where is applied the rule: $(c_1 \Rightarrow c_2)$, the concept node $c_2$ gets media features from concept node $c_1$, where $c_1$ and $c_2$ are called parent and child concept, respectively. The *mereology* association defines a parthood relation, where is applied the rule: $(c_1 \vdash c_2)$, the concept node $c_2$ is part of concept node $c_1$, this association indicates that media from $c_2$ are parts of media of $c_1$.

The K-NCM does not define the rules of associations as first-class entities. They are defined by the self-structural composition of *ConceptNodes*. The hierarchy association, for instance, is defined by the nesting structure of NCM. In NCM, different compositions may contain associations with the same node. Moreover, composite nodes may be nested to any depth, however, a composite node should not recursively contain itself. To identify through which sequence of nested composite nodes the instance of a node $N$ is being observed, NCM introduces the notion of node perspective. The perspective of a node $N$ is a sequence $P = (N_m, \ldots, N_1)$, with $m \geq 1$, such that $N_1 = N$, $N_{i+1}$ is a composite node, $N_i$ is contained in $N_{i+1}$, for $i \in [1, m)$, and $N_m$ is not contained in any other node. Note, in A of Fig. 4.2, for instance, the *hierarchy* rule $(c_1 \Rightarrow c_2)$ is applied, "fruit" concept have three nested "watermelon," "apple," and "orange" sub-concepts, each sub-concept is reified by their respective media objects. This means that: (1) during recognition event, the multimedia engine can infer that "watermelon," "apple," and "orange" concepts also are of "fruit" concept type; (2) the multimedia engine also can interpret that the

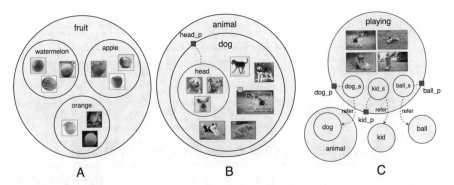

**Fig. 4.2** (**a**) Example of hierarchy association. (**b**) Example of mereology association. (**c**) Example of mereology association that reuses external concepts

"fruit" concept represents an aggregation of all media embeddings that are inside of "watermelon," "apple," and "orange" sub-concepts.

For *mereology* association, it is defined by the *port* of *ConceptNode*. The *port* is a node interface that allows defining mappings between internal sub-concept nodes. The NCM defines a port mapping sequence of a port $p_k$ in a composition $N_k$ the sequence of nodes and interfaces $(N_k, ip_k, \ldots, N_1, ip_1)$ with $k > 1$, such that, for $i \in [1, k)$, where $N_{i+1}$ is a composite node, and $N_i$ is contained in $N_{i+1}$; $ip_i$ is an interface of $N_i$, and $N_i$ and $ip_i$ are the values of the node and interface attributes, respectively, of a port $ip_{i+1}$ of node $N_{i+1}$, this means that $ip_i$ is in the port mapping sequence of $p$. For instance, note in B of Fig. 4.2, that the "dog" concept has: a collection of dogs images, a sub-concept identified as "head," and a *port* identified as "head_p." The port refers to "head" sub-concept, indicating that "head" sub-concept has a mereology association (rule $c_1 \vdash c_2$) with the "dog" concept. This means that when this "head" concept is recognized, then multimedia player can infer that "dog" concept also occurs, because the "head" concept is part of "dog" concept.

In c of Fig. 4.2 is exemplified another example of *mereology* association, but using external mappings. In this example, the "playing" concept represents an activity, where "dog," "kid," and "ball" concepts may be part of it. Examples of valid media that may reify the "playing" concept are a kid playing with a ball; a kid playing with a dog; or yet a dog playing with a ball. Note that the three internal "ball_s," "dog_s," and "kid_s" sub-concepts are empty and they reuse the external "ball," "dog," and "kid" concepts through the *refer* attribute of *ConceptNode*.

K-NCM also enables the use of a part of a media does reify concepts. In NCM, the *ContentNode* has an ordered list of *content anchors* (or area anchor), which has an attribute called *region*. The anchor region specifies a collection of information units of a content node. Any sub-set of content information units may define an anchor and the exact notion of what is an anchor region depends on the node content definition. Every *ContentNode* always has an anchor called *LambdaAnchor*, which is a region that represents the whole content of the node. By default, when a media node only has the *LambdaAnchor* in its anchor list, the whole media content is used to reify the enclosing concept. However, when a media node has other content anchors (besides *LambdaAnchor*), the *LambdaAnchor* is ignored, and these content anchors are used to reify the concept. That way, if an object just occupies a part of an image, an anchor that bounds the object can be used to reification, as shown in b of Fig. 4.2 (blue rectangle).

### 4.4.2 Semantic Anchor

The *SemanticAnchor* represents the concept occurrences in part media node's content. Both the *ContextNode* and *ContentNode* may contain *SemanticAnchors*, but specifically, when a *SemanticAnchor* is within the *ContextNode*, it represents the concept occurrences in all media nodes' content which are within that *ContextNode*. The *SemanticAnchor* is a type of NCM *Virtual Anchor*. This means that the

*SemanticAnchor* relies with the semantic evaluation of media' content in run-time. A *SemanticAnchor s* is defined as a 4-tupla, i.e., $s \equiv$ <*knowledge, score, filter, recognitions*>, where *knowledge* $\in \mathbb{P}(C)$ is a set of concepts that may be detected. The *score* is an attribute that defines the confidence threshold (real number between 0 and 1) to trigger a recognition event. The *filter* is an attribute that defines a expression to select a sub-set of the referred *knowledge*. The *ContentAnchor* refers part of media node's content (in time and space) where a concept is detected, while the *ConceptAnchor* refers part of knowledge that explicitly describes the media node's content. The *knowledge* attribute defines a reference to a knowledge (concept composition) with the elements that will be recognized.

Figure 4.3 illustrates an example of *SemanticAnchor* where recognition occurs in three timestamps ($S = \{t_1, t_2, t_3\}$) of a video scene. The first timestamp represents the recognition of "goldenfish" concept. Next, the second timestamp represents the recognition of "duck" concept. Finally, the third timestamp represents the recognition of "iguana" concept. Each item has a *ContentAnchor* that refers the area/region of the video where the recognized concept occurs, and it also has a *ContentAnchor* that refers to the explicit part of knowledge that describes the content. Note that the *ContentAnchor* ending of third element is not defined, this is because the "iguana" concept still is recognized during run-time.

Traditionally, the NCM focuses its efforts on the definition of selection and presentation events. The K-NCM introduces a new event type, named recognition event. The recognition event represents a transition in recognition state of a concept that is referred by a *SemanticAnchor*. This transition is mapped into a new conditional role called *RecognitionRole*. When the *RecognitionRole* triggers

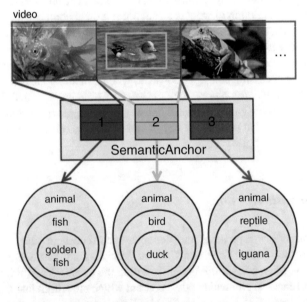

**Fig. 4.3** Example of three concepts occurrences in a video's scene

a recognition event, it receives properties related to referred *SemanticAnchor*: (1) *index*, which is the index of current recognition event in the *SemanticAnchor*'s recognition list; (2) *time*, which is the event trigger timestamp; (3) *concept*, which is the identifier of the recognized concept; (4) *contentArea*, which represents the *ConceptAnchor* of *SemanticAnchor* (part of media node's content) where the recognized concept appears; (5) *knowledgeArea*, which represents the *ConceptAnchor* (part of knowledge) that explicitly describes the *contentArea'* content; (6) *coords*, rectangular area that bounds the *contentArea*. Figure 4.4 illustrates an example of three recognition events. Inside of a context node, there is a *SemanticAnchor*

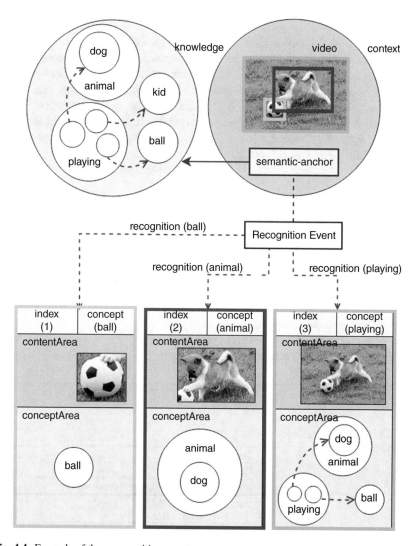

**Fig. 4.4** Example of three recognition events

that refers a knowledge about the playing activity (same c of Fig. 4.2). So, three recognition events are triggered: the first event represents a recognition of "ball" concept; the second, a recognition of "animal" concept; and the third, a recognition of "playing" concept.

## 4.5   K-NCM Instantiation

The previously proposed entities were instantiated in NCL. Table 4.1 shows the XML elements with their new corresponding attributes and child elements, which can be used in NCL documents.

The *ConceptNode* is instantiated using <concept> element. It is defined inside the <body> element and has the *id* attribute, which identifies the concept. The <concept> may contains <port> (NCM *port*), <media> (NCM *ContentNode*), and other <concept> elements as children. Listing 4.1 exemplifies part of the implementation of knowledge B in Fig. 4.2. The root <concept> element identified as "animal" has a *hierarchy* association with its child <concept> element identified as "dog." Next, "dog" concept has a *mereology* association with the <concept> element identified as "head," through the <port> element identified as "head_p." Note that each <concept> contains the <media> elements that reify the concept itself.

**Listing 4.1**  Usage example of <concept> element in NCL

```
<concept id="animal">
  <concept id="dog">
    <port id="head_p" interface="head" />
    <media src="dog1.png"/>
    <media src="dog2.png"/>
    ...
    <concept id="head">
      <media src="dog_head1.png"/>
      <media src="dog_head2.png"/>
      ...
```

**Table 4.1** NCL elements related to the K-NCM

| Element | Attributes | New child elements |
|---------|-----------|--------------------|
| Concept | id | *(concept | port | media)∗* |
| Context | id | *(semantic)∗* |
| Media | id, src, descriptor | *(semantic)∗* |
| Semantic | id, knowledge, score, filter | *empty* |

The *SemanticAnchor* is instantiated using <semantic> element. It is defined inside <context> (NCM *ContextNode*) or <media> element, and it has *id*, *knowledge*, *score*, and *filter* attributes. The expression defined by *filter* attribute is a combination of the *AND*, *OR*, and *NOT* logical operators, and comparison conditions that use the *typeOf* and *partOf* attributes, to select *hierarchy* and *mereology* associations, respectively.

Listing 4.2 exemplifies the usage of <semantic> element. Inside of the <media> element identified as "video1," is defined as a <semantic> element. This element has a *knowledge* attribute that refers a knowledge named "animals," a *score* attribute set with "0.9," and a *filter* attribute set with "typeof=frog OR typeof=dog." That means that only concept that has hierarchy associations with "frog" or "dog" concepts can be recognized in "video1" media, if the concept recognition score has at least of 90% of confidence.

**Listing 4.2** Usage example of <semantic> element in NCL

```
<media id="video1" src="videos/dog.mp4" />
  <semantic knowledge="animals" score="0.9"
     filter="typeof=frog OR typeof=dog"/>
</media>
```

Using NCL *Link* is possible to create a causal recognition event through the *RecognitionRole*. Listing 4.3 exemplifies the implementation of a recognition event. The link identified as "l1" refers to a causal connector named "RecognizeStart" to define that when a concept referred by "s_anchor1" semantic anchor occurs in "video1" media object, then the "textDog" media node is started.

**Listing 4.3** Usage example of a link with the "Recognition" role

```
<link id="l1" xconnector="RecognizeStart">
  <bind role="recognize" component="video1"
     interface="s_anchor1"/>
 <bind role="start" component="textDog"/>
</link>
```

To offer a way to retrieve the properties from recognition events, we define a recognition event handler in Lua script. To do this, we extend the "ncl" class of NCLua API [11] with a new event type called "recognition." Additionally, we define two new event fields: *semantic* and *action*. The *semantic* field refers to a semantic anchor in NCL document. While the *action* field defines the callback behavior of handler function. The *action* field may be defined as "starts," "ends," or "update." The "starts" and "ends" actions define that the handler function will be called when the recognition event of a concept begins or ends, respectively. The "update" action defines that the handler function will be called when any property of recognition event is changed in run-time. When a recognition event triggers, the handler function receives a Lua table[10] with the six event properties described in last section: *index*, *time*, *concept*, *contentArea*, *knowledgeArea*, and *coords*.

Listing 4.4 shows an example of recognition event handling in NCLua. The *event.register* function registers a handler function that waits for a recognition event of "s1" semantic anchor in "m1" media node. The *action* field with "update" value defines that the handler is always called when a property of recognition event is updated (e.g., content anchor, coords). The *handler* function (lines 1–4) prints the recognized concept name and its current *coords*.

**Listing 4.4** Recognition event handler in NCLua

```
1 function handler(evt)
2     print("Concept name:", evt.concept)
3     print("Current coords:", evt.coords)
4 end
5
6 event.register (handler, {class='ncl',
      semantic='m1.s1', type='recognition',
      action='update'})
```

## 4.6 Usage Scenario

To evaluate our approach, we introduce a usage scenario to highlight how K-NCM supports the development of content-aware multimedia presentations. To achieve this, in this section we develop step-by-step a hypermedia application that uses the presented features of K-NCM.

The application is a *Learning Object* (LO) called "African Animals." It is composed of three scenes: the first one, presents information about lions; the second one, presents information about giraffes, and the last one, presents information about elephants. Our objective is to create a smart LO that automatically creates an interactive menu based on which animal appears in scenes.

To allow the execution of this usage scenario, we developed an extension to NCL that incorporates the new proposed NCL/NCLua entities. More precisely, we extended the Ginga reference implementation.[11] To perform learning and recognition tasks, we implement two CNN models: the YOLOv3 [10] to perform object detection, and FaceNet [12] for face recognition. Besides, to allow the running of these models in real-time, we also connect the Ginga set-top-box (iDTV receptor) to a computer with a GeForce GTX 180 Ti GPU.[12]

---

[10]https://www.lua.org/pil/2.5.html.

[11]https://github.com/TeleMidia/ginga.

[12]https://www.nvidia.com/en-us/geforce/products/10series/geforce-gtx-1080-ti.

Section 4.6.1 presents details about the application *knowledge*. In sequence, Sect. 4.6.2 shows how to debug and validate the specified semantic anchors. And finally, Sect. 4.6.3 shows how to create an interactive dynamic menu using the recognition event properties.

## 4.6.1  Application Knowledge

According to K-NCM, the application must contain knowledge that describes the concepts which may be recognized. In this scenery, we want to recognize animals and face of teachers that are in video scenes. To do this, we need to collect the media data that reifies these concepts. So, to reify the concepts of each animal and person, we use a sub-set of COCO [5] dataset. Next, to reify the general face concept, we use a sub-set of the WiderFace [16] dataset. And to reify the individual teachers' faces, we use five facial images of each teacher.

Listing 4.5 shows the knowledge structure of the application. The "wild_animal" concept has the "elephant," "giraffe," and "zebra" sub-concepts. Next, the "person" concept has a "face_p" port that defines a mereology association with "face" concept. Next, the "face" concept has the individual face concept for each teacher: "lany_face," "tony_face," and "jony_face."

**Listing 4.5** "African Animals" knowledge structure

```
<concept name="af_knowledge" >
 <concept id="wild_animals">
  <concept id="elephant"> <!--media set--> </concept>
  <concept id="giraffe"> <!--media set--> </concept>
  <concept id="zebra"> <!--media set--> </concept>
 </concept>
 <concept id="person">
   <!--media set-->
   <port id="face_p" interface="face">
   <concept id="face">
    <!--media set-->
    <concept id="lany_face"> <!--media set--> </concept>
    <concept id="tony_face"> <!--media set--> </concept>
    <concept id="jony_face"> <!--media set--> </concept>
   </concept>
 </concept>
</concept>
```

### 4.6.2  Debugging Recognition Events

The highlighting of recognition events is an easy way to verify if expected concepts
are being correctly detected. In this section, we define an NCLUA code to highlight
all occurrences of animal and face concepts.

Listing 4.6 shows the implementation of this step. The lines 1–3 represent part
of NCL document that contains the main video, and inside of it, is defined as a
semantic anchor that refers to the knowledge created in the previous section. Note
that the semantic anchor has a *filter* attribute defined with "typeof=animal OR
tyeof=face" value, this mean that only animal and face concepts can be recognized.
In Lua document (lines 5–13), at line 13, the *event.register* function registers the
handler function for the "s1" *semantic anchor* with the *action* attribute set with
"update" value. The *handler* function (lines 5–11) uses the event properties to draw
the concept name and the rectangle that bounds the region where the concept is
recognized. Figure 4.5 shows the highlighted concepts during application running.

**Listing 4.6**  Debugging recognition events

```
1 <media id="m1" src="af_video.mp4">
2   <semantic id="s1" knowledge="af_knowledge"
        score="0.9" filter="typeof=animal OR
        tyeof=face" />
3 </media>
4 -------------------------------------------------
5 function handler(evt)
6     x,y,w,h = evt.coords
7     title = evt.concept
8     canvas:attrColor(generateColor(evt.index))
9     canvas:drawRect ('frame',x,y,w,h)
10    canvas:drawText (x,y, title)
11 end
12
13 event.register (handler, {class='ncl', node='m1.s1',
        type='recognition', action='update'})
```

### 4.6.3  Creating a Dynamic Interactive Menu

In this step, we demonstrate how K-NCM can be used to create a content-aware
interactive menu. It is illustrated in Fig. 4.6. To do this, we develop an NCLua code
that use *NCL edit API* [8] to dynamically creates the menu. We create the menu
elements based on recognition events during application running. Additionally,

**Fig. 4.5**  Highlighting all detected concepts during application running

**Fig. 4.6**  Dynamic menu creation during presentation running

when the user selects a menu button, the application must go to a time where the expected animal concept occurred.

To implement this step, we changed the *filter* attribute of the semantic anchor to select only animal concepts. The author also can create a menu based on the teachers' faces, changing the filter attribute to select only face concepts.

Listing 4.7 shows the implementation of this step. The lines 1–6 represent part of NCL document that contains three media (button1, button2, and button3) and three links (link1, link2, and link3). Note that media does not have the *src* (source) attribute, and links do not have their *binds* elements. The objective is to use the recognition function handler to fill the content of these nodes with information about the first three recognition events. In Lua document (lines 8–15), the *handler* function uses the *index* attribute to build the string-id of target media and link. Next, at line 11, the *injectContent* function injects the *contentArea* data into corresponding media node to fill it content with the image frame of recognized concept. At line 12, the *createBindSelect* function creates a <bind> into target link with the *onSelection* role that refers target button node. Finally, at line 13, the *createBindSet* function creates a <bind> with the "set" role that refers the main video' time and set it with the event *timestamp*.

**Listing 4.7** Creating a Dynamic Interactive Menu" source code

```
1  <media id="button1" descriptor="descr1"/>
2  <media id="button2" descriptor="descr2"/>
3  <media id="button3" descriptor="descr3"/>
4  <link id="link1" xconnector="onSelectionSet_var" />
5  <link id="link2" xconnector="onSelectionSet_var" />
6  <link id="link3" xconnector="onSelectionSet_var" />
7  % ---------------------------------------------
8  function handler(evt)
9    targetMedia = "button" .. tostring(evt.index)
10   targetLink = "link" .. tostring(evt.index)
11   injectContent(targetMedia, evt.contentArea)
12   createBindSelect(targetLink, targetMedia)
13   createBindSet(targetLink, "m1", "time", evt.time)
14 end
15 event.register (handler, {class='ncl', node='m1.s1',
       type='recognition', action='start'})
```

## 4.7  Related Work

Recently, some efforts use or extend NCM/NCL to offer mechanisms to specify knowledge description and/or recognition events in hypermedia documents. In this section, we compare our approach with other three works found in the literature.

Moreno et al. [9] propose the NCM 3.1, an NCM extension that supports the specification of relationships between knowledge descriptions, composing what they call *Hyperknowledge*. Their approach is inspired by knowledge engineering standards, such as RDF and OWL. They propose the use of SPO (subject-predicate-object) and hierarchy relations among *ContentNodes* and a string-based entity called

*ConceptNode*s. To represent both types of relations, NCM 3.1 introduces two new types of connectors: (1) hierarchy connector with hierarchy glue and roles; and (2) SPO connector with SPO glue and roles. To recognize concepts during the presentation of *ContentNode*s, they also propose a new type of role called *InferenceRole*, which defines the content node where an expected concept may be recognized.

Instead of using string-based knowledge descriptors, we opt for a way more closely aligned with the machine learning area. In K-NCM, concept nodes are compositions of multimedia data that may be encapsulated and used as input for the training of machine learning models. Another difference is that in K-NCM the association among concepts is not defined by *Links*, but by the self-composition structure of *ConceptNodes*s. We believe that the design decision of not overloading the *Links* to support concept association makes the modeling more clear and avoids the visualization of "hairball" diagrams.

Guedes et al. [3] extend the NCM to support the development of NCL applications with multimodal interactions. This was the first work to use a virtual anchor that has a recognition event. However, instead of define concepts to be recognized, it defines expected user interactions through multimodal descriptions (e.g., SRGS for voice recognition). These descriptions are used in a new *<input>* element to represent input devices. Such elements may have a virtual anchor, called *RecognitionAnchor*, that trigger recognition event when an expected interaction is recognized from the input device.

Abreu and Santos [1] propose the *AbstractAnchor*, which is an anchor type that represents parts of a content node where concepts are detected. They implement an abstract anchor processor (AAP) that uses an API of image classification to analyze video frames. Then, during the document parsing, the processor analyzes all the media and instantiates the *ContentAnchor*s and *Links* with its attributes relative to time interval where expected concepts are recognized in each media.

In K-NCM, we propose the *SemanticAnchor*, which is similar to *AbstractAnchor* and *RecognitionAnchor*, in the sense that both anchors represent parts of content where specific concepts are detected. Instead of pre-processing the document to mark concept occurrences (like Abreu and Santos), we opt to an approach based on virtual anchors (like Guedes et al.) that allow recognition events in run-time. This way, we also can perform recognition event even in applications of live streams. Additionally, the K-NCM also offers access to properties of recognition events, such as identifier of the recognized event, part of media where that concept appears, time of recognition event trigger, etc. Table 4.2 summarize the features comparison among related work and this work.

## 4.8 Final Remarks

This chapter presented the K-NCM (knowledge-based NCM), an extension to NCM aiming at supporting knowledge description and recognition events. We define a new anchor called *SemanticAnchor*. In contrast to traditional anchors, it allows the

**Table 4.2** Features comparison of related work

| Work | Knowledge description | Virtual anchor | Recognition event |
|---|---|---|---|
| Moreno et al. [9] | • Use string-based concepts <br> • Use link-based associations of SPO and hierarchy <br> • Inspired on RDF and OWL | • Not present | • In run-time |
| Guedes et al. [3] | • Delegate to API or recognition services | • Use RecognitionAnchor <br> • Restricted to input devices | • In run-time <br> • Use recognition properties |
| Abreu and Santos [1] | • Delegate to API or recognition services | • Not present | • Instantiated during document parsing |
| K-NCM | • Use multimedia-based concepts <br> • Use associations of hierarchy and mereology <br> • Use composition based associations | • Use SemanticAnchor <br> • Works in any NCM node | • In run-time <br> • Use recognition properties <br> • Use Lua scripts |

specification of knowledge-based events that rely on the semantic evaluation of media node content. The specification of a *SemanticAnchor* is based on references to a knowledge, that is defined by a new type of *CompositeNode* called *ConceptNode*. This entity defines a related concept and it is used by the machine learning-based engine to recognize concepts inside of content nodes. The *ConceptNode*s also contain a new type of anchor called *ConceptAnchor*, that allows for the explicit identification of concepts sub-set in their knowledge.

To evaluate the K-NCM, we describe a usage scenario of smart *Learning Object*. It recognizes visual components into the content presentation and creates a dynamic menu based on which concept appears in the scenes. To do this, we extended the Ginga reference implementation with the new proposed NCL/NCLua entities and implemented *Deep Learning* models (YOLO and FaceNet), to support the new model features.

As future work, we plan to extend the model to (1) support a greater degree of machine autonomy. It would be interesting to explore the use of the NCL edition commands to allow that cognitive agent can create, edit, and delete presentation elements or inject knowledge in the application and (2) explore the use of interaction events with *SemanticAnchor*. To allow users to assist such cognitive agents and help them to perform online learning.

# References

1. Abreu, R., dos Santos, J.A.: Using abstract anchors to aid the development of multimedia applications with sensory effects. In: Proceedings of the 2017 ACM Symposium on Document Engineering, pp. 211–218. ACM, New York (2017)
2. Blakowski, G., Steinmetz, R.: A media synchronization survey: reference model, specification, and case studies. IEEE J. Sel. Areas Commun. **14**(1), 5–35 (1996). https://doi.org/10.1109/49. 481691
3. Guedes, Á.L.V., de Albuquerque Azevedo, R.G., Barbosa, S.D.J.: Extending multimedia languages to support multimodal user interactions. Multimed. Tools Appl. **76**(4), 5691–5720 (2017)
4. Hershey, S., Chaudhuri, S., Ellis, D.P., Gemmeke, J.F., Jansen, A., Moore, R.C., Slaney, M.: CNN architectures for large-scale audio classification. In: 2017 IEEE International Conference on Acoustics, Speech and Signal Processing (ICASSP), pp. 131–135. IEEE, Piscataway (2017)
5. Lin, T.Y., Maire, M., Belongie, S., Hays, J., Perona, P., Ramanan, D., Zitnick, C.L.: Microsoft coco: common objects in context. In: European Conference on Computer Vision, pp. 740–755. Springer, Cham
6. Liu, W., Anguelov, D., Erhan, D., Szegedy, C., Reed, S., Fu, C.-Y., Berg, A.C.: SSD: single shot multibox detector. In: European Conference on Computer Vision, pp. 21–37. Springer, Berlin (2016)
7. Miech, A., Laptev, I., Sivic, J.: Learnable pooling with context gating for video classification. arXiv:1706.06905 (2017, preprint)
8. Moreno, M.F., Batista, C.E.C.F., Soares, L.F.G.: NCL and ITU-T's standardization effort on multimedia application frameworks for IPTV. In *Workshop on Interactive Digital TV (WTVDI) - Brazilian Symposium on Multimedia and the Web - WebMedia 2010, At Belo Horizonte*. ACM, New York (2010)
9. Moreno, M.F., Brandao, R., Cerqueira, R.: Extending hypermedia conceptual models to support hyperknowledge specifications. Int. J. Semantic Comput. **11**(1), 43–64 (2017)
10. Redmon, J., Farhadi, A.: Yolov3: an incremental improvement. arXiv:1804.02767 (2018, preprint)
11. Sant'Anna, F., Cerqueira, R., Soares, L.F.G.: NCLua: objetos imperativos lua na linguagem declarativa NCL. In: Proceedings of the 14th Brazilian Symposium on Multimedia and the Web, pp. 83–90. ACM, New York (2008)
12. Schroff, F., Kalenichenko, D., Philbin, J.: FaceNet: a unified embedding for face recognition and clustering. In: Proceedings of the IEEE Conference on Computer Vision and Pattern Recognition, pp. 815–823 (2015)
13. Soares, L.F.G., Rodrigues, R.F., de Resende Costa, R.M.: Nested context model 3.0. Monogr. Comput. Sci. PUC-Rio **18**, 5–35 (2005)
14. Soares, L.F.G., Moreno, M.F., Neto, C.D. S.S., Moreno, M.F.: Ginga-NCL: declarative middleware for multimedia IPTV services. IEEE Commun. Mag. **48**(6), 74–81 (2010)
15. Steinmetz, R., Nahrstedt, K.: Documents, Hypertext, and Hypermedia. Multimedia Applications, pp. 87–132. Springer, Berlin (2004)
16. Yang, S., Luo, P., Loy, C.C., Tang, X.: Wider face: a face detection benchmark. In: Proceedings of the IEEE Conference on Computer Vision and Pattern Recognition, pp. 5525–5533 (2016)

**Antonio José G. Busson**, MSc., is Ph.D. candidate working under the guidance of Prof. Sergio Colcher at Pontifical Catholic University of Rio de Janeiro (PUC-Rio). He received a B.S. (2013) and M.S. (2015) in Computer Science from the Federal University of Maranhão (UFMA) on Brazil. His research interests are in multimedia systems, working mainly on the following topics: Coding and Processing of Multimedia Data, Hypermedia Document Models, Pattern Recognition, and Applications such as Web, iDTV, and Games. Currently, he is working on the official Ginga Middleware development project, which is the middleware of the Japanese-Brazilian Digital TV System (ISDB-TB) and ITU-T H.761 recommendation for iPTV services. He also is working on the VideoMR project, one of the selected projects in the Microsoft and RNP A.I. challenge, which aims to detect improper content in videos. Address to access CV: http://lattes. cnpq.br/1857348479447184.

**Álan Livio V. Guedes**, DSc., holds a Ph.D. (2017) from the PUC-Rio, where he acts as post-Ph.D. researcher in TeleMídia Lab. He received his Bachelor (2009) and M.Sc. (2012) degrees in Computer Science from the UFPB, where he worked as researcher in Lavid Lab. In both labs, Álan worked in interactive video and TV research projects, and acquired experience in C++/video development and research writing/publication. At Lavid, he worked in awarded projects such as Ginga Store and Brasil 4D. At TeleMídia, he contribute to the Ginga and N CL specifications which today are standards for DTV, IPTV, and IBB. His research interests include Multimedia, Interactive Video, Immersive Media, and Deep Learning for Multimedia. Lattes: http://lattes.cnpq.br/1481576313942910.

**Sérgio Colcher**, DSc., received B.S. (1991) in Computer Engineer, M.S. (1993) in Computer Science, and Ph.D. (1999) in Informatics, all by PUC-Rio, in addition to the postdoctoral (2003) at ISIMA (Institute Supérieur d'Informatique et de Modelisation des Applications—Université Blaise Pascal, Clermont-Ferrand, France). Currently, he teaches in Informatics Department at Pontifical Catholic University of Rio de Janeiro (PUC-Rio). His research interests include computer networks, analysis of performance of computer systems, multimedia/hypermedia systems, and digital TV. Address to access CV: http://lattes.cnpq.br/1104157433492666.

**Ruy Luiz Milidiú**, DSc., received B.S. (1974) in Mathematics and M.S. (1978) in Applied Mathematics from Federal University of Rio de Janeiro. He also received a M.S. (1983) and Ph.D. (1985) in Operations Research from University of California. Currently, he teaches in Informatics Department at Pontifical Catholic University of Rio de Janeiro (PUC-Rio). He has experience in Computer Science, focusing on Algorithmics, Machine Learning and Computational Complexity. Address to access CV: http://lattes.cnpq.br/6918010504362643.

**Edward Hermann Haeusler** received B.S. (1983) in Mathematics from University of Brasilia. He also received a M.S. (1986) and Ph.D. (1985) in Computer Science from Pontifical Catholic University of Rio de Janeiro (PUC-Rio), he teaches in Informatics Department at. Currently, he teaches in Informatics Department at PUC-Rio. He has experience in Computer Science, focusing on Computability and Computational Models, acting on the following subjects: Proof Theory, Category Theory, Natural Deduction, and Formal Semantics. Address to access CV: http://lattes.cnpq.br/6075905438020841.

# Part II
# Tools and Application Development

# Chapter 5
# Building Models for Ubiquitous Application Development in a Model-Driven Engineering Approach

**Marcos Alves Vieira and Sergio T. Carvalho**

## 5.1 Introduction

A model is a high-level graphic or textual representation of a system, where each of its elements is a virtual representation of a component present in the real system. The relationships and abstractions used in a model are described by a metamodel [67]. Metamodels are generally built to allow the creation of models that express specific concepts of a domain such as electric power distribution systems (called microgrids) [46], CrowdSensing [36], Software Product Lines [6, 20], or ubiquitous computing scenarios [64].

This chapter aims to enable undergraduate and graduate students, as well as practitioners in software engineering, in the construction of a graphical modeling tool for designing models in accordance with a given metamodel.

The concepts are presented directly through widely used tools in this context and a good portion of coding and testing. Readers, therefore, have the opportunity to have contact not only with the definitions and conceptual aspects of the area but also with the step-by-step development of an example scenario of ubiquitous computing.

The chapter is divided into three parts: the first part (Sect. 5.2) presents the theoretical and conceptual foundations necessary for the construction of a metamodel for modeling smart spaces; the second part (Sect. 5.3) presents the technological foundations involved; and the third part (Sect. 5.4), in turn, presents a graphical modeling tool that enables the construction of models based on a particular

M. A. Vieira (✉)
Goiano Federal Institute, Iporá, Brazil
e-mail: marcos.vieira@ifgoiano.edu.br

S. T. Carvalho
Informatics Institute, Federal University of Goiás, Goiânia, Brazil
e-mail: sergio@inf.ufg.br

© Springer Nature Switzerland AG 2020
V. Roesler et al. (eds.), *Special Topics in Multimedia, IoT and Web Technologies*,
https://doi.org/10.1007/978-3-030-35102-1_5

metamodel. This tool was built based on the theoretical, conceptual, and technological concepts presented in the previous sections. Finally, the final considerations
of the chapter are presented in Sect. 5.5.

## 5.2 Theoretical and Conceptual Foundations

This section presents the theoretical and conceptual foundations necessary for the
development of the graphic modeling tool.

### 5.2.1 Ubiquitous Computing

Weiser [68] envisioned the possibility of making the use of computing invisible and
ubiquitous to the user, merging it with everyday elements, meaning that the user did
not need to perceive the technology to take advantage of its benefits. According to
this concept, computing would be permeated in the objects of the user's physical
environment, not requiring traditional computing devices for interaction, such as
keyboard and mouse, for instance. In ubiquitous computing, the user's focus leaves
the computing device he manipulates and moves on to the task or action to be
performed.

It is extremely important that a ubiquitous environment supports mobility, i.e.,
keep the user's computational resources available while moving from one place
to another [35]. Ubiquitous computing systems are found in many domains. A
ubiquitous system for home health care (also known as homecare), for example,
can be used to identify an individual's daily physical activities or to assist in the
treatment of people, indicating the times for taking medications (e.g., [7, 55]),
among other functions related to health care. Ubiquitous learning systems can
enable the formation of groups of students to work together in solving a given
problem proposed by the teacher, each using his or her personal mobile device (e.g.,
[73]), or facilitating participation in virtual classrooms through voice recognition
and gestures (e.g., [50]).

Ubiquitous computing needs to rely on other concepts so that it can be fully
implemented, such as context-aware computing, smart spaces, and smart objects.
These concepts are presented in the following subsections.

### 5.2.2 Context-Aware Computing

In a ubiquitous computing scenario, a ubiquitous application must be minimally
intrusive, which requires a certain knowledge of its execution context, i.e., it must
be possible for the application to obtain information about the state of users and the
execution environment, enabling it to modify its behavior based on this information.

The term "context-aware" was first mentioned by Schilit and Theimer [47] as software that "adapts itself according to its location of use, the set of people and nearby objects, as well as the changes that these objects undergo over time." Chagas et al. [8] state that context-awareness allows "using relevant information about environmental entities to facilitate interaction between users and applications." The definition of context, within the scope of this chapter, is related to that proposed by Abowd et al. [1] and Dey [17]: any information that can be used to characterize the situation of a person, place, or object relevant to the interaction between a user and an application, including the latter two.

Changes in the model of a running software can be triggered by changes in the physical environment where the software is being executed. As an example, we can cite the temperature rise of a room, which causes the software responsible for monitoring that environment to activate the air conditioner. The running system, in this case, reacts to a captured context (temperature rise) and modifies its behavior (air conditioner activation).

## 5.2.3 Smart Spaces

The convergence of mobile technologies and the Internet, driven mainly by the popularization of devices and ease of access through third and fourth generation (3G and 4G) mobile connections, is making the world more connected and with more Internet access available. This, combined with the Web of Things (WoT) [24] and Internet of Things (IoT) [3], brings the potential to interconnect, monitor, and remotely control various everyday devices (TVs, locks, light switches, residential alarms, etc.) strengthening the concept of ubiquitous computing.

The decrease in ubiquitous computing environment scope mitigates integration issues, in particular, due to the possibility of providing some user behavior on the site. Smart spaces use this premise to instrument and design the environmental infrastructure as a means of establishing services to enable ubiquitous computing in a given environment. For instance, when it is needed to identify the entering and exiting of a user in a given room, the ubiquitous computing environment (i.e., smart space) is the room itself. So, this physical space can be added with sensors and actuators in order to provide the necessary means required to monitor user mobility.

Context-aware computing is made possible by smart spaces, as they enable the acquisition of knowledge about the environment and the adaptation of their participants in order to take better advantage of this environment [12]. To this end, the sensors monitor and collect data from the physical environment and certain actions are taken based on decisions made by a reasoning mechanism.

The reasoning mechanisms filter and manage the large amounts of information that pass through the smart spaces on a regular basis. The role of a reasoning mechanism is divided into two fronts: (1) model the collected information into useful abstract knowledge; and (2) reasoning over this knowledge to effectively support users' daily activities [12].

Smart spaces extend computing to physical environments and allow different devices to provide coordinated support to users based on their preferences and the current state of the physical environment (context) [52]. In other words, at a very high level of abstraction, smart spaces can be seen as ubiquitous computing environments that understand and react to human needs [35].

Lupiana et al. [35] analyzed the various definitions of smart spaces, given by different authors, to propose a more comprehensive definition:

> A highly integrated computational and sensory environment that effectively reasons about the physical and spatial user contexts to act transparently based on human desires.

The authors then provide further details on this definition, arguing that an environment is *highly integrated* when it is saturated with ubiquitous computing devices and sensors fully integrated with wireless networks; *effective reasoning* can be achieved by a pseudo-intelligent mechanism for the environment as a whole, and not just for individual devices or components; *user context* refers to individual profiles, policies, current location, and mobility status; and *transparency* is related to human actions and the mobility support without the need for direct user interaction.

Given the vast amount of information that can travel in a smart space, the many smart objects that make it up, and the possibility of entering and exiting users who carry their mobile devices, security is one of the critical aspects of these environments. In [2], the authors list a number of security requirements that smart spaces should be concerned with, including:

- Multi-level access, i.e., providing different levels of access according to pre-defined policies, the current situation of the smart space and the available resources.
- A descriptive, well-defined, flexible, and easy-to-configure access policy.
- Human user authentication, as well as mobile applications and devices that enter and leave the smart space.

Another important aspect to be considered in a smart space is user mobility. Smart spaces should support mobility and integrate computational techniques and devices to enable user interaction with the environment in a transparent and intuitive manner [35].

Research in the area of the smart spaces is quite robust. For more than a decade, researchers have been proposing solutions for the field, such as the work of Johanson and Fox [27], who propose the Event Heap, a collaborative workspace that extends the TSpaces, a tuple space presented by IBM Research [72], in which different applications can publish and receive events of their interest.

Coen et al. [11] present Metaglue, a Java-based programming language developed in the artificial intelligence laboratories of the Massachusetts Institute of Technology (MIT). The goal of Metaglue is to enable the development of smart space applications by supporting a number of specific needs of this type of application, such as interconnecting and managing heterogeneous hardware and software, adding, removing, modifying, and updating components in a system at runtime, as well as controlling the allocation of resources.

More recently, the works in the smart spaces field that have attracted attention are the open source initiatives: openHAB[1] and Smart-M3.[2] The openHAB (open Home Automation Bus) project aims to provide a universal integration platform for home automation. openHAB is a Java solution, completely based on OSGi,[3] which facilitates its goal of enabling the hardware interconnection from several vendors, even if they use different communication protocols. Smart-M3 is a platform that offers distributed applications a shared view of information and services present in ubiquitous environments, based on the blackboard architectural model. Smart spaces are seen as information providers and the applications that make up the smart spaces, in turn, produce and consume information.

The traditional smart spaces discussed in this subsection are referred in this chapter as *fixed smart spaces*. In distinction to them, the concept of *personal smart spaces* is presented as follows.

## 5.2.4  Personal Smart Spaces

There are several initiatives aimed at designing traditional smart spaces, or fixed smart spaces, such as the pioneers Gaia [41], Aura [53], Olympus [40], and the Gator Tech smart home [25]. There are also a number of other more recent works (e.g., [13, 21, 26]). However, all of these proposals focus on providing services in confined and geographically limited spaces, and have a system-centric perspective, in which users are external actors who are not contained in the smart space, i.e., users are merely located in the smart spaces, not being part of them [57]. This view contrasts with the original concept of calm computing introduced by Mark Weiser [69], who has the user as the center of computing.

In addition, programming only fixed smart spaces can lead to islands of ubiquity separated by empty spaces, where the support for ubiquitous computing is limited, as these do not allow devices and services to be shared with other smart spaces [14].

In contrast to traditional smart spaces, which are fixed and limited to a certain logical or physical area, a Personal Smart Space (PSS) is created based on the concepts of ubiquitous computing combined with a body network. The various sensors, actuators, and devices that a user carries constitute a body network [9, 33] and this, in turn, is supported by a software infrastructure designed for this purpose, making up their personal smart space [18].

In their work, Korbinian et al. [44] list the main properties of a PSS:

---

[1]http://www.openhab.org.

[2]http://sourceforge.net/projects/smart-m3/.

[3]http://www.osgi.org/Main/HomePage.

1. **The PSS is mobile**: unlike traditional smart space approaches, the physical boundaries of a PSS move with the user. This functionality enables it to overlap with other smart spaces (fixed or personal).
2. **The PSS has an "owner"**: the owner of a PSS is the person on whom the PSS operates. This enables the PSS to be customizable. The PSS preferences can be taken into account when resolving conflicts, for example, to set the best air conditioning temperature in a room based on the average preferences of the present users.
3. **The PSS should support an *ad-hoc* environment**: a PSS must be able to operate in structured and also *ad-hoc* network environments, promoting the PSS's use as a device integrator.
4. **The PSS must be able to adapt itself**: applications within a PSS must be able to adapt to the current situation. In addition, the PSS should facilitate the interaction of its applications with the environment.
5. **The PSS can learn from the previous interactions**: by mining the stored information, the PSS can detect trends and infer the conditions under which changes in user behavior or preferences are manifested. This allows recommendations to be made when PSS interacts with other PSS or even to act proactively based on the user's intentions.

The first two features allow the PSS to follow its *owner*, being always available and allowing the interaction with other smart spaces, either fixed or personal [56].

Features four and five enable self-improvement, one of the primary objectives of a PSS. Self-improvement is the learning of trends in user behavior, enabling recommendations and predictions so that adaptations to the environment can be made automatically for the user [22]. Thus, context-awareness is a crucial aspect of the proper functioning of a PSS.

A multitude of context sources provide data that needs to be collected, disseminated, and managed efficiently, such as information related to user location and activities, movement patterns, temperature, ambient noise level, among others [45]. In [43], the authors present the characteristics of a context management for personal smart spaces, a component built based on a set of specific requirements for PSS, such as: (1) management of context sources; (2) modeling, managing, storing, and processing of historical context information; and (3) event management mechanisms.

A recent proposal for smart space modeling was presented in [64] and considers the concept of personal smart spaces explored by the PERSIST (Personal Self-Improving Smart Spaces) project [18], which presents the view that personal smart spaces provide an interface between the user and the various services and devices available. This way, a user's personal smart space, composed of smart objects (sensors, actuators, and other devices) that the user carries, can interact with other smart spaces, be they personal or fixed.

The concept of personal smart spaces is considered as an alternative so that computer services are always available to the user, regardless of their movement through environments, minimizing the problem of ubiquitous islands.

## 5.2.5  Smart Objects

The continuous miniaturization of computing devices and the emergence of technologies such as RFID (Radio-Frequency IDentification) have enabled the tracking of everyday objects in confined environments, such as stores or warehouses.

Smart objects are an evolution of these "traceable objects." In this concept, the smart objects are physical/digital entities, increased with sensing, processing, and networking capabilities [32]. A smart object can perceive its environment through sensors and communicate with other nearby objects. These capabilities enable smart objects to work collaboratively to determine context and adapt their behavior [51].

Unlike RFID tags, smart objects can "feel," record, and interpret what is happening to themselves and to the physical environment, act on their own, communicate with other smart objects, and exchange information with people [32].

However, smart objects do not only refer to everyday non-digital objects. Traditional computing devices, such as smartphones, PDAs, music players, etc. can have or be increased with sensitive technologies, such as sensors, actuators, and perception algorithms [28].

Kawsar [28] argues that a smart object must exhibit certain properties to ensure its full functioning and interaction with other smart objects, such as:

- **Unique ID**: it is essential to be able to uniquely identify smart objects in the digital world. The identification can be the network interface address or the application level address, considering the appropriate naming resolution service.
- **Self-awareness**: a smart object is expected to be able to know its operational and situational state, in addition to being able to describe itself.
- **Sociability**: a smart object must be able to communicate with other smart objects and computational entities (e.g., a context-aware application) to share its self-awareness.
- **Autonomy**: a smart object must be able to take certain actions. These actions can be as simple as changing its operating state (e.g., changing from turned off to turned on) or as complex as adapting its behavior through autonomous decision-making.

## 5.2.6  Model-Driven Engineering

The concept of Model-Driven Engineering (MDE) considers that models are the main artifacts in the development of a system. According to this approach, models do not only serve to describe or document a software, but also to act on its development, maintenance, and operation [48, 49]. A model is a high-level graphic or textual representation of a system, where each of its elements is a virtual representation of a component present in the real system. The relationships and abstractions used in a model are described by a metamodel [67]. Metamodels are generally built to allow the creation of models that express specific concepts of a domain such as electric power distribution systems (called microgrids) [46], CrowdSensing [36], Software Product Lines [6, 20], or ubiquitous computing scenarios [64].

MDE techniques such as Model-Driven Development (MDD) and Model-Driven Architecture (MDA) propose the use of abstractions closer to the problem domain as a means to mitigate the existing semantic gap between the problem to be solved and the tool (software) used for such.

The emphasis on the integration between the technological part and the specific knowledge of a given domain is an important aspect of the MDE [19], and the use of its principles increases the quality of software systems, the degree of reuse, and, as an implicit result, the efficiency in their development [4].

Given the models' popularity, came the need for a standardization for the construction of metamodels and models. Thus, the Object Management Group (OMG)[4] presented a four-layer metamodel architecture, called Meta-Object Facility (MOF). In MOF, each element of a lower layer is an instance of an element of an upper layer, as illustrated in Fig. 5.1.

The MOF layers can be described as follows [49]:

- **M3 layer**: represents the MOF meta-metamodel, also called MOF Model, used to create metamodels. The MOF model formalizes its own abstractions, eliminating

**Fig. 5.1** MOF metamodeling architecture layers. Adapted from [67]

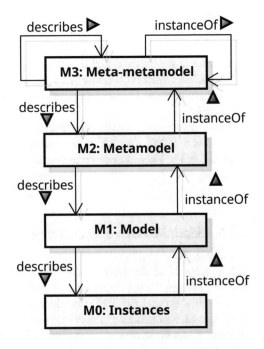

[4]http://www.omg.org.

the need for a higher level. Another example of a member of this layer is Ecore, which is based on MOF.

- **M2 layer**: contains the metamodels that can be used to model specific domain systems. The Unified Modeling Language (UML) is a member example of this layer.
- **M1 layer**: composed of models that describe systems using the definitions contained in their respective metamodels present in M2.
- **M0 layer**: contains the entities or objects that form the runtime system, which is created from the definitions present in M1.

A metamodel can be considered a Domain-Specific Modeling Language (DSML). A DSML is "a textual or graphical language that provides, through appropriate notations and abstractions, expressive power with a focus on a particular problem domain, to visualize, specify, construct, and document artifacts of a software system" [10, 63].

Similar to any language, DSMLs have two main components [20]: syntax and semantics. The syntax of a DSML can be divided into abstract syntax and concrete syntax. The abstract syntax defines its concepts and the relationships between them, while the concrete syntax maps these concepts into visual elements that are used in models. The semantics of a DSML is the meaning of the syntax representations. The abstract syntax is the most important component of a DSML. "It is usual to find DSMLs without formal definitions of their semantics or without a concrete representation, but their abstract syntax is imperative" [20].

In [29], the authors specify a series of general requirements (from 1 to 7) and additional requirements (8 and 9) for building domain-specific languages, as follows:

1. **Compliance**: the constructions must match important concepts of the domain.
2. **Orthogonality**: each language construct should be used to represent exactly one distinct concept of the domain.
3. **Support**: it is important to support the language through tools for modeling and programming management, e.g., code creation, editing and model transformation.
4. **Integration**: the language, and its tools, can be used together with other languages and tools with minimal effort.
5. **Longevity**: it is assumed with this requirement that the domain under consideration persists for a sufficient period of time to justify the construction of the language and its tools.
6. **Simplicity**: a language should be as simple as possible.
7. **Quality**: the language should provide mechanisms for building quality systems.
8. **Scalability**: the language should provide constructs to help manage large-scale descriptions, as well as allowing for the construction of smaller systems.
9. **Usability**: this requirement concerns concepts such as economy, accessibility, and comprehensibility. These characteristics can be partially covered by the general requirements, e.g., simplicity can help in promoting comprehensibility.

## 5.3   Technological Foundation

The following subsections describe the technological concepts involved in the construction of metamodels and in the implementation of their graphic modeling tools.

### 5.3.1   Eclipse Modeling Framework (EMF)

The Eclipse Modeling Framework (EMF) [54] is a modeling framework built on top of the Eclipse Integrated Development Environment (IDE). Widely used (e.g., [23, 34, 38, 64–66]), EMF provides mechanisms for the creation, editing and validation of models and metamodels, in addition to allowing the generation of code from the models. For such, EMF allows the generation of an implementation in Java language, so that each one of the classes of the metamodel (called metaclasses) corresponds to a Java class. This way, these classes can be instantiated to create models in accordance with the metamodel. The EMF also allows creating editors for models in accordance with their metamodels.

The metamodels built in EMF are instances of the Ecore meta-metamodel which, in turn, is based on the MOF meta-metamodel. Thus, Ecore is the central language of EMF [54]. An Ecore based metamodel is defined through instances of: `EClass`, `EAttribute`, `EReference`, `ESuperType`, and `EDataType`. A `EClass` represents a class composed of attributes and references. A `EAttribute` is an attribute that has a name and a type. A `EReference` defines an association between classes and, in the case of a superclass definition, to make use of inheritance concepts, this association is of `ESuperType`. Finally, a `EDataType` is the type of an attribute, whose value can be a primitive type (integer or real number, string, Boolean, etc.), an enumeration `EEnum`, or a reference to a `EClass`.

Figure 5.2 presents an overview of the Ecore meta-metamodel components [37], with their attributes, operations, and relationships. Following is a short description of the elements that compose it:

- `EClass`: models classes. Classes are identified by a name and can contain a number of features, i.e., attributes and references. To enable inheritance support, a class can refer to another class as its supertype. Multiple inheritance is also allowed, in which case different classes are referred to as supertypes. A class can be abstract and thus its instance cannot be created. If a class is defined as an interface, its implementation is not created during code generation.
- `EAttribute`: models attributes, are identified by a name, and have a type. Upper and lower bounds are specified for the attribute multiplicity.
- `EDataType`: models simple types whose structure is not modeled. They act as wrappers that denote a primitive type or an object type defined in Java. They are identified by a name and are most often used as attribute types.

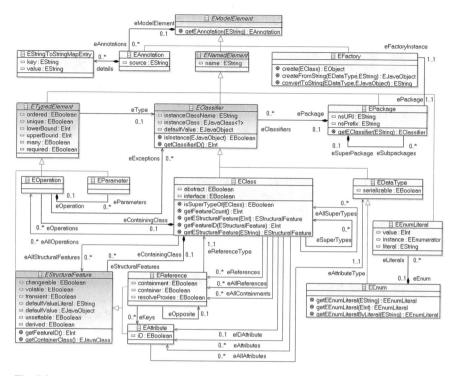

**Fig. 5.2** Ecore meta-metamodel [37]

- **EReference:** models one end of an association between two classes. They are identified by a name and a type, where the type represents the class at the other end of the association. Bidirectionality is supported by pairing a reference with its opposite, i.e., a reference in the class representing the other end of the association. Lower and upper bounds are specified in the reference to denote their multiplicity. A reference can support a strong type of association, called containment, similar to UML's "composition" type association.
- **EModelElement:** models the elements of an Ecore model. It is the abstract root of an Ecore class hierarchy.
- **EPackage:** models packages, containers for classifiers, i.e., classes and data types. A package name does not have to be unique, because its namespace URI is used to identify it. This URI is used in serializing instance documents, along with the namespace prefix, to identify the instance package.
- **EFactory:** models factories for creating object instances. Factories allow the creation of operations to instantiate classes and to convert data values to strings and vice versa.

- EAnnotation: models annotations to associate additional information to a model element.
- EClassifier: models the types of values. It is the common base class for data types and for classes that serve as types of a typed element and is, therefore, the common basis for attributes, references, operations, and parameters.
- ENamedElement: shapes named elements. Most elements in Ecore are models that are identified by a name and therefore extend this class.
- ETypedElement: models typed elements, e.g., attributes, references, parameters, and operations. All typed elements have an associated multiplicity specified by their lower bounds (lowerBound) and upper bounds (upperBound). An undefined lower bound is specified by the -1 value or the ETypedElement.UNBOUNDED _MULTIPLICITY constant.
- EStructuralFeature: models the features that have values in a class. It is the common base class for attributes and references. The following Boolean attributes are used to characterize attributes and references:

  - Changed: indicates whether the feature value can be changed.
  - Derived: indicates whether the value of the feature is to be computed using other related features.
  - Transient: indicates whether the feature value is omitted from the object's persistent serialization.
  - Unsettable: indicates whether the feature value has an undefined state, as opposed to the state that can be defined by any specific value.
  - Volatile: indicates whether the feature does not have a generated storage field in its implementation class.

- EOperation: models operations that can be invoked in a specific class. An operation is defined by a name and a list of zero or more typed parameters, representing its signature. As with all typed elements, an operation specifies a type, which represents its return type, that can be null to represent no return value. An operation can also specify zero or more exceptions specified as classifiers that can represent the types of exceptions that can be thrown.
- EParameter: models an operation's input parameter. A parameter is identified by a name and, like all typed elements, specifies a type, which represents the value type that can be passed as an argument corresponding to that parameter.
- EEnumLiteral: models the members of the literal values enumeration set. A literal enumeration is identified by a name and has an associated integer value, as well as a literal value used during the serialization. The literal value is its own name if this value is null.
- EEnum: models enumeration types, which specify enumeration sets of literal values.

## 5.3.2   Eclipse Graphical Modeling Framework (GMF)

The Eclipse Graphical Modeling Framework (GMF)[5] is a framework based on the Eclipse IDE, which allows the construction of graphical editors to create models that conform to a specific metamodel.

GMF requires that some specific models be created to enable the generation of a graphical editor:

- The **graphic model** (GMFGraph) specifies the graphical elements (shapes, connections, labels, decorations, etc.) used in the editor.
- The **tool model** (GMFTool) specifies the tools for creating elements that will be available in the editor palette.
- The **mapping model** (GMFMap) maps the graphical elements in the graphical model and the building tools in the tool model with the abstract syntax of Ecore's metamodel elements. (classes, attributes, references, etc.)

Once the three models mentioned above have been created, GMF offers features for M2M (model-to-model) transformations to create the generator model (GMFGen), which offers additional customizations for the editor. Then, finally, M2T (model-to-text) transformations produce a new project (.diagram), which contains code in Java language for the editor's instantiation. GMF offers a wizard, called GMF dashboard and presented in Fig. 5.3, for semi-automatic generation of the initial versions of the required models. Figure 5.4 offers an overview of the process of creating these models, in the form of a UML Activity Diagram.

Generated models may require minor customizations. Such customizations are made by manually editing the templates with the help of a text editor or tree editor, both EMF native. Figure 5.5 shows the edition of the GMFMap model using the tree

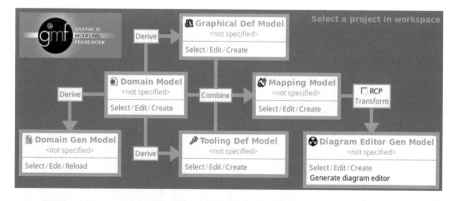

**Fig. 5.3**  GMF dashboard: wizard for creating GMF models

---

[5]https://www.eclipse.org/gmf-tooling/.

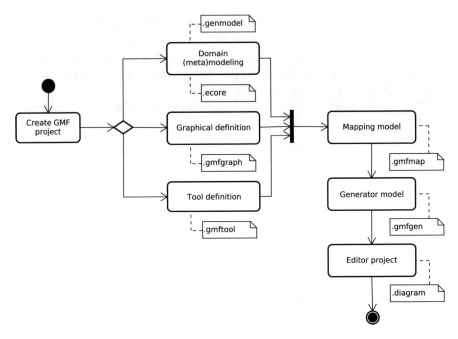

**Fig. 5.4** Process of creating GMF models. Adapted from [62]

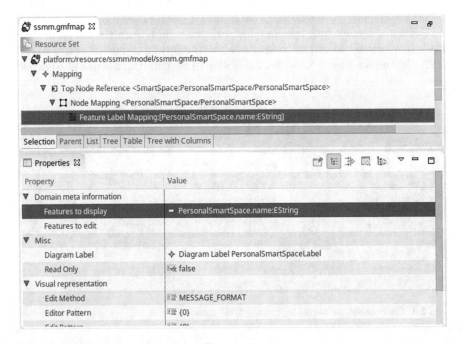

**Fig. 5.5** GMFMap editing using the tree editor

```
 ssmm.gmfmap ⊠                                                              ▭  ◧
 1 <?xml version="1.0" encoding="ASCII"?>
 2 <gmfmap:Mapping
 3     xmi:version="2.0"
 4     xmlns:xmi="http://www.omg.org/XMI"
 5     xmlns:xsi="http://www.w3.org/2001/XMLSchema-instance"
 6     xmlns:ecore="http://www.eclipse.org/emf/2002/Ecore"
 7     xmlns:gmfmap="http://www.eclipse.org/gmf/2008/mappings"
 8     xmlns:gmftool="http://www.eclipse.org/gmf/2005/ToolDefinition">
 9   <nodes>
10     <containmentFeature
11         href="ssmm.ecore#//SmartSpaceDiagram/SmartSpace"/>
12     <ownedChild>
13       <domainMetaElement
14           href="ssmm.ecore#//PersonalSmartSpace"/>
15       <labelMappings
16           xsi:type="gmfmap:FeatureLabelMapping"
17           viewPattern="{0}"
18           editorPattern="{0}"
19           editPattern="{0}">
20         <diagramLabel
21             href="ssmm.gmfgraph#PersonalSmartSpaceLabel"/>
22         <features
23             href="ssmm.ecore#//PersonalSmartSpace/name"/>
24       </labelMappings>
25       <tool
```

**Fig. 5.6** GMFMap editing using the text editor

editor, while Fig. 5.6 shows the model's edition using the text editor. Additionally, with each change in the Ecore metamodel, all GMF models must be regenerated, as the GMF does not offer mechanisms to update its models automatically, unlike the EMF [30].

### 5.3.3 Epsilon

Epsilon[6] is the acronym for Extensible Platform of Integrated Languages for mOdel maNagement [31]. It is a family of widely used languages and tools to support model manipulation activities (e.g., [5, 42, 64–66, 71]), such as code generation, transformation, comparison, joining, refactoring, and model validation.

The following languages constitute Epsilon: Epsilon Object Language (EOL); Epsilon Validation Language (EVL); Epsilon Transformation Language (ETL); Epsilon Comparison Language (ECL); Epsilon Merging Language (EML); Epsilon Wizard Language (EWL); Epsilon Generation Language (EGL); and Epsilon Flock.

For each of these languages, there are development tools based on the Eclipse IDE that offer features such as syntax highlighting and error handling, as well

---

[6]https://www.eclipse.org/epsilon/.

as an interpreter for the language. Epsilon language interpreters can even run independently in Java or Android applications [31], through their Application Programming Interface (API),[7] enabling their use in applications that were not built using the Epsilon development environment.

The following subsections describe the EOL and EVL, in addition to the Eugenia tool, which also composes the Epsilon family. These technologies are used in the construction of the graphical modeling tool, the focus of this chapter. Detailed information on the Epsilon languages can be found at [31].

### 5.3.4   Epsilon Object Language (EOL)

The EOL[8] is the core language of the Epsilon family. All the other languages in this family extend EOL, both in syntax and semantics. Thus, EOL offers a set of functionalities over which the other languages are implemented. In addition, EOL can be used independently, as a general-purpose language for model management, automating tasks that are not specific to other family languages, such as creating, consulting, and modifying EMF models [31].

Among the main characteristics of EOL, the following stand out [59]:

- presence of common constructions in programming, such as while and for loops, variables, etc.;
- possibility to create and make calls to Java object methods;
- support for dynamic addition of metaclasses operations at runtime;
- user interaction support;
- possibility of creating libraries to be imported and used in other Epsilon languages.

Programs written in EOL are organized in modules, as illustrated by Fig. 5.7. Each module defines a body and a number of operations. The body is a block of statements that are evaluated when the module is executed. Each operation defines the type of object to which it is applicable (context), a name, a set of parameters, and an optional return type. Modules can also import other modules.

Besides allowing the construction of operations, the EOL language also offers a series of operations previously defined for each one of its data types, presented in Fig. 5.8, besides allowing the use of native types, defined by the user in his base language, for example, a Java class. Listing 5.1 presents an example of EOL language usage to calculate and print the depth of each tree [31].

---

[7]https://www.eclipse.org/epsilon/download/.

[8]https://www.eclipse.org/epsilon/doc/eol/.

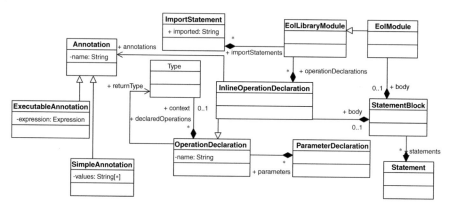

**Fig. 5.7** Module structure of the EOL language [31]

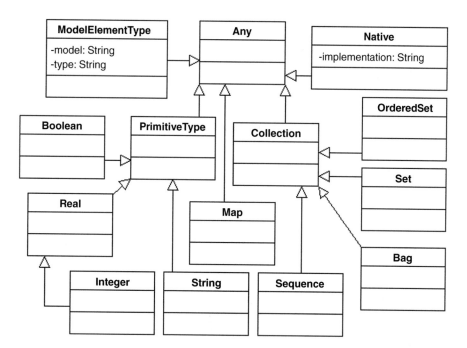

**Fig. 5.8** Overview of the EOL data type system [31]

**Listing 5.1  Example of code in EOL language usage**

```
var depths = new Map;

for (n in Tree.allInstances.select(t|not
    t.parent.isDefined())) {
    n.setDepth(0);
}

for (n in Tree.allInstances) {
    (n.name + " " + depths.get(n)).println();
}

operation Tree setDepth(depth : Integer) {
    depths.put(||self||,depth);
    for (c in ||self||.children) {
        c.setDepth(depth + 1);
    }
}
```

### 5.3.5  Epsilon Validation Language (EVL)

The aim of the EVL[9] is to offer validation features to the Epsilon family. In this way, EVL can be used to specify and evaluate constraints—also called invariants—in models of a specific metamodel. Restrictions written in EVL are similar to OCL (Object Constraint Language) restrictions [39]; however, the EVL language also supports dependencies between constraints (e.g., if constraint A fails, then do not evaluate constraint B), customizable error messages, and the specification of quick fixes that can be triggered to fix inconsistencies [60].

The main characteristics of the EVL language are [60]:

- distinction between errors and warnings during validation;
- quick fixes specification for errors found by restrictions;
- presence of the functionalities offered by the EOL language;
- support for first-order logic operations from OCL (`select`, `reject`, `collect`, etc.);
- user interaction support.

---

[9]https://www.eclipse.org/epsilon/doc/evl/.

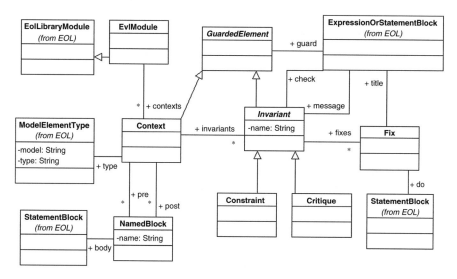

**Fig. 5.9** EVL abstract syntax [31]

In EVL, the validations are organized in modules (EvlModule). In addition to operations, an EVL module can also contain a set of invariants grouped by the context in which they will be applied, along with a number of previous (pre) and posterior (post) blocks. Figure 5.9 illustrates the abstract syntax elements of the EVL language, described below:

- Context: a context specifies the type of instances on which invariants will be assessed. Each context can optionally define a guard that limits its applicability to a smaller subset of instances of a specified type. Thus, if a guard fails for an instance of a specific type, none of its invariants is evaluated.
- Invariant: as in OCL, each EVL invariant defines a name and a body (check). However, it can optionally set a guard. As a way of providing feedback to the user, each invariant can define a message that contains a description of why each constraint has failed on a particular element. To allow semi-automatic bug fixes, an invariant can optionally define one or more (fixes), handled in Eclipse as *"quick fixes."* Each invariant can be a constraint or critique, allowing you to launch *error* or *warning* messages, respectively.
- Guard: guards are used to limit the applicability of invariants.
- Fix: allows semi-automatic correction of errors found during validation. It is possible to define a title and a do block, where the fix functionality will be defined using the EOL language.
- Constraint: restrictions in EVL are used to capture critical errors that invalidate the model. Constraints are a subclass of invariant, thus inheriting all of their characteristics.

- Critique: in distinction to constraints, critiques are used to capture situations that do not invalidate the model, but should be considered to improve its quality. Like constraints, it is a subclass of invariant.
- Pre and Post: contains EOL statements that can be performed before (pre) or after (post) the evaluation of invariants.

To illustrate a usage of an EVL rule, let us suppose that our (already constructed) metamodel allows the modeling of fixed smart spaces and that each of these can have other fixed smart spaces within itself (i.e., sub-fixed smart spaces). However, we need to prevent the fixed smart spaces from having itself as sub-fixed smart space, because it makes no sense. The Listing 5.2 presents an example of an EVL rule that prevents a particular metaclass from having a self-reference, suggesting as *quick fix* deleting the self-referencing found, as illustrated in Fig. 5.10.

**Listing 5.2  Example of code in EVL to prevent self-referencing in a given metaclass**

```
context HasSubFSS {
      constraint CannotSelfReference {
            check : ||self||.source.name <>
                  ||self||.target.at(0).name
            message : 'Cannot make a self reference'
         fix {
           title : "Delete self reference"
           do {
             delete ||self||;
           }
         }
      }
}
```

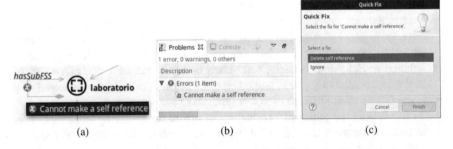

(a)                              (b)                              (c)

**Fig. 5.10** (a) Error found in the model by a rule written in EVL language; (b) Error description; (c) Quick fix suggestion

## 5.3.6 Eugenia

Eugenia[10] is a tool of the Epsilon family that automatically generates the GMFGraph, GMFTool, and GMFMap models, which are necessary for the implementation of a GMF editor, using an annotated Ecore metamodel written in Emfatic[11] language as basis. The Emfatic language allows the representation of Ecore metamodels in textual form and has a syntax similar to the Java language [15, 30]. The Epsilon IDE has features that allow the transformation of Ecore models into Emfatic code and vice versa.

Eugenia's main goal is to reduce the complexity of creating GMF-based graphical modeling tools through high-level annotations made directly on the Emfatic code [16]. Wienands and Golm [70] conducted an industrial experiment and concluded that implementing a graphical editor using pure EMF and GMF is an error-prone process, mainly because it requires developers to write and maintain, at a low level, a series of complex relationships between GMF models. Besides, "more challenging than building a GMF editor, is its maintainability, since GMF, unlike EMF, does not offer mechanisms to update your models automatically when the metamodel is modified" [30].

Eugenia enables automated transformations between annotated Emfatic code, which represents the metamodel, and the low-level models needed to generate the GMF tool, increasing the level of abstraction at which developers must work to build their graphic tools for model editing based on a metamodel [30]. In short, Eugenia offers six categories of annotations [30], which are used in Emfatic codes to guide the creation of the graphical modeling tool. The attributes supported in each type of annotation and their respective list of values will not be covered here; however, they can be obtained from [61]. Below is the list of annotations supported by Eugenia:

- `@gmf.diagram`: specifies the diagram settings, such as the root element type of the template and the file extension of the graphical editor;
- `@gmf.node`: indicates which elements of the abstract syntax will represent nodes (vertices) in the graphical syntax, plus their shape, color, size, label, etc.;
- `@gmf.link`: indicates which elements of the abstract syntax will represent edges in the graphical syntax, in addition to specifying their thickness, color, style, type of arrowheads, labels, etc.;
- `@gmf.compartment`: indicates which nodes can be nested within other nodes in the graphical syntax (e.g., attributes are nested within classes in a UML Class Diagram);
- `@gmf.affixed`: indicates which nodes should be attached to the edge of other nodes in the graphical syntax;
- `@gmf.label`: specifies additional labels for a node in the graphical syntax.

---

[10]https://www.eclipse.org/epsilon/doc/eugenia/.

[11]https://www.eclipse.org/epsilon/doc/articles/emfatic/.

Listing 5.3 brings the Emfatic code of a metamodel to represent file systems [61]. Through this code and its annotations, it is possible to generate a fully functional GMF editor using the Eugenia tool, which is shown in Fig. 5.11.

**Listing 5.3  Emfatic language code of a file system metamodel [61]**

```
@namespace(uri="filesystem", prefix="filesystem")
@gmf
package filesystem;

@gmf.diagram
class Filesystem {
    val Drive[*] drives;
    val Sync[*] syncs;
}

class Drive extends Folder {}

class Folder extends File {
    @gmf.compartment
    val File[*] contents;
}

class Shortcut extends File {
    @gmf.link(target.decoration="arrow", style="dash")
    ref File target;
}

@gmf.link(source="source", target="target",
    style="dot", width="2")
class Sync {
    ref File source;
    ref File target;
}

@gmf.node(label = "name")
class File {
    attr String name;
}
```

Finally, Eugenia allows to make fine adjustments to the appearance of the modeling tool by defining transformation rules in independent models (e.g., ECore2GMF.eol) using the EOL language. These models' rules are executed soon after the derivation of the GMF models by Eugenia. Thus, as opposed to what happens when working directly with GMF, it is not necessary to make adjustments to the appearance of the tool whenever there are new changes in the metamodel.

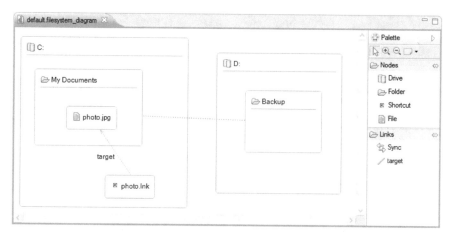

**Fig. 5.11** GMF editor generated with Eugenia tool support [61]

Listing 5.4 presents the contents of the `ECore2GMF.eol` file, whose objective is to remove the edges of the pictures in the models generated in a GMF editor, which was implemented with the support of the Eugenia tool.

**Listing 5.4  Code in EOL language (`ECore2GMF.eol`) to remove the edges of model pictures, in a GMF editor created with the Eugenia support [58]**

```
-- Find the attribute figure
var attributeFigure = GmfGraph!Rectangle.all.
    selectOne(r|r.name = 'AttributeFigure');

-- ... delete its border
delete attributeFigure.border;
```

## 5.4   A Graphical Modeling Tool for Ubiquitous Computing Scenarios

This section presents a graphical modeling tool for ubiquitous computing scenarios, to enable the creation of models in accordance with the metamodel of [64], presented in Fig. 5.12.

The graphics editor was implemented using the Eclipse Graphical Modeling Framework (GMF). The graphics editor was enhanced with the use of Epsilon family languages and its construction was supported by the Eugenia tool, which also integrates the Epsilon family. The technologies used in this subsection were presented in Sects. 5.3.2 and 5.3.3. The source codes presented here are only excerpts.

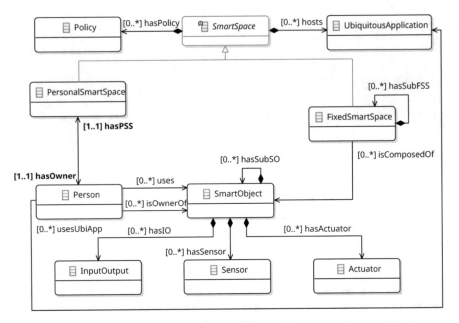

**Fig. 5.12** Metamodel proposed for modeling scenarios composed of personal and fixed smart spaces [64]

Figure 5.13 presents the modeling tool used to configure a ubiquitous computing scenario. The tool window is divided into two parts: (1) and (2). In (1) there is a reserved area for the construction of the model. In (2) are the icons that represent the metamodel concepts, grouped in a toolbar (or palette). The toolbar is divided into two parts: (a) tools for creating elements, i.e., instances of the types defined in the metamodel; and (b) tools for creating associations between the elements.

Models built using the modeling tool can be saved in two XML files with different extensions: .ssmm and .ssmmd. The .ssmm file represents the instance of the metamodel and contains the elements, their attributes and the associations between the elements; the .ssmmd file, on the other hand, is used to indicate the position of each element and association in the graphical diagram, so that its positions are preserved when closing and reopening the model.

The modeling tool allows the validation of the model built to ensure its conformity with its metamodel. If any inconsistency is found, it is pointed out, allowing its correction. To extend the models' validation, rules were defined using the EVL (Epsilon Validation Language) language, allowing to increase the syntactic rules defined by the metamodel with additional restrictions. Table 5.1 presents the EVL rules that were implemented.

Listing 5.5 presents rules RV1, RV3 and part of rule RV4: rule RV1 requires the element to have a name; rule RV3 prevents elements of the same type from having the same names; the excerpt of rule RV4 presented prevents self-referencing to elements of FixedSmartSpace type, that is, prevents an FSS

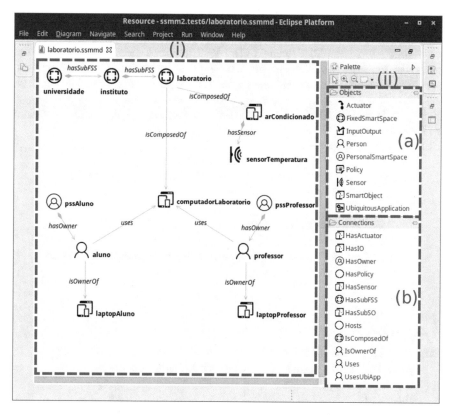

**Fig. 5.13** Modeling tool used to build a ubiquitous computing scenario

**Table 5.1** EVL rules implemented in the graphical modeling tool

| Rule | Type | Description | Element to which it applies | Quick fix(es) |
|------|------|-------------|-----------------------------|---------------|
| RV1 | Error | The element must have a defined name | All | Name the element |
| RV2 | Warn. | The element name must start with a lowercase letter | All | (a) Suggests the name with lowercase initial; (b) Option to rename the element |
| RV3 | Error | There can be no other element of the same type with the same name | All | Option to rename the element |
| RV4 | Error | There can be no self-referencing for the element | `FixedSmartSpace`, `SmartObject` | Remove self-reference |

from being contained in itself. Quick fixes have been defined (indicated in the code by the fix block) which, when activated, perform the correction of the error found in a simplified manner. The RV3 quick fix prompts to enter a new name for the duplicate element and then applies the new name to the element. RV4's quick fix deletes the self-referencing for the node, as presented in Fig. 5.14.

**Listing 5.5  EVL rules: RV1, RV3 and part of RV4 rule**

```
//RV1 rule
constraint HasName {
   check : ||self||.name.isDefined()
   message : 'Unnamed ' + ||self||.eClass().name + '
      not allowed'
   fix {
      title : 'Set a name...'
      do {
         ||self||.name := System.user.prompt('Please
            enter a name');
      }
   }
}
//RV3 rule
constraint CheckUniqueName {
   guard : not ||self||.~checked.isDefined()

   check {
      var others := Actuator.all.select(c|c.name =
         ||self||.name and c <> ||self||);
      if (others.size() > 0) {
         for (other in others) {
            other.~checked := true;
         }
         return false;
      } else {
         return true;
      }
   }
      message : 'Duplicated ' + ||self||.eClass().name
         + ' name'
   fix {
      title : 'Rename...'
      do {
         ||self||.name := System.user.prompt('Please
            enter a new name', ||self||.name);
      }
   }
}
```

```
//RV4 rule (partial)
context HasSubFSS {
    constraint CannotSelfReference {
        check : ||self||.source.name <>
            ||self||.target.at(0).name
        message : 'Cannot make a self reference'
        fix {
            title : "Delete self reference"
            do {
                delete ||self||;
            }
        }
    }
}
```

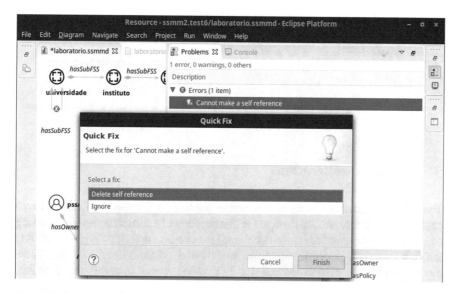

**Fig. 5.14** Suggestion of quick fix for self-referencing not allowed by EVL rules

Finally, fine adjustments were made to the modeling tool to improve the appearance of element labels and associations between the elements of the built models, with the aim of facilitating the reading of the models and avoiding confusion between association labels and element labels. Thus, two rules were written in EOL (Epsilon Object Language) to (1) change the association labels to italics and (2) change the element labels to bold. Listing 5.6 presents the rule that changes the associations' labels to italics.

**Listing 5.6  Transformation rules written in EOL language to stylize the modeling tool**

```
for (c in GmfGraph!Label.all) {
      if(c.name = 'HasActuatorLabelLabel' or
         c.name = 'HasIOLabelLabel' or
         c.name =
            'PersonalSmartSpaceHasOwnerExternalLabel'
            or
         c.name = 'HasPolicyLabelLabel' or
         c.name = 'HasSensorLabelLabel' or
         c.name = 'HasSubFSSLabelLabel' or
         c.name = 'HasSubSOLabelLabel' or
         c.name = 'HostsLabelLabel' or
         c.name =
            'FixedSmartSpaceIsComposedOfExternalLabel'
            or
         c.name = 'PersonIsOwnerOfExternalLabel' or
         c.name = 'PersonUsesExternalLabel' or
         c.name = 'PersonUsesUbiAppExternalLabel'){
         c.font = new GmfGraph!BasicFont;
         c.font.style = GmfGraph!FontStyle#ITALIC;
      }
}
```

## 5.5  Final Considerations

This chapter aims not only to introduce readers to the area of model-driven engineering but also to train them in the construction of a complete model, involving since the conception of the metamodel until the construction of a graphic modeling tool with which it is possible to build models derived from its metamodel. These models can then be used to document and maintain systems from different domains.

## References

1. Abowd, G.D., Dey, A.K., Brown, P.J., Davies, N., Smith, M., Steggles, P.: Towards a better understanding of context and context-awareness. In: Handheld and Ubiquitous Computing, pp. 304–307. Springer, Berlin (1999)
2. Al-Muhtadi, J., Ranganathan, A., Campbell, R., Mickunas, M.D.: Cerberus: a context-aware security scheme for smart spaces. In: Proceedings of the First IEEE International Conference on Pervasive Computing and Communications (PerCom 2003), pp. 489–496. IEEE, New York (2003)

3. Atzori, L., Iera, A., Morabito, G.: The Internet of Things: a survey. Comput. Netw. **54**(15), 2787–2805 (2010). http://dx.doi.org/10.1016/j.comnet.2010.05.010

4. Bézivin, J., Jouault, F., Touzet, D.: Principles, standards and tools for model engineering. In: Proceedings. 10th IEEE International Conference on Engineering of Complex Computer Systems, ICECCS 2005, pp. 28–29. IEEE, Piscataway (2005)

5. Biffl, S., Maetzler, E., Wimmer, M., Lueder, A., Schmidt, N.: Linking and versioning support for automationML: a model-driven engineering perspective. In: 2015 IEEE 13th International Conference on Industrial Informatics (INDIN), pp. 499–506. IEEE, Piscataway (2015)

6. Carvalho, S.T.: Modelagem de Linha de Produto de Software Dinâmica para Aplicações Ubíquas. Ph.D. Thesis, Universidade Federal Fluminense, Niterói (2013)

7. Carvalho, S.T., Copetti, A., Loques Filho, O.G.: Sistema de computação ubíqua na assistência domiciliar à saúde. J. Health Inform. **3**(2), 51–57 (2011)

8. Chagas, J., Ferraz, C., Alves, A.P., Carvalho, G.: Sensibilidade a contexto na gestão eficiente de energia elétrica. In: Simpósio Brasileiro de Redes de Computadores e Sistemas Distribuídos. Anais do XXVIII Simpósio Brasileiro de Redes de Computadores e Sistemas Distribuídos. Gramado: UFRGS pp. 145–158 (2010)

9. Chen, M., Gonzalez, S., Vasilakos, A., Cao, H., Leung, V.: Body area networks: a survey. Mobile Netw. Appl. **16**(2), 171–193 (2011). http://dx.doi.org/10.1007/s11036-010-0260-8

10. Chiprianov, V., Kermarrec, Y., Rouvrais, S., Simonin, J.: Extending enterprise architecture modeling languages for domain specificity and collaboration: application to telecommunication service design. Softw. Syst. Model. **13**(3), 963–974 (2014). http://dx.doi.org/10.1007/s10270-012-0298-0

11. Coen, M.H., Phillips, B., Warshawsky, N., Weisman, L., Peters, S., Finin, P.: Meeting the computational needs of intelligent environments: The metaglue system. In: Managing Interactions in Smart Environments, pp. 201–212. Springer, Berlin (2000)

12. Cook, D.J., Das, S.K.: How smart are our environments? An updated look at the state of the art. Pervasive Mob. Comput. **3**(2), 53–73 (2007)

13. Corredor, I., Bernardos, A.M., Iglesias, J., Casar, J.R.: Model-driven methodology for rapid deployment of smart spaces based on resource-oriented architectures. Sensors **12**(7), 9286–9335 (2012)

14. Crotty, M., Taylor, N., Williams, H., Frank, K., Roussaki, I., Roddy, M.: A pervasive environment based on personal self-improving smart spaces. In: Gerhäuser, H., Hupp, J., Efstratiou, C., Heppner, J. (eds.) Constructing Ambient Intelligence. Communications in Computer and Information Science, vol. 32, pp. 58–62. Springer, Berlin (2009). https://doi.org/10.1007/978-3-642-10607-1_10

15. Daly, C., The Eclipse Foundation: Emfatic language reference (2015). https://www.eclipse.org/epsilon/doc/articles/emfatic/

16. Daly, C., The Eclipse Foundation: EuGENia (2015). https://www.eclipse.org/epsilon/doc/eugenia/

17. Dey, A.K.: Understanding and using context. Pers. Ubiquit. Comput. **5**(1), 4–7 (2001)

18. Dolinar, K., Porekar, J., McKitterick, D., Roussaki, I., Kalatzis, N., Liampotis, N., Papaioannou, I., Papadopoulou, E., Burney, S.M., Frank, K., Hayden, P., Walsh, A.: PERSIST deliverable D3.1: detailed design for personal smart spaces (2008). http://www.ict-persist.eu/?q=content/persist-deliverables-and-publications

19. Favre, J.M., Nguyen, T.: Towards a megamodel to model software evolution through transformations. Electron. Notes Theor. Comput. Sci. **127**(3), 59–74 (2005)

20. Ferreira Filho, J.B.: Leveraging model-based product lines for systems engineering. Ph.D. Thesis, Université Rennes 1, Paris (2014)

21. Freitas, L.A., Costa, F.M., Rocha, R.C., Allen, A.: An architecture for a smart spaces virtual machine. In: Proceedings of the 9th Workshop on Middleware for Next Generation Internet Computing, p. 7. ACM, New York (2014)

22. Gallacher, S.M., Papadopoulou, E., Taylor, N.K., Williams, M.H.: Putting the 'Personal' into personal smart spaces. In: Proceedings of Pervasive Personalisation Workshop, vol. 2010, pp. 10–17 (2010)

23. Gascueña, J.M., Navarro, E., Fernández-Caballero, A.: Model-driven engineering techniques for the development of multi-agent systems. Eng. Appl. Artif. Intell. **25**(1), 159–173 (2012). http://dx.doi.org/10.1016/j.engappai.2011.08.008
24. Guinard, D., Trifa, V., Pham, T., Liechti, O.: Towards physical mashups in the web of things. In: Proceedings of INSS 2009 (IEEE Sixth International Conference on Networked Sensing Systems), pp. 196–199. Pittsburgh (2009)
25. Helal, S., Mann, W., El-Zabadani, H., King, J., Kaddoura, Y., Jansen, E.: The Gator Tech Smart House: A programmable pervasive space. Computer **38**(3), 50–60 (2005)
26. Honkola, J., Laine, H., Brown, R., Tyrkko, O.: Smart-M3 information sharing platform. In: The IEEE symposium on Computers and Communications, ISCC, pp. 1041–1046 (2010)
27. Johanson, B., Fox, A.: The Event Heap: a coordination infrastructure for interactive workspaces. In: Proceedings Fourth IEEE Workshop on Mobile Computing Systems and Applications, pp. 83–93 (2002). https://doi.org/10.1109/MCSA.2002.1017488
28. Kawsar, F.: A document-based framework for user centric smart object systems. Ph.D. in Computer Science, Waseda University (2009)
29. Kolovos, D.S., Paige, R.F., Kelly, T., Polack, F.A.: Requirements for domain-specific languages. In: Proceedings of the First ECOOP Workshop on Domain-Specific Program Development (2006)
30. Kolovos, D.S., García-Domínguez, A., Rose, L.M., Paige, R.F.: Eugenia: towards disciplined and automated development of GMF-based graphical model editors. Softw. Syst. Model. **16**, pp. 229–255 (2015). https://doi.org/10.1007/s10270-015-0455-3
31. Kolovos, D.S., Rose, L.M., García-Domínguez, A., Paige, R.F.: The Epsilon Book (2015). https://www.eclipse.org/epsilon/doc/book/
32. Kortuem, G., Kawsar, F., Fitton, D., Sundramoorthy, V.: Smart objects as building blocks for the Internet of Things. IEEE Internet Comput. **14**(1), 44–51 (2010)
33. Latré, B., Braem, B., Moerman, I., Blondia, C., Demeester, P.: A survey on wireless body area networks. Wireless Netw. **17**(1), 1–18 (2011). http://dx.doi.org/10.1007/s11276-010-0252-4
34. López-Fernández, J.J., Cuadrado, J.S., Guerra, E., de Lara, J. (2015). Example-driven meta-model development. Softw. Syst. Model. **14**(4), 1323–1347 (2015). http://dx.doi.org/10.1007/s10270-013-0392-y
35. Lupiana, D., O'Driscoll, C., Mtenzi, F.: Taxonomy for ubiquitous computing environments. In: First International Conference on Networked Digital Technologies, NDT '09, pp. 469–475 (2009). https://doi.org/10.1109/NDT.2009.5272068
36. Melo, P.C.F.: CSVM: Uma Plataforma para CrowdSensing Móvel Dirigida por Modelos em Tempo de Execução. Master's Thesis, Instituto de Informática - Universidade Federal de Goiás, Goiânia-GO (2014)
37. Merks, E., Sugrue, J.: Essential EMF. https://dzone.com/refcardz/essential-emf (2009)
38. Monperrus, M., Jézéquel, J.M., Baudry, B., Champeau, J., Hoeltzener, B.: Model-driven generative development of measurement software. Softw. Syst. Model. **10**(4), 537–552 (2011)
39. Object Management Group: Object constraint language (OCL) (2015). http://www.omg.org/spec/OCL/
40. Ranganathan, A., Chetan, S., Al-Muhtadi, J., Campbell, R.H., Mickunas, M.D.: Olympus: a high-level programming model for pervasive computing environments. In: Third IEEE International Conference on Pervasive Computing and Communications, PerCom 2005, pp. 7–16. IEEE, Piscataway (2005)
41. Román, M., Hess, C., Cerqueira, R., Campbell, R.H., Nahrstedt, K.: Gaia: a middleware infrastructure to enable active spaces. IEEE Pervasive Comput. **1**, 74–83 (2002)
42. Rose, L., Guerra, E., De Lara, J., Etien, A., Kolovos, D., Paige, R.: Genericity for model management operations. Softw. Syst. Model. **12**(1), 201–219 (2013)
43. Roussaki, I., Kalatzis, N., Liampotis, N., Frank, K., Sykas, E.D., Anagnostou, M.: Developing context-aware personal smart spaces. In: P. Alencar, D. Cowan (eds.) Handbook of Research on Mobile Software Engineering: Design, Implementation, and Emergent Applications, chap. 35, pp. 659–676. IGI Global, Hershey (2012)

44. Roussaki, I., Kalatzis, N., Liampotis, N., Papaioannou, I., Pils, C., Crotty, M., AlanWalsh, Frank, K., Whitmore, J., McKitterick, D., Taylor, N., McBurney, S., Papadopoulou, E., Williams, H., Dolinar, K., Porekar, J., Venezia, C., Bucchiarone, A.: PERSIST deliverable D2.1: scenario description and requirements specification (2008). http://www.ict-persist.eu/? q=content/persist-deliverables-and-publications
45. Roussaki, I., Kalatzis, N., Liampotis, N., Kosmides, P., Anagnostou, M., Sykas, E.: Putting personal smart spaces into context. In: V.G. Díaz, J.M.C. Lovelle, B.C.P. García-Bustelo (eds.) Handbook of Research on Innovations in Systems and Software Engineering, chap. 27, pp. 710–730. IGI Global, Hershey, PA (2015)
46. Sampaio Junior, A.R.: Controle de Microgrids Dirigido por Modelos. Master's Thesis, Instituto de Informática - Universidade Federal de Goiás, Goiânia-GO (2014)
47. Schilit, B.N., Theimer, M.M.: Disseminating active map information to mobile hosts. IEEE Netw. **8**(5), 22–32 (1994). http://dx.doi.org/10.1109/65.313011
48. Schmidt, D.C.: Guest editor's introduction: model-driven engineering. Computer **39**(2), 0025–31 (2006)
49. Seidewitz, E.: What models mean. IEEE Softw. **20**(5), 26–32 (2003)
50. Shi, Y., Xie, W., Xu, G., Shi, R., Chen, E., Mao, Y., Liu, F.: The smart classroom: merging technologies for seamless tele-education. IEEE Pervasive Comput. **2**(2), 47–55 (2003)
51. Siegemund, F.: A context-aware communication platform for smart objects. In: Pervasive Computing, pp. 69–86. Springer, Berlin (2004)
52. Smirnov, A., Kashevnik, A., Shilov, N., Teslya, N.: Context-based access control model for smart space. In: 2013 5th International Conference on Cyber Conflict (CyCon), pp. 1–15. IEEE, Piscataway (2013)
53. Sousa, J.P., Garlan, D.: Aura: an architectural framework for user mobility in ubiquitous computing environments. In: Bosch, J., Gentleman, M., Hofmeister, C., Kuusela, J. (eds.) Software Architecture. IFIP - The International Federation for Information Processing, vol. 97, pp. 29–43. Springer, New York (2002). http://dx.doi.org/10.1007/978-0-387-35607-5_2
54. Steinberg, D., Budinsky, F., Merks, E., Paternostro, M.: EMF: Eclipse Modeling Framework. Pearson Education (2008). https://books.google.com.br/books?id=sA0zOZuDXhgC
55. Sztajnberg, A., Rodrigues, A.L.B., Bezerra, L.N., Loques, O.G., Copetti, A., Carvalho, S.T.: Applying context-aware techniques to design remote assisted living applications. International Journal of Functional Informatics and Personalised Medicine **2**(4), 358–378 (2009)
56. Taylor, N.: Personal eSpace and personal smart spaces. In: Second IEEE International Conference on Self-Adaptive and Self-Organizing Systems Workshops, SASOW 2008, pp. 156–161 (2008). https://doi.org/10.1109/SASOW.2008.23
57. Taylor, N.: Personal smart spaces. In: A. Ferscha (ed.) Pervasive Adaptation: The Next Generation Pervasive Computing Research Agenda, pp. 79–80. Institute for Pervasive Computing, Johannes Kepler University Linz, Linz (2011)
58. The Eclipse Foundation: Customizing a GMF editor generated by EuGENia (2015). https://www.eclipse.org/epsilon/doc/articles/eugenia-polishing/
59. The Eclipse Foundation: Epsilon object language (2015). https://www.eclipse.org/epsilon/doc/eol/
60. The Eclipse Foundation: Epsilon validation language (2015). https://www.eclipse.org/epsilon/doc/evl/
61. The Eclipse Foundation: EuGENia GMF tutorial (2015). https://www.eclipse.org/epsilon/doc/articles/eugenia-gmf-tutorial/
62. The Eclipse Foundation: Graphical modeling framework documentation (2015). https://wiki.eclipse.org/Graphical_Modeling_Framework/Documentation/Index
63. Van Deursen, A., Klint, P., Visser, J.: Domain-specific languages: an annotated bibliography. SIGPLAN Not. **35**(6), 26–36 (2000)
64. Vieira, M.A.: Modelagem de espaços inteligentes pessoais e espaços inteligentes fixos no contexto de cenários de computação ubíqua. Master's Thesis, Universidade Federal de Goiás, Goiânia, Goiás (2016)

65. Vieira, M.A., Carvalho, S.T.: Addressing the concurrent access to smart objects in ubiquitous computing scenarios. In: Proceedings of the 22nd Brazilian Symposium on Multimedia and the Web, Webmedia'16, pp. 79–82. ACM, New York (2016). http://doi.acm.org/10.1145/2976796.2988166

66. Vieira, M.A., Carvalho, S.T.: (Meta)Modelagem de Espaços Inteligentes Pessoais e Espaços Inteligentes Fixos para Aplicações Ubíquas. In: Proceedings of the 8th Simpósio Brasileiro de Computação Ubíqua e Pervasiva, VIII SBCUP, pp. 1056–1065. SBC, Porto Alegre (2016)

67. Völter, M., Stahl, T., Bettin, J., Haase, A., Helsen, S.: Model-Driven Software Development: Technology, Engineering, Management.Wiley, Hoboken (2013)

68. Weiser, M.: The computer for the 21st century. Sci. Am. **265**(3), 94–104 (1991)

69. Weiser, M., Brown, J.S.: The coming age of calm technology. In: Beyond Calculation, pp. 75–85. Springer, Berlin (1997)

70. Wienands, C., Golm, M.: Anatomy of a visual domain-specific language project in an industrial context. In: Model Driven Engineering Languages and Systems, pp. 453–467. Springer, Berlin (2009)

71. Williams, J., Poulding, S., Rose, L., Paige, R., Polack, F.: Identifying desirable game character behaviours through the application of evolutionary algorithms to model-driven engineering metamodels. In: International Symposium on Search Based Software Engineering. Lecture Notes in Computer Science (including subseries Lecture Notes in Artificial Intelligence and Lecture Notes in Bioinformatics), vol. 6956, pp. 112–126 (2011). https://doi.org/10.1007/978-3-642-23716-4_13

72. Wyckoff, P., McLaughry, S.W., Lehman, T.J., Ford, D.A.: T spaces. IBM Syst. J. **37**(3), 454–474 (1998)

73. Yau, S.S., Gupta, S.K., Karim, F., Ahamed, S.I., Wang, Y., Wang, B.: Smart classroom: enhancing collaborative learning using pervasive computing technology. In: ASEE 2003 Annual Conference and Exposition, pp. 13633–13642 (2003)

**Marcos Alves Vieira**, MSc., is a professor at the Federal Institute of Education, Science and Technology Goiano—Campus Iporá, where he teaches Computer Science subjects in technical and higher education courses. He holds a Bachelor degree in Informatics from the Federal Institute of Education, Science and Technology of Goiás (IFG) and a Master's degree in Computer Science from the Institute of Informatics (INF) of the Federal University of Goiás (UFG), where he developed research focusing on Ubiquitous Computing Smart Spaces and Model-Driven Engineering. He is currently a Ph.D. student in Computer Science from INF/UFG.

**Sergio T. Carvalho**, DSc., is a professor at the Institute of Informatics, Federal University of Goiás (UFG), Brazil, since 2006, where he works in the Postgraduate Program in Computer Science (Master and Doctoral Advisor) and teaches courses in Computer Science, Information Systems, and Software Engineering. He has taught in various colleges and university centers in Computer Science area. For several years he served mainly as software project coordinator, and held positions such as Director of the Information Systems, responsible for the development and maintenance of systems, and Director of Technology Support, responsible for hardware and software infrastructure. For over 17 years, he served as IT professional on various public and private companies, exercising activities on software development, database management, and network and systems management. He holds a BSc in Computer Science from the UFG, an MSc, and a Ph.D. in Computer Science, both from the Fluminense Federal University (UFF). He has experience in Distributed Systems and Software Engineering areas, and his main fields of activity are ubiquitous computing, with focus on health care applications, software architecture, and self-adaptive architectures.

# Chapter 6
# Authoring Hypervideos Learning Objects

**André Luiz Brandão Damasceno, Antonio José G. Busson,
Thacyla Sousa Lima, and Carlos Salles Soares Neto**

## 6.1 Introduction

Due to innovations in information and communication technologies (ICTs), teaching and learning processes have undergone many changes in recent years. In particular, ICT-enhanced education is continuing to support improved activities both inside and outside the classroom. For instance, multimedia resources such as slideshows, videos, and games have been increasingly used in distance and face-to-face education, promoting new experiences that can help the students to assimilate the educational content.

In such a context, education-based multimedia authoring environments are essential to provide teachers with the technological support they need. Such environments help teachers in creating and managing the multimedia content used in education. Moreover, when well integrated with e-learning and distributing platforms, they can help in the process of assessing the learning evolution of the students and in providing feedback for the teacher, which allow him/her to improve his/her educational content.

The aforementioned multimedia resources used for educational purposes are commonly referred to as *Learning Object*s (LOs). More precisely, an LO is any entity, digital or non-digital, that can be used, reused, or referenced during a learning or training process supported by computer(s) [29]. A specific, and nowadays very

A. L. B. Damasceno · A. J. G. Busson (✉)
Pontifical Catholic University of Rio de Janeiro (PUC-Rio), Rio de Janeiro, Brazil
e-mail: andre@telemidia.puc-rio.br; busson@telemidia.puc-rio.br

T. S. Lima · C. S. Soares Neto
Federal University of Maranhão (UFMA), Maranhão, Brazil
e-mail: csalles@deinf.ufma.br

© Springer Nature Switzerland AG 2020
V. Roesler et al. (eds.), *Special Topics in Multimedia, IoT and Web Technologies*,
https://doi.org/10.1007/978-3-030-35102-1_6

popular, type of LO is the hypervideo-based LO, or *hypervideo LO*. Hypervideos are non-linear videos whose playback can be influenced by hyperlinks embedded in elements contained within the video stream [15, 22]. Using these additional elements one can specify complex behaviors to LOs such as playing video lectures in sequence, synchronizing lecture videos and additional elements through temporal and spatiotemporal links, and providing different navigation modes over video lectures [29].

In general, the development of hypervideo LOs is complex, expensive, and time-consuming, usually requiring a multidisciplinary team [11]. Software developers are required to develop the source code; designers help to provide a common visual identity across related LOs; and education experts create and measure the teaching goals. Furthermore, as a central role in the production team, there is the content specialist (e.g., teacher or tutor), who provides the subject to be taught and the structure of the course.

To provide a less complex environment, in which teachers can create the multimedia educational content by themselves, with less intervention or support from a whole multidisciplinary team, new authoring tools (with higher levels of abstraction) are needed. These tools must be designed to be used by non-programmers and with minimalist and easy-to-use interface metaphors. As part of such a context, the main contributions of this chapter are:

- a comprehensive list of requirements for hypervideo LO authoring tools (gathered from a literature review, a user-oriented participatory design, and a review of current LO authoring tools);
- a conceptual model (named SceneSync) and its XML-based instantiation for authoring hypervideo-based LOs;
- an easy-to-use authoring tool (named Cacuriá [1]) that instantiates the proposed authoring model following a WYSIWYG (What You See Is What You Get) approach; and
- a usability evaluation study of the Cacuriá authoring tool.

To discuss each contribution, the remainder of the chapter is structured as follows. Section 6.2 presents the main requirements for hypervideo-based LOs, which were mainly gathered by: (1) surveying the LO-related literature; (2) performing participatory design activities; and (3) analyzing previous LOs authoring tools. Section 6.3 presents both the interface design process for Cacuriá tool and its underlying SceneSync model, created as a document engineering solution for hypervideo LOs. Section 6.4 presents the evaluations we conducted of the SceneSync model and of the Cacuriá authoring tool, which include a case study, a usability test, and an analysis of the requirements coverage. Finally, Sect. 6.5 concludes the chapter with some final remarks and directions for future work.

---

[1] Cacuriá is the name of a Brazilian dance that is popular in the state of Maranhão.

## 6.2   Authoring Requirements for Hypervideo LOs

To better understand the hypervideo LOs domain and its authoring requirements, we started with a brief *literature review* (Sect. 6.2.1) aiming at precisely defining the hypervideo LOs, then we proceeded to a *participatory design* activity (Sect. 6.2.2) with stakeholders, and, finally, we performed a comparative analysis (Sect. 6.2.3) of previous authoring tools based on the previous findings.

Since there are good recent systematic reviews on "hypervideos" and "interactive video" [15], and on the application of hypervideos to the educational context [21], we opted not to perform yet another systematic review on these terms in this chapter. Instead, we built on these recent works and validate their results within a participatory design approach with authors and to conduct a comparative analysis of authoring tools for LOs. Indeed, those two steps allowed us to analyze and refine the requirements gathered from the literature review, and to define not only the functional requirements but also non-functional requirements that are important from the authors' point of view.

As discussed in Sects. 6.3.2 and 6.3.1, the requirements gathered from those three steps were used as the basis for the creation of a conceptual model (SceneSync) and an authoring tool (Cacuriá) for hypermedia LOs.

### *6.2.1   Definition and Features*

Since hypervideos were first proposed by Sawhney et al. [22] the concept has been used in different contexts by different researchers, which has caused some confusion. To address this issue, some recent work tries to provide a precise definition for hypervideo, highlighting the functional features hypervideos should support.

Meixner [15], for instance, defines hypervideo as:

"video-based hypermedia that combines nonlinear video structuring and dynamic information presentations. Video information is linked with different kinds of additional information (like text, pictures, audio files, or further videos). Users can interact with sensitive regions having spatial and temporal characteristics. These are shown in video scenes or separately but are synchronized with the video. They provide access to additional information (heterogeneous hypervideos) or allow jumps to other scenes (homogeneous hypervideos)."

The main features of hypervideos identified by the Meixner's literature review are: *hyperlinks* (to scenes or additional information), usually represented by hotspots or sensitive regions that depend on space and time in the main video; *(linear) heterogeneous hypervideos*: composed of video and additional information like text images, audio files, animations, and other videos; *homogeneous hypervideos*: videos linked to other videos; *hybrid hypervideos*: videos linked to other videos and to additional information, in a graph structure.

Focused on the educational domain, Sauli et al. [21] define hypervideos as:

> "a non-linear video that presents both classical (e.g. play, pause, stop, and rewind/forward buttons) and more complex (e.g. table of contents and index) functions to control the navigation of the video stream (corresponding respectively to micro- and macro-level activities), and it is enriched with hyperlinks giving access to additional material (e.g. documents, audio files, images, etc.) through specific markers or hotspots."

Sauli et al. also recognize that a hypervideo can

> "also be provided with a variety of exchange options, which include the possibility to be directly annotated within the interface showing the video, both individually or collaboratively; . . . Finally, hypervideos allow the users to receive feedback through the above-mentioned communication tools or automatically from the system (e.g. through a quiz feature)."

The main hypervideo features identified by Sauli et al.'s literature review are divided into basic and additional features. The *basic features* include *dynamism*, *control*, and *hyperlinks*. *Dynamism* is related to the in-motion dimension of the video images (in contrast to the static nature of pictures). *Control* features represent the idea that hypervideos can be watched or "navigated" through a non-linear path, which includes typical features of linear video, such as play/pause/stop and rewind/forward buttons, and more complex such as indexes, menus, or markers on which one can click and which are linked to other resources. *Hyperlinks*, i.e., clickable markers that give access to additional material such as text, pictures, web pages, and audio. The *additional features* include *individual video annotation*, *collaborative video annotation*, and *quizzes*.

Although there are some differences in the above definitions and hypervideo features, there is some consistency at least in the *basic features* as defined by Sauli et al.'s work. Other researchers have investigated how these and other hypervideo LO features are perceived by students, which may also be useful from the authoring point of view.

For instance, Vieira et al. [26] highlight the importance of the students' interaction and the promotion of their participation in video-oriented e-learning environments. By comparing different e-learning patterns, Vieira et al.'s work identifies fundamental requirements that should be taken into account when developing such environments. The analyzed patterns were: *Lecture Capture* (recording of a class or lecture); *Talking Head* (top recording of the instructor talking to the camera); *Voice Over Presentation* (slides presentation complemented with narration); and *Interactive Video* (video presentation enriched with multimedia content and interaction features). The identified requirements were: *the usage of short videos, soft transitions, hyperlinks support*, and *content summarization* (for selective viewers).

Zhang et al. [30] studied the preferences of the students and their learning satisfaction on e-learning environments. Zhang et al. [30] analyzed four different environments: (1) use of interactive videos; (2) use of non-interactive videos; (3) without videos; and (4) traditional classroom. They concluded that students are significantly better satisfied and they have better learning performances in the first environment, which uses interactive videos. Indeed, by providing an individualized control for content access through an organized content index, the student can learn at his or her own pace.

Brecht [4] measured the benefits of using video lectures to complement face-to-face classes by analyzing three different LO designs. The first design is characterized by the lack of attention to relief and change-of-pace elements (this is similar to the previously mentioned *Lecture Capture* from [26]). The second one included graphics/cartoons and sound/music clips, which were used to provide relief from fatigue during the class. Finally, the third design uses a significantly reduced number of graphics and sounds that were subtly presented in a way that they did not call too much of the students' attention. By comparing those designs, Brecht found that the second design (which uses graphics/cartoons and sound/music clips) had presented the best performance (i.e., the best learning rate and the lowest dropout rate of the students) of the three.

Mujacic et al. [18] evaluated the performance of two groups of students in e-learning environments using hypervideo LOs. The first group undertook the course using the traditional model of lectures, while the second group used the hypervideo LOs. By interviewing the students, the researchers verified that the introduction of the hypervideo LOs, provided to the second group, gave them better insight into the activities, and enabled a higher level of interaction and control over the contents. The LO model features used by Mujacic et al. include *scenes composition, timeline-based synchronism,* and *spatiotemporal links.*

Interactivity and multimedia content are also important for including impaired children and improving their learning experience. Focused on mathematics and pre-calculus, Munoz-Soto et al. [19] presented an LO model for children diagnosed with autism spectrum disorders (ASD). Through a preliminary evaluation of the proposed model, Munoz-Soto et al. verified that the ASD children approved the interaction features and the use of multimedia content to add learning value. Becerra et al. [2] presented an LO for children with language impairments that uses multiple sounds synchronized with other multimedia. The goal of their proposal was to use sound elements to stimulate children's phonological awareness.

## 6.2.2 Participatory Design

The main goal of the participatory design (PD) activities we conducted was to understand what authors and teachers consider to be good learning objects, and what features they need (or believe are important) in such a domain. The PD activities involved three techniques: *focus group* and *card sorting*, used in a meeting to explore and gather requirements, and *paper prototyping*, used to evaluate the concepts and clarify the requirements.

In total, 18 stakeholders of the authoring tool participated in the PD sessions: 3 undergraduate students and 5 master's students in Design, 6 undergraduate students and 1 master's student in Computer Science, 2 high schoolteachers, and 1 pedagogue.

### 6.2.2.1 Focus Group and Card Sorting

*Focus group* is a qualitative technique that uncovers feelings, beliefs, and opinions about the subject investigated through a kind of moderated collective interview, usually guided by a predefined script or list of topics [23]. In general, the aim of this technique is not to get the consensus of ideas, but to collect a range of opinions on a particular topic. The results are not analyzed as percentages or statistics and should not be generalized to a population [23]. Figure 6.1a shows the focus group setting.

*Card sorting* consists of writing topics on small cards, which are then distributed to a group of users (5 to 15 people) who must categorize them in a way that makes sense to them [20]. This technique promotes a better understanding of the users' mental models, i.e., how they think about the concepts in a given application domain.

The card sorting sessions began with a presentation of LOs to level the knowledge of the group. Then, participants were asked about the characteristics of a good LO, and what criteria an authoring tool should meet to create a good LO. At the end of the session, the participants reported the main features an authoring tool should have and grouped them in small paper cards (see Fig. 6.1b).

We observed that the predefined script for the focus group yielded objective and relevant discussions. Most participants had some knowledge about LOs and had already used them to teach or to study.

Following the focus group script, participants started talking about what they knew about LOs and which models of learning objects they use in their teaching and learning processes. Most of them pointed out that the use of video and the possibility of the student to interact with the LO would improve and increase student focus on the LO content. Indeed, soon they converged for many of the features previously discussed as in Sect. 6.2.1 functional requirements for hypervideos but also discussed interesting non-functional features. For instance, an interesting point raised by the first group was the creation of an LO repository, in order to allow teachers be able to reference and reuse the content in LMSs (Learning Management Systems). However, for the stakeholders, sharing LOs in a repository raises copyright violation concerns.

Participants were unanimous in determining that an authoring tool *should not require programming skills* to build an LO. Both groups set as a requirement a

(a)                                    (b)                                    (c)

**Fig. 6.1** Participatory design sessions. (**a**) Focus group. (**b**) Card sorting. (**c**) Paper prototyping

**Table 6.1** Results obtained from card sorting

| | |
|---|---|
| Interaction | Interactivity (does it help to learn?); interaction (student×teacher); interaction (student×student) |
| Ubiquity | Mobile version; desktop version; different environments (in class×distance learning); study Anywhere |
| Engagement | Learning curve (adjustment period); choosing the moment to study; abandonment, commitment, acceptance and withdrawal, lack of interest of the student; demotivation of the student, content revision; strategy to attract and engage |
| Ethics | Content copyright |
| Reliability | Few errors; no error interruptions |
| Usability | Minimalist aesthetic; fewer buttons; easy to use; cover basic needs; have a media library with drag-and-drop functions; clean workspace; timeline; dynamic; simple edition tools |
| Resources | Power point; videos; 3D; text; slides; quiz; images; tutorial; animation; references; movies and documentaries |
| Functionalities | Remove; download content; creation and edition tools; insert image; cut; audio volume control; resizing; add subtitles; navigation tools; URL links; recording tool; related images listing; video tools; text tools |

minimalist interface, with few buttons and easy to use. Also, they agreed that the tool should support the inclusion of media objects such as image, text, PDF, audio, and video files. Lastly, the second group reported that for a user to have a good experience and to feel motivated to create LOs, the tool should be *reliable* and not *error-prone*.

Additional relevant information was obtained from the card sorting session. Table 6.1 shows an overview of the stakeholders' categorization of the important features that must be supported in an authoring tool. Some requirements for the design of authoring tools were obtained as a result of this phase.

### 6.2.2.2 Design and Prototyping

The next step in PD involved paper prototyping. A prototype can be seen as a draft design and aims to conduct tests for user interface evaluation. This kind of prototyping is considered low precision because it uses materials such as paper and cardboard, but tends to be simpler and faster to produce [24]. Its main goal is to evaluate design options early, thus helping to find problems before implementation starts.

The same participants of the previous activities were divided into 2 groups of 9 people. Each group was responsible for creating the user interface of an LO authoring tool based on the requirements obtained from the focus group and card sorting sessions (see Fig. 6.1c). After finishing the prototype, one member of each team presented it, along with its underlying design vision and the types of LOs the proposed authoring tool would support creating. Then, they demonstrated the LO creation process and the possibilities of interaction and system feedback through the user interface.

The adopted PD process allowed the stakeholders to freely and easily explore diverse user interface solutions by assembling and disassembling user interface prototypes. In addition, it allowed them to find problems and easily solve them by themselves. When a problem was found, they would redesign the user interface and test it again. During the prototype tool demonstration, the groups presented good ideas, features, and a user interface which was easy to understand. The main results achieved were the interactive designs with fewer usability problems, which avoid later rework and thus save time in implementing the authoring tool.

The first and the second group described minimalist interfaces. Both of them presented the video as the main media and the initial step for the creation of an LO. Another common decision was to use temporal and spatial views. The goal of the spatial view is to make it easy to position and scale the media object. Nevertheless, there were some differences in the temporal view. The first group made a "slide switch" in which each slide had a main video and the timeline referred to a video frame. Meanwhile, the second group created a single timeline referencing all videos of the LO. Timelines could contain markers (which participants called sync points). The first group proposed two kinds of markers (start and end) to show the temporal relationship among media (e.g., video, audio, text, and image), whereas the second group made just a start marker to represent the beginning of all videos.

The first group also had the idea of a library view. This view allows authors to add a media object to the project and then use it in the spatial view (for instance, via drag-and-drop interactions). This group also added a widgets concept to their user interface. The intention behind widgets is to allow authors to include extensions in the LO such as quiz, slideshow, and menu.

In general, both groups believed that the tool should have few buttons, be easy to use, and allow the inclusion of different media objects and formats (image, audio, and text). A number of users with experience using video-editing tools pointed out the importance of a temporal view to have a better time control of media such as video and audio.

The paper prototyping technique helped to improve the understanding of the requirements collected in the previous phases, by allowing participants to explore concrete solutions to meet and refine those requirements.

## 6.2.3   Comparative Analysis

Finally, we conducted a comparative analysis of existing authoring tools for LOs. Each tool was briefly described in a table and compared with the results obtained in the previous activities. The purpose of analyzing similar authoring tools is to identify the characteristics of existing solutions and investigate the authoring approaches they support. Moreover, this activity also helped to find out whether and to what extent existing tools already fulfilled the requirements gathered in the literature review and PD activities.

Figure 6.2 shows the main authoring tools for learning objects found were: CourseLab [28]; DITV-Learning [7]; eXeLearning [5]; HotPotatoes [13]; Microsoft LCDS [17]; MARKER [8]. Most of them use SCORM (Shareable Content Object Reference Model), which is a set of specifications defining a content aggregation model, a sequence model, and a model for executing LOs on the Web [3]. Table 6.2 presents a summary of the LO authoring tools.

The user interface of CourseLab [28] resembles Microsoft PowerPoint. It uses a WYSIWYG (What You See Is What You Get) approach in order to facilitate the creation of LOs by nondevelopers. The tool supports various file formats, such as video, audio, text, Java applets, and Flash. In addition to content structuring, it is possible to assign actions to objects, such as animations on a clickable image. However, it does not allow editing the source code of LOs for advanced functionality. CourseLab also allows creating interactive activities such as questions with single and multiple choices, true or false; sorting items; filling gaps in sentences; and linking items. Moreover, its contents can run on various LMS, such as Moodle, ATutor, and Oracle iLearning.

DITV-Learning [7] automates the creation of LOs for interactive TV by professionals who have little knowledge of programming. The tool supports various file formats of video, audio, image, and text objects. DITV-Learning allows users to create LOs as a quiz, bonus (content in the form of slides), and extra (add-ons that can be triggered interactively during an application execution). The LOs generated by the tool run only on devices with the Ginga-NCL middleware.

eXeLearning [5] is a Web-based tool for the creation of LOs in HTML, which can also be used in LMS. It provides interactive features to users, such as text reading, multiple choice questions, true or false questions, Java applets, YouTube videos, and Wikibooks articles. The authoring tool has seven editable templates, an LO that describes how to use the tool, iDevices creation, and an HTML editor of LOs.

HotPotatoes [13] is a desktop tool designed for the production of interactive exercises in LMS, such as Moodle. It consists of five types of interactive exercises: quiz, fill the gaps, crosswords, matching columns, and sorting of words in the text. When you create an activity you can enter questions and answers, but you cannot use animations. The tool allows grouping activities into a package.

Microsoft LCDS [17] is a desktop tool for creating LOs, which includes templates for authoring LOs and a software manual. It supports various file types of text, images, and video objects. It allows the production of page sequences, but it does not allow resizing the page. The LO in HTML format generated by the LCDS does not follow the SCORM model and does not allow editing.

MARKER [8] is a desktop tool and, like DITV-Learning, it is intended for authoring LOs which can run on interactive TV with the Ginga-NCL middleware embedded. It allows the user to create markers on the main video in order to replace them for other media objects (e.g., audio, video, image, text). The user can also define interactions related to those objects. For instance, pressing the blue button on the remote, an image can be resized, a video can be paused, etc.

**Fig. 6.2** Screenshots of the analyzed Learning Objects authoring tools. (**a**) CourseLab. (**b**) DITV Learning. (**c**) eXeLearning. (**d**) HotPotatoes. (**e**) Microsoft LCSD. (**f**) MARKER

## *6.2.4 Summary*

Table 6.3 summarizes the functional and non-functional requirements we have gathered for creating hypervideo-based LOs through the LO literature review, the PD activities, and the analysis of previous learning objects authoring tools.

**Table 6.2** Summary of LO authoring tools

| | CourseLab | DITV-learning | eXe learning | HotPotatoes | Microsoft LCDS | MARKER |
|---|---|---|---|---|---|---|
| Interactive videos as LOs | x | x | | | x | x |
| Mobile compatible LOs | x | | | | | |
| Desktop multiplatform | | x | x | x | | x |
| Few buttons (minimalist) | | x | | | x | x |
| Multimedia content manipulation (WYSIWYG) | x | | | | | |
| Non-linear LOs | x | | x | | x | x |
| Timeline | x | | | | | x |
| Programing knowledge Not-required | x | x | x | x | x | x |

**Table 6.3** Requirements for a hypervideo model for designing LOs extracted from the literature review

| FR# | Functional requirements |
|---|---|
| FR1 | Use multiple short videos instead of a single video (split into scenes) [6, 18, 26] |
| FR2 | Support for internal and external hyperlinks [6, 10, 19, 26, 30] |
| FR3 | Additional information: video enriched with images, texts, animations, other videos, audios, etc. [2, 4, 6, 10, 19] |
| FR4 | Clickable areas, button panels, questions or quizzes. [6, 10, 19, 26, 30] |
| FR5 | Non-linear structure: no predefined course of playback, but a graph structure of scenes [6, 19, 26, 30] |
| FR6 | Timeline-based synchronism paradigm: media items are placed along a time axis, but possibly on different tracks [6, 18] |
| FR7 | Temporal links: jump labels on a timeline of a scene [6, 18]. Additional functional requirements |
| FR8 | Content summarization |
| FR9 | Individual annotation |
| FR10 | Collaborative annotation |

| NF# | Non-functional requirements |
|---|---|
| NF1 | Transition effects: presentation effect used when the formatter starts or finishes displaying a media [26] |
| NF2 | Interoperability: run on the Web, Mobile, iDTV [6, 10] |
| NF3 | Adaptability: adaptation to different contexts [4, 10] |
| NF4 | Accessibility [10] |
| NF5 | Durability: resist technological changes without the need for recoding [10] |
| NF6 | Reusability: reuse of components [6, 10] |
| NF7 | Reliability: reliable and without errors [6] |

## 6.3   Cacuriá Authoring Tool

As shown in Table 6.2, existing tools are aimed at creating LOs without requiring
users to have programming skills. However, none of them fulfills all the requirements uncovered in the PD activities. This motivated the development of Cacuriá,[2]
a novel multimedia authoring tool for creating LOs.

### 6.3.1   Interface Design

The user interface was designed based on the concepts identified in the solutions
obtained in the gathering requirement activities (Sect. 6.2) and on the comparative
analysis (Sect. 6.2.3).

#### 6.3.1.1   User Interface Design

To satisfy the desired requirements for the tool, the user interface design was
conceived considering both the results obtained in the paper prototyping activity
and on user interfaces and system features present in the tools identified in the
comparative analysis.

The user interface was designed with six views to manage media, as seen in
Fig. 6.3. In the *Menu View* (1), users can add media, visualize the project, and

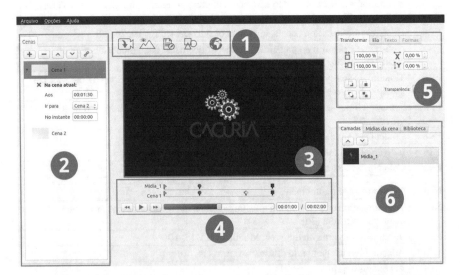

**Fig. 6.3** Cacuriá's user interface

---

[2]Available at https://goo.gl/inxv1N.

publish the LO. In the *Scenes View* (2), users can add, remove, edit, and select a scene, templates, and automatic links among scenes. In the *Layout View* (3), users can view the position and size the media over time, as well as add, remove, and edit media. In the *Temporal View* (4), users can run the LO and manipulate the time of the scene, as well as view, move, and remove the temporal markers of each media in a scene. In the *Feature View* (5), users can visualize and edit the properties of the selected media. In the *Library View* (6), users can list, rename, and edit the order of media objects in the project.

Cacuriá[3] is a WYSIWYG (What You See Is What You Get) tool, in which all the viewed content and the one that is being modified resemble the final application generated by the tool. The tool does not require the user to have specific previous knowledge about the specification language used to develop interactive applications. This turns out to be quite useful for end users who do not have specific programming knowledge, but who are interested in creating LOs. It can be useful also to casual users, who do not want to spend too much time learning a language or technology to create LOs.

The abstraction adopted by the tool for creating LOs is based on the media synchronization in a composite node. This same abstraction is used in several tools [1, 16, 28]. In this chapter, the composite nodes are called *scenes*. Each scene is composed of one or more media objects (videos, image, text, and shapes) synchronized with the timeline. In order to create interactive, non-linear content, the tool provides ways to navigate between scenes and to open additional content such as web pages, which are triggered by links anchored on certain media objects. The tool also features the use of *scene templates*, which predefine the position and size of media objects, leaving for the user only the work of choosing media objects that will be used in the template. Therefore, as shown in Table 6.4, Cacuriá covers all the requirements gathered in the PD activities.

**Table 6.4** Requirements covered by Cacuriá

|                                              | Cacuriá |
| -------------------------------------------- | ------- |
| Interactive videos as LOS                    | x       |
| Mobile compatible LOs                        | x       |
| Desktop multiplatform                        | x       |
| Few buttons (minimalist)                     | x       |
| Multimedia content manipulation (WYSIWYG)    | x       |
| Non-linear LOs                               | x       |
| Timeline                                     | x       |
| Programing knowledge not-required            | x       |

---

[3] Available at https://goo.gl/inxv1N.

## 6.3.2  The SceneSync Model

Although it is possible to develop hypervideo LOs using declarative multimedia languages—such as SMIL [27], HTML, XMT [14], and NCL [25]—those languages are designed for general-purpose interactive multimedia presentations and do not implement specific features of the educational domain. When using such broad-spectrum models, teachers must rationalize all the complexity of the model to be able to define new LOs. In contrast, Cacuriá implements its own declarative model to specify hypervideo documents in the educational domain, named SceneSync. The SceneSync Model (SSM) (see Fig. 6.4) was designed taking into account the requirements described in Sect. 6.2. Also, SSM is not designed to be used directly by end users, but to be used by authoring tools and players, or converted to one of the aforementioned multimedia languages. The remainder of this subsection details SSM's entities.

A *Content* entity can be a *Scene* or a *Media object*. The *Scene* entity is used as an abstraction for representing multimedia compositions (FR1 and FR3 requirements). A *Scene* entity instance has, as its content, a collection of *Media objects* and *Synchronization anchors* (*Sync*). To simplify the LOs modeling, a *Scene* entity cannot contain other scene objects, i.e., SSM does not allow nesting compositions.

The timeline abstraction is used for providing synchronism among *Media objects* (FR6 requirement) in the same *Scene*. Every *Content* object (*Scene* or *Media*) has an internal clock that can be used as a reference for defining temporal anchors on the scene. An anchor is defined by the *Sync* entity, and has, as its content, a collection of *Action* objects.

An *Action* defines the relationships between the *Anchor* and *Content* objects, and can be of one of the following five types: *Start*, which starts the presentation of a media object; *Stop*, which stops the presentation of a media object; *Set*, which sets

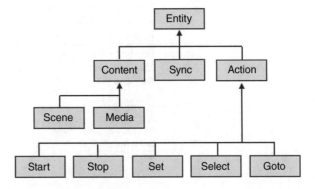

**Fig. 6.4** Class hierarchy of the SSM entities

the properties of a media object; and *Select* and *Goto*, which redirect the presentation to another time point or scene node. The difference between the *Select* and *Goto* actions is that the *Select* action is triggered via the user interaction (requirements FR2, FR4, and FR7), whereas the *Goto* action is triggered when the scene reaches a specific time point. In particular, these actions enable modeling non-linear LOs (FR5 requirement).

## 6.3.3 The SceneSync Language

The SSM model is instantiated in XML by the SceneSync language, which is specified using a modular approach in XML Schema [9]. Table 6.5 details the three modules of the language: *Structural*, *Content*, and *Synchronization*. In this table, "?" denotes an optional element and "*" denotes any number of that element.

**Table 6.5** SceneSync language modules, elements, and attributes

| Element | Attributes | Child elements |
|---------|-----------|----------------|
| *Structure module* | | |
| Scenesync | id, xmls | (Head?, body) |
| Head | – | meta? |
| Body | – | (Scene—media—sync)* |
| *Content module* | | |
| Scene | id | (Image, text, audio, video, sync)* |
| Audio | id, src, volume | Sync* |
| Image | id, src, left, top, width, height, transparency, layer | Sync* |
| Video | id, src, left, top, width, height, transparency, volume, layer | Sync* |
| Text | id, src, left, top, style, align, color, fontfamily, fontsize, transparency, layer | Sync* |
| *Synchronization module* | | |
| Sync | id, time | (Start, stop, set, select, goto)* |
| Start | id, target | – |
| Stop | id, target | – |
| Set | id, target | property* |
| Goto | id, target, timeevent | – |
| Select | id, target, timeevent, key | – |
| Property | id, name, value | – |

#### 6.3.3.1   Structure Module

The structure module defines three main elements: `<scenesync>`, `<head>`, and `<body>`. The root element of the language is `<scenesync>`; it has the `<head>` and `<body>` elements as children. It also has the *id* and *xmls* attributes, which identify the application and the standard scheme, respectively. The `<head>` element may have an optional `<meta>` element that allows authors to specify metadata about the document. The `<body>` element has as children the elements that describe the presentation content, such as media and synchronism objects.

#### 6.3.3.2   Content Module

A SceneSync presentation is composed of one or more scene nodes, represented by the `<scene>` element. Besides the identifier, a `<scene>` has a collection of media objects and synchronization elements as children. Each media object type is represented by a different first class element with their proper attributes: `<Chap6/image>`, `<text>`, `<audio>`, or `<video>`. Media objects have as attributes: *id*, a unique identifier of the media object; *src*, which defines the media object contents *URI*; and other attributes that define presentation characteristics, such as *top*, *left*, *width*, *height*, and *transparency*. Media objects also contain a list of synchronism objects (`<sync>` elements, discussed next).

#### 6.3.3.3   Synchronization Module

The synchronization among the media objects and scenes is defined by the `<sync>` element. The `<sync>` element has the *id* and *time* attributes. The *id* attribute identifies a `<sync>` element unambiguously in the document. The *time* attribute defines a temporal anchor in its parent element timeline (a `<scene>` or a media object). The children actions of the `<sync>` element will be fired when the parent element presentation reaches the time specified by the *time* attribute.

In the SceneSync language, every possible action over a `<scene>` or media object is represented by a different element. The `<start>` and `<stop>` elements represent actions that, respectively, start or stop the presentation of a `<scene>` or media object. The `<set>` element represents an action that changes the property of a media object. The `<goto>` and `<select>` elements represent actions to redirect the multimedia presentation to another moment in time or to another `<scene>`. The difference between the `<goto>` and `<select>` actions is that the former is always triggered when the presentation reaches the specified time, whereas the latter is only triggered by a user interaction (such as a key press or mouse click).

Besides their identifiers, action objects also have a *target* attribute, which defines the target object of the action. In particular, the `<set>` element has a list of `<property>` elements. A `<property>` element specifies the property that will be modified (*name* attribute) and the new value to be defined (*value* attribute). The `<select>` element has the *key* attribute, which defines a key that triggers the action. The *timeEvent* attribute, which may be specified in a `<select>` and `<goto>`, defines the time anchor to which the scene node will be redirected.

## 6.3.4 Modeling an LO Using SceneSync

To help understand the SceneSync language, this subsection presents a step-by-step development of a simple hypervideo LO, the "Sorting Algorithms" LO. This LO begins with the video of a teacher introducing general concepts related to sorting algorithms. At some point during his lecture, the teacher asks the viewer to choose whether he or she wants to learn more about the *InsertSort* or the *QuickSort* sorting algorithm. The LO then presents a specific lecture (about *InsertSort* or *QuickSort*) based on the user choice.

To implement the "Sorting Algorithms" LO, we divide it into three `<scene>` elements:

1. *IntroductoryScene*, which contains:

    (a) one introductory video about sorting algorithms;
    (b) one image that represents the *InsertSort* option; and
    (c) one image that represents the *QuickSort* option.

2. *InsertSortScene*, which contains:

    (a) one background image;
    (b) one video about the *InsertSort* algorithm; and
    (c) one image that illustrates an example of the *InsertSort* algorithm.

3. *QuickSortScene*, which contains:

    (a) one background image;
    (b) one video about the *QuickSort* algorithm; and
    (c) one image that illustrates an example of the *QuickSort* algorithm.

Listing 6.1 shows part of the "Sorting algorithm" source code, highlighting the `<scene>` and media objects, organized as above. Next, we discuss the behavior specification of each `<scene>` element.

The *IntroductoryScene* starts with the "vid_alg" video. This can be modeled with a `<sync>` element containing a child object of action `<start>` pointing to a video object (as shown in lines 3–5 of Listing 6.2). Note that we do not need to provide the value of the *time* attribute, which is 0 by default.

**Listing 6.1** Scenes and media objects of the "Sorting Algorithm" LO

```
1  <scene id="IntroductoryScene">
2    <video id="vid_alg" src="intro.mp4" width="100%"
        height="100%" />
3    <image id="img_insert" src="img1.png" left="30%"
        top="80%" width="30%" height="20%" />
4    <image id="img_quick" src="img2.png" left="65%"
        top="80%" width="30%" height="20%" />
5    ...
6  </scene>
7  <scene id="InsertSortScene">
8    <video id="vid_insert" src="video1.mp4"
        width="100%" height="100%" />
9    <image id="back_insert" src="back.png"
        width="100%" height="100%" />
10   <image id="img_alg_insert" src="img2.png"
        left="65%" width="80%" width="30%" height="20%"
        />
11   ...
12 </scene>
13 <scene id="QuickSortScene">
14   <video id="vid_quick" src="video1.mp4"
        width="100%" height="100%" />
15   <image id="back_quick" src="back.png" width="100%"
        height="100%" />
16   <image id="img_alg_quick" src="img2.png"
        left="65%" width="80%" width="30%" height="20%"
        />
17   ...
18 </scene>
```

Moreover, when the teacher invites the viewer to choose the next lecture (*InsertSortScene* or *QuickSortScene*), two images are displayed, illustrating those options to the viewer. It is also necessary to enable the user interactions that will lead to the selection of the respective scenes. To do this, we create a new <sync> element (lines 6–11 of Listing 6.2) with the *time* attribute set to "45s" (the time the teacher asks the user to interact). Inside this <sync> we define two <start> actions, the first one created to start the "img_insert" object, and the second one created to start the "img_quick" object. To enable user interaction, we define two <select> actions, which enable the key interaction feature.

Finally, when the main video of the *IntroductoryScene* ends (65s), the scene presentation should go back to 45s, and stay in a loop until the user chooses an option. We use the `<goto>` element to implement such behavior (lines 12–14 of Listing 6.2). The `<goto>` element is used with *target* and *timeEvent* attributes set as "IntroductoryScene" and "45s," respectively. Figure 6.5b shows the preview and temporal view of the *IntroductoryScene*.

---

**Listing 6.2** Source code defining the temporal behavior of *IntroductoryScene* of the "Sorting Algorithm" LO

```
1 <scene id="IntroductoryScene">
2 ...
3  <sync>
4   <start target="vid_intro" />
5  </sync>
6  <sync time="45">
7   <start target="img_insert" />
8   <start target="img_quick" />
9   <select key="1" target="InsertSortScene"/>
10  <select key="2" target="QuickSortScene"/>
11 </sync>
12 <sync time="65s">
13  <goto target="IntroductoryScene" timeEvent="45s"/>
14 </sync>
15 </scene>
```

---

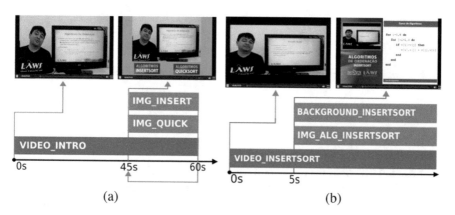

**Fig. 6.5** Preview (top) and temporal view (bottom) of (**a**) *IntroductoryScene* and (**b**) *InsertSortScene*

The second (*InsertSortScene*) and third (*QuickSortScene*) scenes have a similar behavior. Therefore, we discuss only the second scene here. The *InsertSortScene* starts by displaying the video about the *InsertSort* algorithm. For that, a `<sync>` element is defined containing a `<start>` action referring the video presentation "vid_insert" (Listing 6.3, lines 3–5). As an additional behavior of this scene, at 5 s: (1) the main video must be resized and moved to the upper left corner; (2) a background image must be started (behind the video and occupying the entire scene); and (3) the image containing an example of the *InsertSort* algorithm must be displayed on the right side of the screen. To implement that, we used the `<sync>` element defined in Listing 6.3, lines 6–15. Figure 6.5b shows the preview and temporal view of the *InsertSortScene*.

**Listing 6.3** Source code defining the temporal behavior of *InsertSortScene* of the "Sorting Algorithm" LO

```
1  <scene id="InsertSortScene">
2  ...
3   <sync>
4    <start target="vid_insert" />
5   </sync>
6   <sync time="5s">
7    <start target="img_back_insert" />
8    <start target="img_alg_insert" />
9    <set target="vid insert">
10    <property name="left" value="5%" />
11    <property name="top" value="5%" />
12    <property name="width" value="17%" />
13    <property name="height" value="10%" />
14   </set>
15   </sync>
16  </scene>
```

## 6.4 Evaluation

This section describes the evaluation study, which comprised two steps: a *case study* and an *usability test*. The first step aimed to evaluate what kinds of interactive applications experts are able to build with Cacuriá. The second one aimed to evaluate the usability of Cacuriá and to investigate whether end users can successfully create an interactive application.

This section presents the results of both studies, which show the effectiveness and efficiency of the authoring tool Cacuriá. The participants' feedback raised new requirements and recommendations for refining the tool.

### 6.4.1   Case Study

The goal of the case study was to identify a range of applications that can be created using Cacuriá. We therefore analyzed the tool and identified the models of learning objects that could be created with it.

To illustrate the development process of an interactive application, we describe here the process of authoring an application about tourist spots in Rio de Janeiro. The application is called "Roteiro do dia" (Tour of the day) and, as Fig. 6.6 shows, it is composed of four images and five videos. It starts with an introduction video describing some places in Rio. Then, the video offers the possibility of getting to know more about two locations (Central do Brasil and Copacabana). At the end of whichever video the user may choose, two additional locations are offered (Gafieira Estudantina and Jardim Botânico) for users to obtain more information.

The synchronization with the video happens in the exhibition of the images "Central do Brasil.png," "Copacabana.png," "Gafieira Estudantina.png," and "Jardim Botânico.png," which are shown in the final seconds of each video. The non-linear authoring is characterized by offering

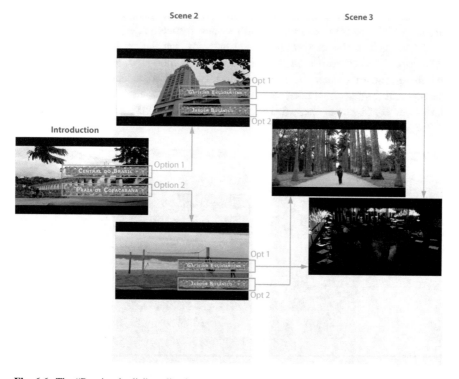

**Fig. 6.6** The "Roteiro do dia" application

a choice of place about which the student may want to obtain further information. This choice may appear to users as a kind of customized experience.

Based on the results obtained during the participatory design, user interface design, and implementation phases [6], we defined and developed Cacuriá as a tool to support users in generating non-linear LOs composed of synchronized media (e.g., video, image, and text). The "Roteiro do dia" application was used to illustrate the content model generated by the tool and some other features the tool offered, such as the synchronism between media objects and the insertion of links on the scenes to demonstrate the nonlinearity of content. As the study involved skilled users, there was no need to follow the step-by-step task script provided to users in the usability testing activity.

When Cacuriá is run, the first action to be taken is to click on the video icon to choose the first video for the scene. Then, the video is added in the Library View and its first frame is shown in the Layout View. In addition, the timeline of the Temporal View receives the total duration of the video and the options in the Properties View are enabled.

Next, four scenes are added through the option "add scene" located in the Scene View. Then, the second scene is selected in the same view, in order to add the "Central do Brasil.mp4" video. Similarly, the "Copacabana.mp4," "Gafieira Estudantina.mp4," and "Jardim Botânico.mp4" videos are inserted in the third, fourth, and fifth scenes, respectively.

Then, back to the first scene to add and position the "Central do Brasil.png" and "Copacabana.png" images on the video. Next, the links from the first scene are created. The images recently added are selected and links to the second and third scene are set in the Properties View, as Fig. 6.7 illustrates. Similarly, the "Gafieira Estudantina.png" and "Jardim Botânico.png"

**Fig. 6.7** Cacuriá's interface

images are inserted and positioned in both the second and third scenes. Lastly, a link is also configured for each image to trigger the fourth and fifth scenes, respectively.

### 6.4.2 Usability Test

The usability evaluation was conducted with 44 teachers distributed in sessions of 6 to 10 participants (Fig. 6.8). They had little or no experience in using authoring tools. The overall goal of the usability test was to evaluate user satisfaction, effectiveness, and efficiency of the tool, and to investigate whether the prototype supports teachers in the creation of interactive content.

The tests were carried out using desktop computers containing a software for capturing the participants' actions and the authoring tool Cacuriá for creating LOs. A folder in each computer contained a shortcut to access the tool and the media to be used when building the application. Moreover, a 30-step task script for the construction of the application presented in Sect. 6.4.1 was given to the participants.

Each session started with a brief introduction about the authoring tool. Then the "Roteiro do dia" application was run. Finally we asked participants to build the application using Cacuriá. After developing the application, each teacher answered

**Fig. 6.8** Test settings for the tool evaluation

an online multiple choice questionnaire, based on version 7.0 of the Questionnaire for User-Interaction Satisfaction (QUIS),[4] whose objective is to measure user satisfaction [12]. The questionnaire was adapted so as not to be long and to assess just what was relevant for the tool. It therefore included only 44 of the 126 QUIS questions. Moreover, the original scales were reduced from 9 to 5 points, ranging from 1, representing the user's dislike, to 5, representing the user's satisfaction with the corresponding aspect.

The questionnaire used in the evaluation was divided into 6 sections. The first section was related to the user identification and contains fields to enter the name, occupation, experience as a teacher or tutor, as well as programming skills. Next, the participants should answer questions to assess their overall perception of the tool. The third section aimed to evaluate the tool interface. The fourth section contained questions related to terminology and system information. The fifth section consisted of questions focused on the evaluation of learning to use the tool. The sixth and final section was associated with system capabilities such as speed, response time, correcting typos, etc. At the end of each section, participants could make free-form textual comments about the aspects of the tool addressed in the corresponding section.

### 6.4.2.1   Results

The usability test was performed in 7 days. Only 6 of the 44 participants failed to perform all the tasks. We noticed a certain degree of difficulty to start the application development: the average learning time was around 10 min. Most participants built the application in less than 40 min, which was the expected time. Although the tool still requires improvements in its efficiency, the results demonstrate that an adequate degree of effectiveness was achieved.

The results are presented through graphs with percentages of agreeing and disagreeing responses to each question. The use of color in the graphs aims to make it easy to identify where there are agreements on the proposed model and what problems were found in the tool. The evaluation analysis also includes the comments provided by the participants at the end of each stage. The results considered satisfactory are those for which the participant chose option 4 or 5 (green color) on the scale. But when option 1, 2, or 3 (red and gray color) was selected, the result is classified as a problem and considered a feature to be improved.

Figure 6.9 shows the results of the general impressions that the participants had after using Cacuriá. It can be observed that most users believed Cacuriá to be a useful tool (Q1). Furthermore, participants found the tool motivating for the construction of LOs (Q2). More than half of the participants assessed the tool features as sufficient (Q4), and both its use (Q3) and the options offered to make

---

[4]Available in: http://lap.umd.edu/quis/.

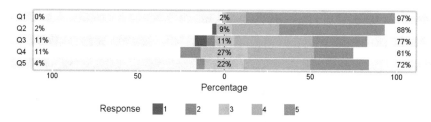

**Fig. 6.9** General impressions of the tool

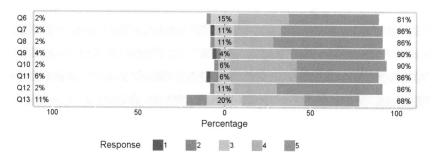

**Fig. 6.10** Overall results about the user interface

the activities (Q5) were deemed satisfactory. Based on these data, we notice overall positive general impressions of the tool.

According to Fig. 6.10, over half of the users rated the letters used in the tool interface as easy to identify (Q6), with adequate font sharpness (Q7) and good readability (Q8). In addition, most of them thought it was easy (Q10) to find the media properties and (Q9) to identify the corresponding icons to add video, image, text, shapes, as well as to publish a learning object. Regarding system colors (Q11), although they were considered appropriate in general, some users found them a little confusing. Meanwhile, most participants reported as adequate the arrangement of information (Q12) and the progression of work-related tasks (Q13).

The results regarding the terminology and system information are shown in Fig. 6.11. Most of the participants perceived as consistent the system terminology (Q14), the messages displayed on the user interface (Q19), and the terms related to the task (Q15) and the computer (Q16). They also agreed that performing an operation in Cacuriá leads to a predictable results (Q22). Moreover, the computer terms used in the tool (Q17) and displayed on the system interface (Q18) were evaluated as appropriately and precise. However, the feedback messages issued by the tool can be improved. The participants found somewhat unsatisfactory the instructions for correcting errors (Q20); whether the system keeps the user informed about what it is doing (Q21); issues regarding the error messages (Q23), the phrasing of error messages (Q25), and if error messages clarify the problem (Q24).

As can be seen in Fig. 6.12, the results obtained in the evaluation of learning demonstrate that Cacuriá was perceived as easy to operate (Q26). Most of the partic-

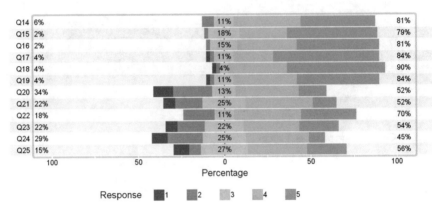

**Fig. 6.11** Overall results about the terminology and system information

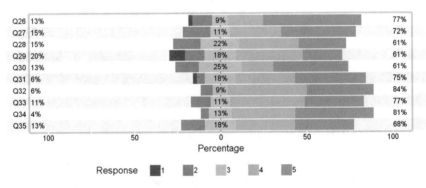

**Fig. 6.12** Overall results about the learning

ipants positively assessed issues regarding getting started (Q27), learning advanced features (Q28), time to learn to use the system (Q29), exploration of features by trial and error (Q30), discovery of new features (Q31), straightforwardness of tasks performance (Q32), number of steps per task (Q33), logical sequence of steps to complete a task (Q34), and feedback on the completion of steps (Q35).

Some participants made comments regarding the ease, simplicity, and speed in learning to use the tool. A participant reported that: "for people like me who have worked with some video editor or even Microsoft PowerPoint, learning is not time-consuming because the symbols follow the same standard and were well applied in Cacuriá". Despite the satisfactory results, participants also gave interesting suggestions for the user to learn to operate Cacuriá more efficiently. The main suggestions were related to the use of a manual and videos embedded in the tool to demonstrate system features.

Figure 6.13 shows the evaluation results of system capabilities. Satisfactory results were obtained on issues related to system speed (Q36), response time for most operations (Q37), rate at which information is displayed (Q38), correcting

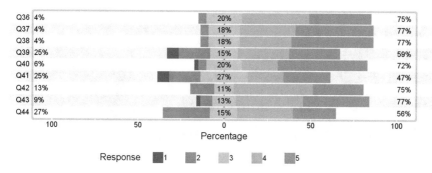

**Fig. 6.13** Overall results about system capabilities

typos (Q40), whether the ease of operation depends on the user's level of experience (Q42), and whether the user could accomplish tasks knowing only a few commands (Q43). Most users considered it easy to correct their mistakes (Q39) and to use shortcuts to perform actions (Q44). Nevertheless, the support to undo operations (Q41) was classified as inadequate. Despite satisfactory results in Q39 and Q44, they were also considered as features to be improved due to the number of participants' suggestions. In addition, many participants remarked that the tool needs to offer users an option to undo, triggered by the "Ctrl + Z" key combination, as well as more shortcuts to perform functions.

## 6.4.3 Analysis

To show the feasibility of using the SceneSync model we have asked for 142 stakeholders (teachers and educational content creators) to develop LOs using the concepts provided by SceneSync. To allow them to use the SceneSync concepts and create an executable LO, we have used Cacuriá, which is an authoring tool that graphically implements the SSM concepts. The LOs were created as part of seven workshops and one technical session held in five Brazilian cities during 3 years of a research project. Here, we summarize and analyze those results with regards to the underlying SceneSync model.

Both in the workshops and in the technical session, we first presented to the participants the process of authoring LOs using SceneSync concepts and the Cacuriá authoring tool. Then, we asked them to develop an LO about some topic of their interest (in the workshops) or a predefined LO (in the technical session). In total, 32 LOs[5] (Fig. 6.14) were specified in SceneSync using the Cacuriá tool.

Table 6.6 summarizes the developed LOs, with their respective disciplines and identified functional requirements. Note that all the functional requirements that

---

[5] Available at https://goo.gl/I6SyKu.

**Fig. 6.14** Examples of hypervideo LOs developed by stakeholders

guided us in the development of SceneSync were successfully explored by the authors of LOs.

All LO authors were able to use the following features successfully: multimedia compositions (FR1) through the `<scene>` element; additional video information such as images, texts, animations, another videos, and audio (FR3); timeline-based synchronism (FR6), through the `<sync>` and `<action>` elements; clickable areas (FR4) and non-linear narrative structures (FR5), through the `<sync>` and `<select>` elements; temporal links, spatial-temporal links (FR7), `<sync>`, `<goto>`, and `<select>` elements.

Cacuriá supported the external hyperlinks (FR2) feature only in the last workshop. Thus, only three LOs ("05-Citation," "08-Scientific Work," and "15-Game of Thrones quiz") have used it. Probably, if that functionality had been provided before, more LOs would have been created using this feature.

## 6.5 Conclusion

In this work we have introduced Cacuriá, a hypervideo tool for interactive non-linear educational videos. First, we started with a brief literature review in order to raise concepts about hypervideo LOs. These concepts were used to perform a participatory design process with stakeholders to gather authoring requirements for hypervideo LOs and improve our understanding of users' needs. Besides, we conducted a comparative analysis of previous authoring tools for LOs to identify the characteristics of existing solutions and investigate the authoring approaches they support. As a result, none of them fulfills all the requirements uncovered in the PD process.

This chapter also presents a hypervideo model for LOs, named SceneSync, and its instantiation in XML for specifying hypervideo LOs. Compared to other approaches designed to implement hypervideo LOs, such as using a general-purpose multimedia languages directly, SSM allowed Cacuriá to make use of abstractions close to the hypervideo LOs domain. Furthermore, the final artifact created using SSM can be converted to other lower-level languages, such as HTML (to run on

**Table 6.6** Functional requirements used by every LO's authors

| # | Title | Discipline | FR1 | FR2 | FR3 | FR4 | FR5 | FR6 | FR7 |
|---|-------|-----------|-----|-----|-----|-----|-----|-----|-----|
| 01 | Nephrology | Medicine | x | | x | x | x | x | x |
| 02 | Plagiarism | Education | x | | x | x | x | x | x |
| 03 | Scientific methodology | Philosophy | x | | x | x | x | x | x |
| 04 | LIBRAS (Brazilian sign language) | Accessibility | x | | x | x | x | x | x |
| 05 | Citation | Education | x | x | x | x | x | x | x |
| 06 | Cupcake recipe | Culinary | x | | x | x | x | x | x |
| 07 | Thyroid | Medicine | x | | x | x | x | x | x |
| 08 | Scientific work | Education | x | x | x | x | x | x | x |
| 09 | Recycling actions | Recycling | x | | x | x | x | x | x |
| 10 | Tourist points of "Urbano Santos" | Turism | x | | x | x | x | x | x |
| 11 | Knowledge | Philosophy | x | | x | x | x | x | x |
| 12 | Importance of bees | Biology | x | | x | x | x | x | x |
| 13 | "Boa Hora" river | Geography | x | | x | x | x | x | x |
| 14 | PGASS elaboration | Management | x | | x | x | x | x | x |
| 15 | "Game of Thrones" quiz | Entertainment | x | x | x | x | x | x | x |
| 16 | Social control in SUS | Health | x | | x | x | x | x | x |
| 17 | Princess abduction | Entertainment | x | | x | x | x | x | x |
| 18 | Sucupira platform | Technology | x | | x | x | x | x | x |
| 19 | Aedes aegypti | Biology | x | | x | x | x | x | x |
| 20 | Geometry in the square | Mathematics | x | | x | x | x | x | x |
| 21 | Elderly health | Health | x | | x | x | x | x | x |
| 22 | Sedentary lifestyle | Health | x | | x | x | x | x | x |
| 23 | HCI | Design | x | | x | x | x | x | x |
| 24 | Communicability | Design | x | | x | x | x | x | x |
| 25 | Dishes | Culinary | x | | x | x | x | x | x |
| 26 | Route of the day | Turism | x | | x | x | x | x | x |
| 27 | Life cycle of bryophytes | Biology | x | | x | x | x | x | x |
| 28 | Empiricism | Philosophy | x | | x | x | x | x | x |
| 29 | Physical education | Health | x | | x | x | x | x | x |
| 30 | Scientific text | Education | x | | x | x | x | x | x |
| 31 | Cybersecurity | Technology | x | | x | x | x | x | x |
| 32 | Wifi help | Technology | x | | x | x | x | x | x |

the Web) or NCL (to run in iDTV platforms). We highlight that HTML has a major advantage of being supported on many platforms. As future work, we plan to investigate the reusability degree that we can achieve when using SSM together with the SCORM standard for VLE integration.

Based on the results presented in Sect. 6.5, we are very confident that SceneSync model is useful to express a broad range of features for hypervideo LOs. In addition, the integration of users at the core of the design process incorporates mechanisms for iteratively evaluating and redesigning the prototypes to improve the Cacuriá tool. Indeed, the evaluation of the current version of Cacuriá achieved satisfactory results regarding its effectiveness. The tool proved to be useful for teachers building classes for distance learning and supplementary content for classroom teaching. The main positive results of the usability tests were related to its ease of use and reduced learning time. However, some improvements would be welcome, related both to the colors used at the user interface and the feedback messages issued by the tool.

Both requirements gathered in our research and methods described in this chapter (e.g., paper prototyping, card sorting) can be reused to support the design of other multimedia authoring tools. Moreover, based on the development experience of Cacuriá, it seems that its effectiveness was achieved in the first cycle. However, more cycles are necessary to improve the tool's efficiency.

For future work, we plan to perform a qualitative study of the communicability and usability of the SSM model without the interposing of a graphical tool. We also want to investigate the reusability degree that we can achieve when using SSM together with the SCORM standard.

Still focused on reusability, we plan to extend the SSM features by providing native support for designing new concepts in the model through templates. Templates can improve the reuse of the specification of LOs and help to create a visual identity among sets of LOs.

Finally, another future work is related to the identification and analysis of design patterns that could be useful in the scope of hypervideo LOs. The goal will be to find recurrent structures and best practices that authors can reuse when authoring new LOs in Cacuriá tool. The definition of design patterns can be useful in at least two ways: (1) for defining authoring guidelines and (2) for providing new concepts, which can be used to extend the model.

**Acknowledgements** This work was supported by RNP, the National Research and Educational Network from Brazil, and was developed in the context of the RNP Working Groups program, during the cycles 2012–2013, 2013–2014, and 2015. The authors also thank CAPES, FAPEMA, and CNPq for their additional support.

# References

1. Azevedo, R.G.A., Araújo, E.C., Lima, B., Soares, L.F.G., Moreno, M.F.: Composer: meeting non-functional aspects of hypermedia authoring environment. Multimed. Tools Appl. **70**(2), 1199–1228 (2014). https://doi.org/10.1007/s11042-012-1216-8
2. Becerra, C., Noel, R., Munoz, R., Quiroga, I.: Explorando aprendo: learning object to enhance language development in children with specific language impairment. In: Latin American Conference on Learning Objects and Technology (LACLO), pp. 1–5. IEEE, Piscataway (2016)

3. Bohl, O., Scheuhase, J., Sengler, R., Winand, U.: The sharable content object reference model (SCORM)-a critical review. In: International Conference on Computers in Education Proceedings, pp. 950–951. IEEE, Piscataway (2002)
4. Brecht, H.D.: Learning from online video lectures. J. Inf. Technol. Educ. **11**, 227–250 (2012)
5. Community, e.: exelearning. https://exelearning.org. Accessed March 2018
6. Damasceno, A.L.D.B., Soares Neto, C.S., Barbosa, S.D.J.: Integrating participatory and interaction design of an authoring tool for learning objects involving a multidisciplinary team. In: Proceedings of the International Conference on Human-Computer Interaction (2017)
7. de Sousa Neto, F.A., Bezerra, E.P., Dias, D.D.S.F.: ITV-learning: a tool for construction of learning objects for interactive digital television. In: Proceedings of the IADIS International Conference of the Future of Education, pp. 486–490 (2012)
8. de Sousa, S.W.F., Bezerra, E.P., Soares, I.M., Brennand, E.G.D.G.: Marker: a tool for building interactive applications for T-learning. In: Proceedings of the 19th Brazilian Symposium on Multimedia and the Web - WebMedia'13, pp. 281–284. Salvador (2013). https://doi.org/10.1145/2526188.2526236. http://www.scopus.com/inward/record.url?eid=2-s2.0-84889596806&partnerID=tZOtx3y1
9. Fallside, D.C., Walmsley, P.: Xml Schema Part 0: Primer Second Edition. W3C Recommendation vol. 16 (2004)
10. Gadelha, B.F., Castro, Jr., A.N., Fuks, H.: Representando objetos de aprendizagem funcionais para tvdi. In: SET2007–Congresso da Sociedade Brasileira de Engenharia de Televisão, São Paulo (2007)
11. González-Videgaray, M., Hernández-Zamora, G., Jesús, H.: Learning objects in theory and practice: a vision from Mexican university teachers. Comput. Edu. **53**(4), 1330–1338 (2009)
12. Harper, B.D., Slaughter, L.A., Norman, K.L.: Questionnaire administration via the www: a validation & reliability study for a user satisfaction questionnaire. In: WebNet, vol. 97, pp. 1–4 (1997)
13. H.S. Inc.: Hotpotatoes suite. https://hotpot.uvic.ca. Accessed March 2018
14. Kim, M., Wood, S., Cheok, L.T.: Extensible MPEG-4 textual format (XMT). In: Proceedings of the 2000 ACM Workshops on Multimedia, pp. 71–74. ACM, New York (2000)
15. Meixner, B.: Hypervideos and interactive multimedia presentations. ACM Comput. Surv. **50**(1), 9:1–9:34 (2017). https://doi.org/10.1145/3038925
16. Meixner, B., Matusik, K., Grill, C., Kosch, H.: Towards an easy to use authoring tool for interactive non-linear video. Multimed. Tools Appl. **70**(2), 1251–1276 (2014)
17. Microsoft: Microsoft learning content development system (LCDS). https://www.microsoft.com/en-us/learning/lcds-tool.aspx. Accessed March 2018
18. Mujacic, S., Debevc, M., Kosec, P., Bloice, M., Holzinger, A.: Modeling, design, development and evaluation of a hypervideo presentation for digital systems teaching and learning. Multimed. Tools Appl. **58**(2), 435–452 (2012)
19. Munoz-Soto, R., Becerra, C., Noël, R., Barcelos, T., Villarroel, R., Kreisel, S., Camblor, M.: Proyect@ matemáticas: a learning object for supporting the practitioners in autism spectrum disorders. In: Latin American Conference on Learning Objects and Technology (LACLO), pp. 1–6. IEEE, Piscataway (2016)
20. Nielsen, J.: Card sorting: how many users to test. Jakob Nielsen's Alertbox (2004). https://www.nngroup.com/articles/card-sorting-how-many-users-to-test/
21. Sauli, F., Cattaneo, A., van der Meij, H.: Hypervideo for educational purposes: a literature review on a multifaceted technological tool. Technol. Pedagog. Educ. **27**115–134 (2017). https://doi.org/10.1080/1475939X.2017.1407357
22. Sawhney, N., Balcom, D., Smith, I.: Hypercafe: narrative and aesthetic properties of hypervideo. In: Proceedings of the Seventh ACM Conference on Hypertext, pp. 1–10. ACM, New York (1996)
23. Simonsen, J., Robertson, T.: Routledge International Handbook of Participatory Design. Routledge, London (2012)
24. Snyder, C.: Paper Prototyping: The Fast and Easy Way to Design and Refine User Interfaces. Morgan Kaufmann, Burlington (2003)

25. Soares, L.F.G., Rodrigues, R.F., Costa, R.R., Moreno, M.F.: Nested context language 3.0: Part 9–NCL live editing commands. Monografias em Ciência da Computação do Departamento de Informática, PUC-Rio **6**, 36 (2006)
26. Vieira, I., Lopes, A.P., Soares, F.: The potential benefits of using videos in higher education. In: Proceedings of EDULEARN14 Conference, pp. 0750–0756. IATED Publications, Valencia (2014)
27. W3C Consortium, et al.: Synchronized multimedia integration language–SMIL 3.0 specification, w3c recommendation. Tech. Rep. (2008)
28. W. Ltd.: Courselab. http://www.courselab.com/view_doc.html?mode=home. Accessed March 2018
29. Wiley, D.A.: Connecting learning objects to instructional design theory: a definition, a metaphor and a taconomy. In D. A. Wiley (Ed.), The instructional use of learning objects. Bloomington, IN: Agency for Instructional Technology and Association for Educational Communications and Technology. http://members.aect.org/publications/InstructionalUseofLearningObjects.pdf. Accessed December 2018
30. Zhang, D., Zhou, L., Briggs, R.O., Nunamaker, J.F.: Instructional video in e-learning: assessing the impact of interactive video on learning effectiveness. Inf. Manage. **43**(1), 15–27 (2006)

**André Luiz Brandão Damasceno**, MSc., is PhD candidate working under the guidance of Prof. Simone Diniz Junqueira Barbosa at Pontifical Catholic University of Rio de Janeiro (PUC-Rio). He received a BS (2013) and MS (2015) in Computer Science from the Federal University of Maranhão (UFMA) on Brazil. He is researcher member at IDEIAS & DASLab—PUC-Rio. His research interests include Multimedia Systems, Data Science, and Machine Learning, working mainly on the following topics: Educational Data Mining and Learning Analytics. Currently, he is working on models to develop dashboards to support instructors understand logs from Virtual Learning Environment in order to predict the students' performance and identify behavior patterns. He also took part on the development of the GT-VOA in partnership with RNP, the National Research and Educational Network in Brazil, which was developed in the context of the RNP Working Groups program, during the cycles of 2012–2013, 2013–2014, and 2015. This work resulted in publications on conferences and symposiums such as CBIE 2014, SBGames 2016, WebMedia 2015 and 2016, ACM Hypertext 2017, and HCI 2017. Address to access CV: http://lattes.cnpq.br/0969337931297570.

**Antonio José G. Busson**, MSc., is PhD candidate working under the guidance of Prof. Sergio Colcher at Pontifical Catholic University of Rio de Janeiro (PUC-Rio). He received a BS (2013) and MS (2015) in Computer Science from the Federal University of Maranhão (UFMA) on Brazil. He is researcher member at Telemidia Lab—PUC-Rio and research collaborator at the Laboratory of Advanced Web Systems (LAWS)—UFMA. His research interests are in multimedia systems, working mainly on the following topics: Coding and Processing of multimedia data; Hypermedia Document models, Pattern Recognition, and applications such as Web, iDTV, and Games. Currently, he is working on the official Ginga Middleware development project, which is the middleware of the Japanese–Brazilian Digital TV

System (ISDB-TB) and ITU-T H.761 recommendation for iPTV services. He also took part on the development of the GT-VOA in partnership with RNP, the National Research and Educational Network in Brazil, which was developed in the context of the RNP Working Groups program, during the cycles of 2012–2013, 2013–2014, and 2015. This work resulted in publications on conferences and symposiums such as CBIE 2014, SBGames 2016, WebMedia 2015 and 2016, and ACM Hypertext 2017. Address to access CV: http://lattes.cnpq.br/1857348479447184.

**Thacyla Sousa Lima**, MSc., received a BS (2016) and MS (2019) in Computer Science from Federal University of Maranhão (UFMA). She is researcher member at Telemidia Lab—UFMA. Her research interests are in multimedia systems, working mainly on the following topics: Hypermedia Document models, authoring and applications such as Web and iDTV. She took part on the development of the GT-VOA in partnership with RNP, the National Research and Educational Network in Brazil, which was developed in the context of the RNP Working Groups program, during the cycles of 2012–2013, 2013–2014, and 2015. This work resulted in publications on conferences and symposiums such as CBIE 2014, SBGames 2016, WebMedia 2015 and 2016, and ACM Hypertext 2017. Address to access CV: http://lattes.cnpq.br/5822658991850778.

**Carlos Salles Soares Neto**, DSc., received a BS (2000) in Computer Science from Federal University of Maranhão (UFMA), MS (2003) and PhD (2010) in Computing at Pontifical Catholic University of Rio de Janeiro (PUC-Rio). He is currently an adjunct professor at the UFMA where he is coordinator of TeleMidia Lab—UFMA and is associate researcher at the TeleMidia Laboratory of PUC-Rio. He has experience in Computer Science area, with emphasis on Hypermedia, working mainly in multimedia applications, iDTV and Hypermedia Document models. He also took part on the development of the GT-VOA in partnership with RNP, the National Research and Educational Network in Brazil, which was developed in the context of the RNP Working Groups program, during the cycles of 2012–2013, 2013–2014, and 2015. This work resulted in publications on conferences and symposiums such as CBIE 2014, SBGames 2016, WebMedia 2015 and 2016, ACM Hypertext 2017, and HCI 2017. Address to access CV: http://lattes.cnpq.br/1512846862093142.

# Part III
# Data Collection and Analysis

# Chapter 7
# A Basic Approach for Extracting and Analyzing Data from Twitter

**Clarissa Castellã Xavier and Marlo Souza**

## 7.1 Introduction

Social media has a strong position in people's lives, particularly in Brazil. Thus, understanding users behavior is an important task for any organization. However, all these data are difficult to manage and this difficulty stems mainly from the fact that this information is in an unstructured or semi-structured format, such as text, images, and web pages.

Twitter[1] is a microblogging and social networking service launched in late 2006 in which users post messages up to 280 characters. In the first quarter of 2019, the service had an average of 330 million active users per month.[2]

According to [20], in Brazil, Twitter is characterized as an informative medium, i.e., users engage with the platform more for collecting and sharing information than for engaging in social interactions such as conversations. According to this study, about 62% of tweets have informational content and 48% are conversational, with 10% having both characteristics. Regarding the texts with an informative profile, about 25% have opinion content, that is, the user expresses opinions or feelings. In fact, according to a study on the global news access profile [16], 72% of Brazilians living in urban areas use social media as their news source, and 13% of them use Twitter as a news source (15% in the population under 35).

It is clear that the amount of available information significantly increased owing to the new ways of information indexing and new distribution resources. Due to this

---

[1] https://twitter.com/.

[2] https://www.statista.com/statistics/282087/number-ofmonthly-active-twitter-users/.

---

C. C. Xavier (✉) · M. Souza
Institute of Mathematics and Statistics, Federal University of Bahia (UFBA), Salvador, Brazil
e-mail: msouza1@ufba.br

large amount of data, however, it is not easy or even manageable to find and exploit strategical or relevant information. This difficulty lies in the unstructured nature of the data since its computational treatment is not trivial. In this context, information technologies and in particular text analysis might be employed to facilitate Web data collection effort.

Text Analysis, similarly Natural Language Processing (NLP), studies how to apply computational intelligence methods to automatically extract structured information from unstructured documents [2]. For [2], this area aims to develop solutions to eight major problems: Information Retrieval, Text Categorization and Grouping, Entity Recognition, Nominal Co-Reference, Text Summarization, Information Extraction, Sentiment (Polarity) Analysis, and Question Answering Systems. In this work, we focus on two relevant issues to dealing with the Twitter micro-texts: Polarity Classification and Entity Recognition.

Polarity classification is a well-known NLP task. Given a text, its purpose is to identify if there is a subjective content in it and obtain the polarity of the sentiment (or subjective orientation, i.e., polarity) conveyed by the information. For example, if the text fragment expresses a positive, negative, or neutral sentiment. Given the extensive use of informal and specialized language in the context of Twitter (and, in fact, other social media), performing polarity classification in it has become a unique task, with its particular challenges.

Entity Extraction (EE) (also known as Named Entity Recognition (NER)) is a sub-task of the Information Extraction area. Its purpose is to locate and sort named entities in the text. EE is often one of the first stages of the information extraction pipeline. Like other NLP tasks, the brief, informal, and noisy style of Twitter presents challenges to systems and methods developed for EE in other text styles and, as such, require specialized methods to deal with its specific characteristics. In this work, we study different approaches to detect entities cited in a tweet.

In this chapter, we present different semantic data extraction and classification techniques for obtaining information from Twitter. Additionally, we talk about tools that implement these techniques and view how to use these features in practice. We also show how to apply these skills in a case study to practice important data manipulation skills, learning how to use different forms of data analysis.

All cases and examples are extracted from Brazilian users Twitter accounts written in the Portuguese language. However, every method and tool is language-independent, except for the Entity Extractor.

## 7.2 Extracting Data from Twitter

Twitter is a microblogging tool launched in late 2006 where users post messages up to 280 characters called tweets. Only registered users can post, but those who are not registered can read them. Twitter can be accessed through its website interface, short message service (SMS), or mobile app.

It is possible to collect information from Twitter using its public API,[3] as well as using alternative applications and libraries. We will present Twitter API and Twint library[4] and learn how to use them to perform data extraction.

## 7.2.1 Twitter API

Tweets are freely available to software developers via public APIs. The APIs can be classified into two types [8]:

1. REST APIs: use a pull strategy to retrieve data. That is, the user must explicitly make a request to gather information.
2. Streaming APIs: use push strategy for data recovery. That is, the API provides a continuous stream of updates after a request for information, without requiring any further requests.

Twitter APIs include a wide variety of endpoints classified into five main groups: Accounts and users; Direct Messages; Ads; Publisher tools and SDKs; Tweets and replies. We will focus on the last group.

The Tweets and Replies API makes tweets and public responses available for developers. It also allows posting tweets. Developers can access tweets by searching for specific keywords or by requesting content from specific accounts [21].

### 7.2.1.1 API Access

In order to access Twitter API, it is required to register an application. By default, applications can access only public information. Some applications, such as those responsible for sending or receiving direct messages, require additional permissions [21].

It is necessary to get an API access key, a token and a consumer key at http://dev. twitter.com/apps.

The API requests authentication is performed using open authentication (OAuth). Figure 7.1 summarizes this task steps [8]:

1. The application (consumer) registers at Twitter (http://dev.twitter.com). In this process, it receives a key and a token used to authenticate itself.
2. The application uses the key and the token to create a unique Twitter link which directs the user for authentication. The user authorizes the application by authenticating to Twitter. Twitter verifies his identity and provides an OAuth (PIN) checker.
3. The user enters the application PIN. The application uses the PIN to request a unique user token and access key.

---

[3]https://developer.twitter.com/.

[4]https://github.com/twintproject/twint.

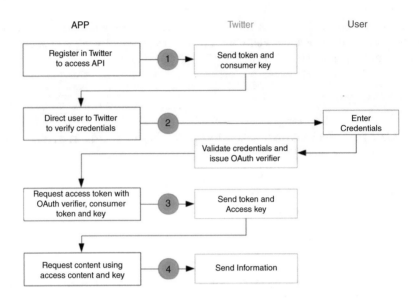

**Fig. 7.1** OAuth stream to get Twitter API access token. Adapted from [8]

4. Using the token and the access key the application authenticates the user on Twitter and calls the API on behalf of the user.

The user token and access key cannot be changed and can be cached by the application for future requests. This way, this process runs only once.

The Python code reproduced in Listing 7.1 implements the OAuth stream to access Twitter API presented in Fig. 7.1. As we can see, it uses Oauth2[5] library, dealing with all the OAuth 2.0 protocol steps required to make API calls.

**Listing 7.1  Python code to access Twitter API**

```
import oauth2
def oauth_req(url, ACCESS_KEY, ACCESS_TOKEN,
    http_method="GET", post_body="", http_headers=None):
    token = oauth2.Token(key=ACCESS_KEY,
        secret=ACCESS_TOKEN)
    consume = oauth2.Consumer(key=CONSUME_KEY,
        secret=CONSUME_TOKEN)
    client = oauth2.Client(consume, token)
    resp, content = client.request( url,
        method=http_method, body=post_body,
        headers=http_headers )
    return content
```

---

[5]https://pypi.org/project/python-oauth2.

## 7.2.2   Collect Data Without Accessing the API

There are other approaches to collect Twitter data besides the API. One option is Twint tool, implemented in Python. It uses Twitter search operators to capture specific users' tweets for specific topics, hashtags, or trends. It also makes special Twitter inquiries, allowing to get a user's followers, tweets, and follows.

## 7.2.3   Practical Examples

Next, we present examples of how to use Twitter API and Twint to extract the following information: User information; User followers; Whom the user follows; Tweets; Search results. All examples deal with texts in Brazilian Portuguese. However, the presented methods are not tied to a specific language and can be used in any idiom.

### 7.2.3.1   User Information

API

Twitter's main API is responsible for handling and querying data. Any method of this API is preceded by the URI http://api.twitter.com/version/, where version is the API version (currently 1).

Each user is associated to an identifier, also called screen name (*screen_name*) and an ID (*user_id*).

The *users/show*[6] returns the user profile information. It accepts a valid username as a parameter and returns the user's Twitter profile.

Listing 7.2 shows a Python code for getting data from a profile. An example of how to call the method created in Listing 7.2 code would be: `user_info('twitterbrasil')`. A typical user object is formatted as Listing 7.3.

---

[6]https://developer.twitter.com/en/docs/accounts-and-users/follow-search-get-users/api-reference/get-users-method-show.html.

---

**Listing 7.2  Python code to call *users/show* API**

```
def user_info(user):
    GET_USR_URL =
        "https://api.twitter.com/1.1/users/show.json?
        screen_name="+user
    req = oauth_req(GET_USR_URL,ACCESS_TOKEN,ACCESS_KEY)
    return req
```

---

**Listing 7.3  Part of the JSON object returned by method *user_info('twitterbrasil')***

```
{...
    "created_at": "Thu Mar 10 22:54:23 +0000 2011",
    "description": "Bem-vindos \u00e0 conta oficial do
        Twitter Brasil! Precisa de ajuda? Acesse
        https://t.co/Nu5ZS0w4UD",
    "favourites_count": 1537,
    "followers_count": 2181337,
    "id": 263884490,
    "lang": "pt",
    "location": "Brasil",
    "name": "Twitter Brasil",
    "screen_name": "TwitterBrasil",
    "statuses_count": 7434,
    "time_zone": null,
    "translator_type": "regular",
    "url": "http://t.co/GuzHOnaY84",
    "verified": true
...}
```

---

Twint tool does not provide a functionality to get user profile information.

### 7.2.3.2  User Followers

API

Method *followers/list*[7] returns a collection of user objects representing the users that follow the profile entered as a parameter. Results are provided in groups of 20 and multiple results pages can be browsed using the value *next_cursor* in subsequent requests.

---

[7]https://developer.twitter.com/en/docs/accounts-and-users/follow-search-get-users/api-reference/get-followers-list.html.

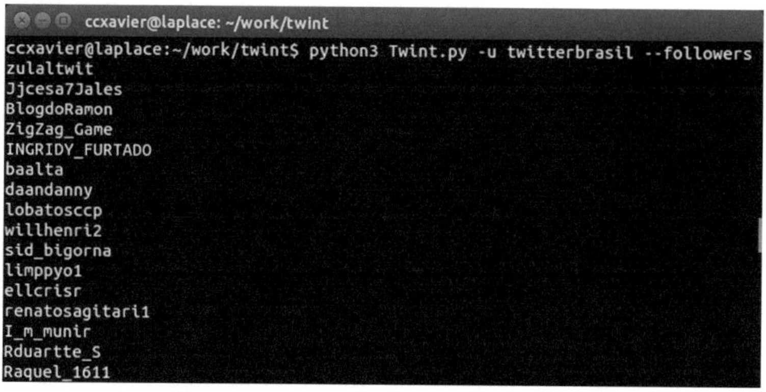

**Fig. 7.2** Results of the command for listing users following an user account

Listing 7.4 shows the Python code to get followers of a profile.

**Listing 7.4  Python code to call *followers/list* API**

```
def user_followers(user):
    GET_URL =
        "https://api.twitter.com/1.1/followers/list.json?cursor=
        -1&skip_status=true&include_user_entities=false&
        screen_name="+user
    req = oauth_req(GET_URL,ACCESS_TOKEN,ACCESS_KEY)
    return req
```

Twint

The following command lists users following a certain account:
python3 Twint.py -u [usuário] -followers.

Figure 7.2 shows the command python3 Twint.py -u twitterbrasil -followers call and return.

### 7.2.3.3   Who the User Follows

API

Method *friends/list*[8] returns a collection of user objects containing users followed by the profile entered as a parameter. Results are provided in groups of 20 users and

---

[8]https://developer.twitter.com/en/docs/accounts-and-users/follow-search-get-users/api-reference/get-friendsmethod-list.

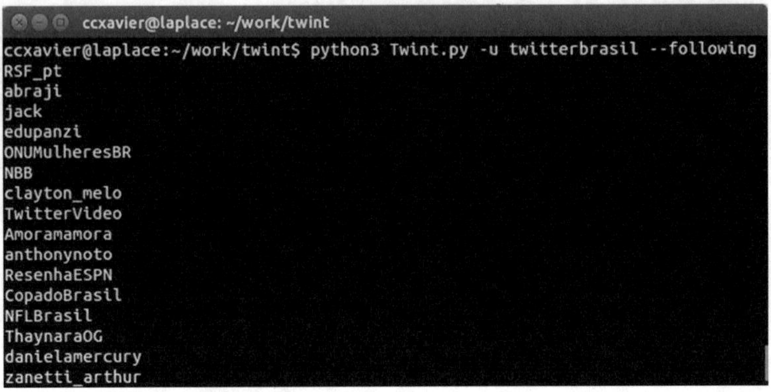

```
⊗ ● ⊙   ccxavier@laplace: ~/work/twint
ccxavier@laplace:~/work/twint$ python3 Twint.py -u twitterbrasil --following
RSF_pt
abraji
jack
edupanzi
ONUMulheresBR
NBB
clayton_melo
TwitterVideo
Amoramamora
anthonynoto
ResenhaESPN
CopadoBrasil
NFLBrasil
ThaynaraOG
danielamercury
zanetti_arthur
```

**Fig. 7.3** Results of the command for listing the users followed by an user account

multiple results pages can be browsed using the value *next_cursor* in subsequent requests.

Listing 7.5 shows the Python code for getting the friends list of an user.

**Listing 7.5  Python code to call *friends/list* API**

```python
def user_friends(user):
    GET_URL =
        "https://api.twitter.com/1.1/friends/list.json?cursor=-1
        &skip_status=true&include_user_entities=false&
        screen_name="+user
    req = oauth_req(GET_URL,ACCESS_TOKEN,ACCESS_KEY)
    return req
```

Twint

Command `python3 Twint.py -u [user] -following` returns the list of users who follow the user entered as a parameter. Figure 7.3 shows the command call and return
`python3 Twint.py -u twitterbrasil -following`.

#### 7.2.3.4   Get Tweets

API

A tweet can be written by the user or a special type of Tweet, called Retweet, reproduces a tweet from other user. A user's tweets can be retrieved using the REST and streaming APIs.

The *statuses/usertimeline*[9] method returns a collection of tweets recently posted by a user using the REST API. Timelines belonging to protected users can only be requested when the authenticated user "owns" the timeline or is an approved follower.

This method returns up to 3200 of a user's most recent tweets. The results are provided in groups and multiple result pages can be browsed using the next_cursor value in subsequent requests. Each page returns up to 200 tweets. The parameter *max id* is used to paginate. To retrieve the next page, the oldest TweetType ID in the list is used as a parameter in the subsequent request. Then, the API will only retrieve tweets whose IDs are below the given value.

Listing 7.6 shows Python code for getting the last tweet from a profile.

**Listing 7.6  Python code to call *statuses/usertimeline* API**

```python
def user_tweets(user):
    GET_URL =
        "https://api.twitter.com/1.1/statuses/user_timeline.json?
        count=1&screen_name="+user
    req = oauth_req(GET_URL,ACCESS_TOKEN,ACCESS_KEY)
    return req
```

Method *statuses/filter*[10] returns a collection of tweets that match one or more filter parameters using streaming. It allows the client to use a single connection while persisting the API connection.

Listing 7.7 shows the Python code for creating a POST request to the API and fetch the search results. The parameter is the term that will be followed. For example, if the term parameter is "twitter," the method will print the tweets containing this term publicly created on the platform. The code calls the auxiliary libraries oauth2, JSON[11], and urllib2.[12]

---

[9]https://developer.twitter.com/en/docs/tweets/timelines/api-reference/get-statuses-user_timeline. html.

[10]https://developer.twitter.com/en/docs/tweets/timelines/api-reference/get-statuses-user_timeline. html.

[11]https://docs.python.org/2/library/json.html.

[12]https://docs.python.org/2/library/urllib2.html.

**Listing 7.7  Python code to call *statuses/filter* API**

```
def follow_tweets(term):
    url =
        "https://stream.twitter.com/1.1/statuses/filter.json?
            track="+term
    http_method="POST"
    post_body=""
    http_headers=None
    token = oauth2.Token(key=ACCESS_KEY, secret=ACCESS_TOKEN)
    consume = oauth2.Consumer(key=CONSUME_KEY,
        secret=CONSUME_TOKEN)
    client = oauth2.Client(consume, token)
    headers = {}
    req = oauth2.Request.from_consumer_and_token(
      client.consumer, token=client.token,
      http_method="POST", http_url=url)
    req.sign_request(client.method, client.consumer,
        client.token)
    headers.update(req.to_header())
    body = req.to_postdata()
    headers['Content-Type'] =
        'application/x-www-form-urlencoded'
    req = urllib2.Request(url, body, headers=headers)
    try:
      f = urllib2.urlopen(req)
    except urllib2.HTTPError, e:
      data = e.fp.read(1024)
      raise Exception(e, data)
    for line in f:
      d = json.loads(line)
      try:
          print d["user"]["name"], d["text"]
      except:
          print d.get("id")
```

## Twint

The following command returns all tweets from the user timeline: python3
Twint.py -u [user]. Figure 7.4 shows the command call and return
python3 Twint.py -u twitterbrasil.

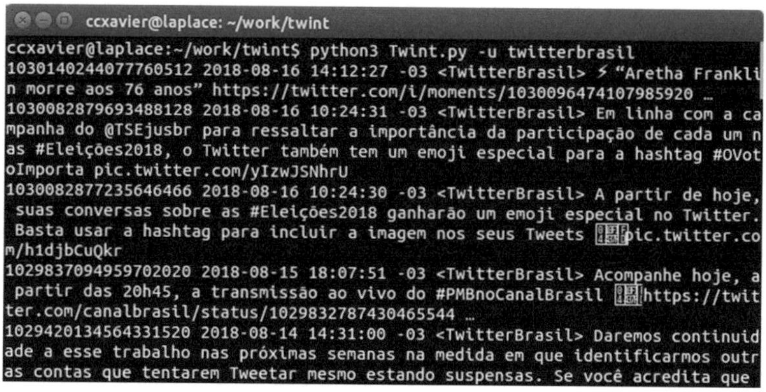

**Fig. 7.4** Results of the command for listing all tweets from a user account

### 7.2.3.5 Search Results

API

Method *search/tweets*[13] returns tweets corresponding to the search parameters. These parameters may include keywords, hashtags, phrases, regions, usernames, or ids.

Listing 7.8 shows the Python code for getting tweets containing the keyword informed as the "search" parameter.

**Listing 7.8 Python code to call *search/tweets* API**

```
def search_tweets(search):
    GET_URL =
        "https://api.twitter.com/1.1/search/tweets.json?q="+
        search
    req = oauth_req(GET_URL,ACCESS_TOKEN,ACCESS_KEY)
    return req
```

Twint

The command returns all tweets containing the keyword informed as a parameter
`python3 Twint.py -s [keyword]`. Figure 7.5 shows the Twint command
and its return for searching "eniac" keyword.

---

[13] https://developer.twitter.com/en/docs/tweets/search/api-reference/get-search-tweets.html.

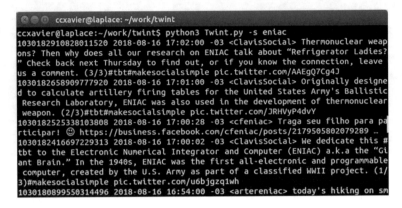

**Fig. 7.5** Results of the command for searching tweets containing a certain keyword

## 7.3 Polarity Analysis

According to [5], Polarity Analysis (including Sentiment Analysis) is a type of text classification based on the feeling orientation of the opinion. In our opinion, this task is one of the most interesting Text Analysis applications.

Sentiment Analysis main task at the sentence level is to find its polarity. For example, a positive feeling is attributed when the tweet indicates happiness, excitement, or sympathy. A negative feeling is related to anger, sadness or difficult situations. When no emotion is suggested, the text can be classified as neutral [9].

Due to its informal and specific language, tweets polarity analysis is a unique task. Post classification according to the sentiment expressed has several applications in political science, social sciences, market research, etc. [13–15]. Pak and Paroubek [17] present reasons for using Twitter as a corpus for sentiment analysis and opinion mining:

- Microblogging platforms are used by many people to express their point of view on different topics, being a valuable source of opinions.
- Twitter contains a large number of text posts that grows every day. In this way, the collected corpus can be quite large.
- The Twitter audience ranges from ordinary users to celebrities, business representatives, politicians, and country presidents. Therefore, it is possible to collect text messages from users of different social groups and interests.
- The Twitter audience is represented by users from several countries.

To exemplify how polarity classification of tweets works, Table 7.1 shows examples of positive and negative classification.

**Table 7.1** Tweets polarity classification example

| User | @ivetesangalo |
|------|---------------|
| Tweet | I am very happy and very thankful for all this love *V V V*[a] |
| Polarity | Positive |
| User | @EPTC_POA |
| Tweet | At this point, the bus station access in Vespasiano Julio Veppo square, from Conceição tunel is very complicate[b] |
| Polarity | Negative |

[a]Original text in Portuguese: Estou muito feliz e muito agradecida por todo esse amor *V V V*
[b]Original text in Portuguese: Neste momento, bem complicado o acesso a Rodoviária no Largo Vespasiano Julio Veppo, pelo Túnel da Conceição

## 7.3.1  Approaches

The main approaches for this task are:

### 7.3.1.1  Rule-Based Approach

In this approach patterns or rules are defined to understand the opinions about the text. Behavior [5]:

- For each sentence:

  - Tokenize.
  - Start with neutral punctuation (0).
  - For each pattern found, apply a rating (punctuation).

- The sentence is considered positive if the final polarity score is greater than zero or negative if the overall score is lower than zero.

### 7.3.1.2  Lexical-Based Approach

Lexicon-based techniques assume that the polarity or feeling expressed by a sentence or document can be identified by the polarities of the lexical units composing it.

According to [6], the lexical unit (lexical item) is the unit of meaning in the mental lexicon, which serves as a vehicle for language culture and can be composed of one or more words (head, umbrella, dirty money, etc.).

In order to perform the sentiment analysis using lexical methods, it is necessary, initially, to preprocess the texts. This step aims to reduce the volume of data before beginning the execution of the analysis steps. After preprocessing, the sentiment analysis method must represent each text and its words. In these representations, each word is represented by a weight. This weight may simply be its frequency, or, for example, the TF-IDF value. The weight of the positive or negative word increases proportionally as the number of occurrences of it increases in the document. This value can be balanced by the inverse of the frequency defined for each term. With this, it is possible to distinguish the fact that some terms are generally more common than others in the positive or negative context [4].

### 7.3.1.3 Machine Learning-Based Approach

This approach strategies work through the application of a training algorithm. This algorithm first trains itself using a set of training data and then performs the learning itself. Thus, machine learning techniques first train the algorithm with some specific inputs and then work with new unknown data [5].

We will focus on this approach to perform tweets polarity classification. In this way, we will evaluate the following classifiers:

- Maximum Entropy: Ratnaparkhi [19] says that "*according to the maximum entropy principle, the correct distribution is the one that maximizes the entropy or uncertain subject to the constraints that represent the "evidence," that is, the facts known by the experimenter.*" This principle is often invoked in modelling, assuming that the observed data itself is testable information.
- Naive Bayes is a probability model that assumes independence between the input resources, based on the application of Bayes' theorem. It assumes that the presence of a specific feature does not relate to the existence of any other feature [7].
- Support Vector Machine (SVM) is a supervised classification algorithm extensively and successfully used for text classification [18]. Given a set of training examples, each one marked as belonging to a category, the SVM training algorithm creates a template that assigns new examples to a category. An SVM model is a representation of the examples as points in a hyperplane. The algorithm calculates a line of separation (hyperplane) between two classes of data (represented in Fig. 7.6). This line aims to maximize the distance between the nearest points in relation to each class [3].

**Fig. 7.6** Hyperplane graphic
representation (central line)

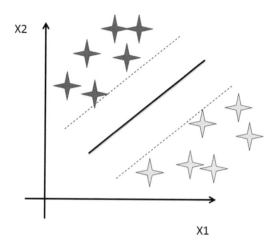

## 7.3.2   Practical Example

In order to understand how these concepts work in practice, we will review a polarity classifier implemented in Python using the NLTK library.[14]

NLTK Python library implements tools for natural language processing. It provides interfaces to corpora and lexical resources such as WordNet, along with a set of word processing libraries for sorting, tokenization, stemming, texting, parsing, and semantic analysis [1].

Classification is the task of applying the correct label to a particular entry. In basic classification tasks, each entry is considered isolated from all other entries and the label set is defined in advance. In this example, we will consider polarity analysis as a classification task where tweets can be classified as Positive, Negative, or Neutral.

We will work with supervised classification. A classifier is called supervised when it uses a training corpus. Figure 7.7 represents its framework which is divided into two defined steps: training and learning, as detailed below.

1. Training: the features extractor converts each input value into a feature set. Pairs of feature sets and labels feed the machine learning algorithm to generate a model.
2. Features are fed into the model, which generates the new labels (classification), which is used to convert new entries (not present in feature sets).

---

[14]http://www.nltk.org/.

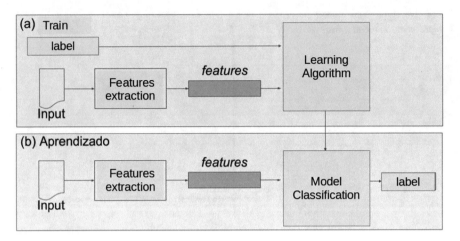

**Fig. 7.7** Supervised classifier framework. Based on [1]

Machine learning classifiers usually require text input represented as a fixed-length vector. Probably the most common of these vectors is the bag-of-words due to its simplicity, efficiency, and precision [10]. In this model, the text is represented as a bag or set of words, disregarding grammar and even word order, but maintaining multiplicity. The bag-of-words vector example for the sentence Ana likes Zeca, Zeca likes Lia and Lia does not like anyone would be ["Ana":1, ''like":3, "Zeca":2, "Lia":2, "and":1, "does":1, "not":1, "anyone":1]

Our experiments use this model as the feature set.

### 7.3.2.1   Feature Extraction

In Listing 7.9, we can see the Python code that implements the extraction of features, that is, the input vector creation in the bag-of-words model, which will be used both by the algorithm of learning as by the classification model, as shown in Fig. 7.7.

Function split() receives as input a sentence vector and returns a word vector for each sentence from the input vector. For instance, considering the input vector:

["Accented traffic in both directions of Carlos Gomes Avenue x Campos Sales."][15],

---

[15]Original in Portuguese: Trânsito acentuado nos dois sentidos da Av. Carlos Gomes x Campos Sales.

the function returns the output:

```
['accented', 'traffic', 'in', 'both', 'directions', 'of',
    'Carlos', 'Gomes', 'Avenue','x', 'Campos', 'Sales'].
```

The function described in Listing 7.9 creates the bag-of-words vector.

**Listing 7.9   Python code implementing features extraction**

```
def split(data):
    data_new = []
    for word in data:
        word_filter = [i.lower() for i in word.split()]
        data_new.append(word_filter)
    return data_new[0]

def bag_of_words(words):
    return dict([(word, words.count(word)) for word in
        words])
```

#### 7.3.2.2   Training

Listing 7.10 shows the Python code that implements training of three types of supervised classifiers using the NLTK library: SVM, Naive Bayes, and Maximum Entropy.

The training data are @EPTC_POA[16] tweets manually labelled as "pos" (positive), "neg" (negative), and "neu" (neutral). These data are available for download at https://github.com/clarissacastella/twittercourse/.

The function uses the bag-of-words features generated by function listed at Listing 7.9 and returns a trained model for each of the three sorting algorithms.

---

[16]https://twitter.com/EPTC_POA.

**Listing 7.10  Python code implementing classifiers training**

```python
def train_classifiers():
    posdata = []
    with
        open('./traindata/train_EPTC_POA_v3nbal_1.data',
        'rb') as myfile:
        reader = csv.reader(myfile, delimiter=',')
        for val in reader:
            posdata.append(val[0])
    negdata = []
    with
        open('./traindata/train_EPTC_POA_v3nbal_0.data',
        'rb') as myfile:
        reader = csv.reader(myfile, delimiter=',')
        for val in reader:
            negdata.append(val[0])
    neudata = []
    with
        open('./traindata/train_EPTC_POA_v3nbal_2.data',
        'rb') as myfile:
        reader = csv.reader(myfile, delimiter=',')
        for val in reader:
            neudata.append(val[0])
    negfeats = [(bag_of_words(f), 'neg') for f in
        split(negdata)]
    posfeats = [(bag_of_words(f), 'pos') for f in
        split(posdata)]
    neufeats = [(bag_of_words(f), 'neu') for f in
        split(neudata)]
    train = negfeats + posfeats+ neufeats

    #Maximum Entropy
    classifierME = MaxentClassifier.train(train, 'GIS',
        trace=0, encoding=None, labels=None,
        gaussian_prior_sigma=0, max_iter = 1)

    #SVM
    classifierSVM = SklearnClassifier(LinearSVC(),
        sparse=False)
    classifierSVM.train(train)

    # Naive Bayes
    classifierNB = NaiveBayesClassifier.train(train)
    return ([classifierME,classifierSVM,classifierNB])
```

### 7.3.2.3 Classification

The three models created by `treina_classificadores` function are used in the code presented at Listing 7.11 for the function that classifies an input sentence (in this case a Tweet), presented in Fig. 7.7.

**Listing 7.11 Python code implementing a polarity classifier**

```python
def polarity_classification(sentences, classifiers):
    ret = []
    for s in sentences:
        c = split([s])
        feats= bag_of_words(c[0])
        classification = []
        classification.append(classifiers[1].classify(feats))
        classification.append(classifiers[2].classify(feats))
        classification.append(classifiers[0].classify(feats))
        ret.append(classification)
    return ret
```

For instance, when `polarity_classification` function receives sentences "`Flow too congested in Osvaldo Aranha at tunnel access. Now, it's also raining. So, attention! Do not use the cell phone at the wheel, 80% of your attention is diverted`"[17] as input vector, it returns the result vector `[['neg', 'pos ',' neg '], [' neu ',' neu ',' neu ']]`.

In this way, the first tweet was classified as negative by the Entropy classifier, positive by SVM and negative by Naive Bayes. That is, Entropy and Naive Bayes classifiers correctly categorized the text and the SVM classifier did not. The second tweet was correctly classified as neutral by all classifiers.

For further details, the complete polarity classifier implementation can be found at https://github.com/clarissacastella/twittercourse.

## 7.4 Entity Extraction

Entity Extraction (EE), also known as Named Entity Recognition (REN), is an information extraction task that consists of identifying references made to certain entities and their classification. This task is often one of the semantic analysis first steps since the mentioned entities transmit much information about the content of the text itself.

---

[17]Original in Portuguese: Fluxo muito congestionado na Osvaldo Aranha no acesso para o Túnel. Agora, tá chovendo também. Então, atenção!, Não use o celular ao volante, 80% da sua atenção é desviada.

Twitter posts small format poses some difficulties in its processing. For this reason, EE methods that applied to other types of text may not have the same precision in tweets. For example, [12] shows that a state-of-the-art annotator, such as Stanford NER,[18] has its performance quite reduced when applied to Twitter texts.

Short texts offer little contextual information for entities identification. In addition, important features to identify proper names, such as capitalization, are not strictly used on Twitter. Sub-capitalization is very common, that is, no word is capitalized, as well as super-capitalization, where several or all words are capitalized, usually with intention of denoting intensity. Thus, EE methods should generally be adapted to this context.

To demonstrate how to perform EE on tweets, the following example shows which entities can be extracted from the @EPTC_POA post listed in Table 7.1 "At this point, the bus station access in Vespasiano Julio Veppo square, from Conceição tunnel is very complicated"[19]. using the format `[entity (classification)]`.

```
[bus station (LOC)] [Vespasiano Julio Veppo square(LOC)]
   [Concei\c{c}\~{a}o Tunel(LOC)]
```

Recent EE systems use machine learning techniques, in a way that it becomes the main approach, in contrast to older systems that used manually coded and heuristic rules. In this way, EE has been treated as a sequential labelling task [22].

Twitter EE tools, in general, use state-of-the-art techniques associated with optimization strategies such as preprocessing heuristics, or semi-supervised learning methods, or semi-supervised methods [11] that explore the large amount of non-annotated data available.

### 7.4.1 Practical Example

Aiming to apply these concepts in practice, let us explore a machine learning solution that extracts entities from tweets implemented in Python using spaCy[20] library, an open-source library for advanced natural language processing. SpaCy is a deep learning-based solution that interacts with the Python artificial intelligence ecosystem libraries. The library uses a statistical EE system, which assigns labels to contiguous extensions of tokens.[21]

---

[18]https://nlp.stanford.edu/software/CRF-NER.shtml.

[19]Neste momento, bem complicado o acesso a Rodoviária no Largo Vespasiano Julio Veppo, pelo Túnel da Conceição.

[20]https://spacy.io/.

[21]Tokens usually correspond to the lexical units of a text, i.e., approximately the words of the text. For instance, the sentence "complicate traffic" tokens are `[complicate] [traffic]`.

In the presented implementation we create the spaCy model pre-trained for Portuguese language. Currently spaCy provides support for more than 20 languages,[22] such that the presented techniques can be implemented in other languages.

### 7.4.1.1   Training

The library generates statistical models. Every decision, like if a word is an entity, is a prediction. This prediction is based on the examples learned during the training. To train a model, it is required a set of data consisting of text samples and labels that must be predicted by the model. Model training is not just examples memorization, but patterns generation to generalize other examples. For this reason, training data must be representative.

Listing 7.12 shows the Python code for changing the training data contained in ./data/dataTrainingLoc.txt file into the model input format. Function create_training_data transforms a list of tweets and the locations quoted in them into a vector containing a tuple. Table 7.2 shows the function operation. The Input line consists of an excerpt from the input file and the Output line represents the tuple corresponding to the excerpt within the output vector.

**Listing 7.12  Python code that formats training data**

```
def data_training(file='./data/dataTrainingLoc.txt'):
  data\_training = []
  fin = open(file, 'rb')
  n=0
  post = u''
  for val in fin:
    d = {}
      n = n + 1
      if (n % 2 == 1) :
      post = val.replace('\n','')
    else :
      d['entities']=ast.literal_eval(val.replace('\n',''))
      data_training.append((post, d))
  fin.close()
  return data_trainning
```

Listing 7.13 presents the Python code that creates a new spaCy model to perform EE and trains it with the data imported by the function data_training (Listing 7.12) by following these steps:

---

[22]https://spacy.io/usage/models#languages.

**Table 7.2** Function `data_training` operating example

| Input | 5:53 pm—ATTENTION! Car and motorcycle accident on Dom Pedro II St, south/north direction, near Barão do Cotegipe St. [(48,63,'LOC'), (94,114,'LOC')] |
|---|---|
| Output | { [...(5:53 pm—ATTENTION! Car and motorcycle accident on Dom Pedro II St, south/north direction, near Barão do Cotegipe St.', ( {'entities': { [(48,63,'LOC'), (94,114,'LOC')] } } ] } |

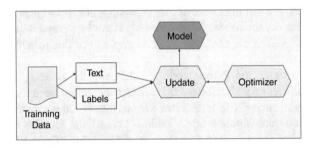

**Fig. 7.8** EE training flow. Adapted from [23]

- Create a blank template.
- Add NER pipeline to the model, responsible for EE.
- Read the training data.
- Train Model.

The training data is shuffled before each iteration, as represented in Fig. 7.8. Training data is shuffled in each iteration, in order to avoid generalizations based on the order of the examples . A loss rate is set to "discard" individual resources and representations at random. For example, a drop of 0.25 means that each feature or internal representation has a chance of 1/4 of chance of being dropped.

**Listing 7.13   Code for training a new EE model**

```
path = "./modelEE" # create blank model
path = Path(path)
nlp = spacy.blank('pt') #working with Portuguese
    Language
path.mkdir()
ner = nlp.create_pipe('ner')
nlp.add_pipe(ner, last=True)

import data_training as tr
data_training = tr.data_training('./data/test.txt')

for _, annotations in data_training:
    for ent in annotations.get('entities'):
        ner.add_label(ent[2])

# train EE
optimizer = nlp.begin_training()
n_iter = 5 #iteractions
for itn in range(n_iter):
    c = 0
    losses = {}
    random.shuffle(data_training) #shuffles to avoid
        bias
    for text, annotations in data_training:
        c = c + 1
        nlp.update(
            [unicode(text)], # text batch
            [annotations], # annotation batch
            drop=0.25,
            sgd=optimizer,
            losses=losses)
    print(losses)

nlp.to_disk(path) #save model
```

#### 7.4.1.2   Learning

Listing 7.14 presents the Python code that performs EE from the previously generated spaCy model by following these steps:

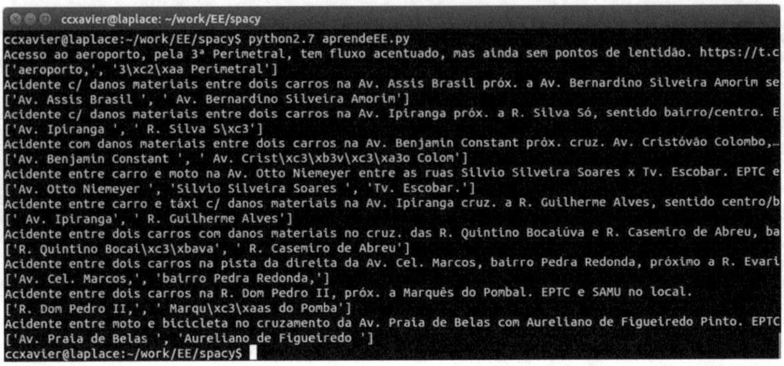

**Fig. 7.9** $ `python2.7 learnEE.py` call and return

- Load model.
- Read posts file.
- For each post: apply EE model.

---

**Listing 7.14 Code that performs EE from the previously generated SpaCy model**

```
model_path = Path ("./modelEE" )
model = spacy.load(model_path) # roda modelo
fin = open('./data/posts.txt', 'rb')
for text in fin:
        doc_model = model(unicode(text))
        locs = []
        for ent in doc_model.ents:
            aux = (ent.start_char, ent.end_char,
                str(ent.label_))
            locs.append(text[ent.start_char:ent.end_char])
        print (text,locs)
```

---

Figure 7.9 shows the program call and corresponding return to the code listed in Listing 7.14.

For further details, the EE implementation is available at https://github.com/clarissacastella/twittercourse.

## 7.5 Twitter Text Processing Challenges

Twitter messages are limited in length to 280 characters. For this reason, tweets can be characterized as short text, similar to other media texts such as short text messages (SMS) or telegram messages.

Short texts have unique characteristics like informal writing, abbreviations, slang, etc. Such characteristics make their processing harder. Also, its understanding is difficult for human readers sometimes. In addition, short texts do not provide important contextual information commonly exploited by various text analysis tools.

In addition, since coming from a real-time internet service, data from Twitter has some unique characteristics, such as large volume, uncertain context distributed in different messages (flow structure or stream).

Different strategies have been used to deal with tweets particularities, such as:

- Text normalization: use of automatic parsing techniques to convert Twitter's noisy text into more formal language, such as correcting spelling errors;
- Tweets grouping: automatic group tweets dealing with the same subject, or contextually linked, to create texts capable of providing more relevant contextual information to the text analysis tools;
- Time series: since tweets have a flow structure, i.e., they are time-shifted, some methods for tweet processing use time series-based modelling trying to organically capture the context of tweets from its temporal information;
- Specific tools: some methods and tools require specific strategies for dealing with tweets, taking into account the contextual poverty and their lexical variations.

Each strategy has its own advantages and disadvantages and there is no established solution for the problem. For instance, textual normalization allows the use of well-developed techniques and tools that are specialized in more formal textual styles, such as journalistic texts; however, normalization methods are still quite inaccurate and do not overcome the lack of context difficulties.

## 7.6   Conclusion

Twitter is a valuable source of information about people opinions and feelings about a wide range of topics. For this reason academy, industry, and media organizations are seeking ways to extract knowledge from it.

This chapter presented different approaches to collecting tweets information. First, we saw how to collect information from Twitter using the public API as well as Python Twint library. To perform the extraction and semantic classification of this data, we used Natural Language Processing and Machine Learning techniques. We focused our study on two text analysis tasks: Polarity Analysis and Entity Extraction.

# References

1. Bird, S., Klein, E., Loper, E.: Natural Language Processing with Python: Analyzing Text with the Natural Language Toolkit. O'Reilly Media, Sebastopol (2009)
2. Dale, R.: Where is text analytics today. In: Presentation to Sydney Data Miners Meeting (2008)
3. D'Andrea, E., Ducange, P., Lazzerini, B., Marcelloni, F.: Real-time detection of traffic from twitter stream analysis. IEEE Trans. Intell. Transp. Syst. **16**(4), 2269–2283 (2015)
4. de Souza, K.F., Pereira, M.H.R., Dalip, D.H.: Unilex: Método léxico para análise de sentimentos textuais sobre conteúdo de tweets em português brasileiro. Abakós **5**(2), 79–96 (2017)
5. Devika, M., Sunitha, C., Ganesh, A.: Sentiment analysis: a comparative study on different approaches. Proc. Comput. Sci. **87**, 44–49 (2016)
6. Gómez Molina, J.R.: La subcompetencia léxico-semántica. Vademécum para la formación de profesores. Enseñar español como segunda lengua (L2)/lengua extranjera (LE), Madrid, SGEL, pp. 491–510 (2004)
7. John, G.H., Langley, P.: Estimating continuous distributions in Bayesian classifiers. In: Proceedings of the Eleventh Conference on Uncertainty in Artificial Intelligence, pp. 338–345. Morgan Kaufmann Publishers, San Francisco (1995)
8. Kumar, S., Morstatter, F., Liu, H.: Twitter Data Analytics. Springer Publishing Company, Incorporated, New York (2013)
9. Lalrempuii, C., Mittal, N.: Sentiment classification of crisis related tweets using segmentation. In: Proceedings of the International Conference on Informatics and Analytics, p. 89. ACM, New York (2016)
10. Le, Q., Mikolov, T.: Distributed representations of sentences and documents. In: International Conference on Machine Learning, pp. 1188–1196 (2014)
11. Liu, B.: Sentiment analysis and subjectivity. Handb. Nat. Lang. Process. **2**, 627–666 (2010)
12. Locke, B.W.: Named entity recognition: adapting to microblogging. Technical report, University of Colorado (2009)
13. Martínez-Cámara, E., Martín-Valdivia, M.T., Urena-López, L.A., Montejo-Ráez, A.R.: Sentiment analysis in twitter. Nat. Lang. Eng. **20**(1), 1–28 (2014)
14. Mejova, Y., Weber, I., Macy, M.W.: Twitter: a digital socioscope. Cambridge University Press, Cambridge (2015)
15. Nakov, P., Ritter, A., Rosenthal, S., Sebastiani, F., Stoyanov, V.: SemEval-2016 task 4: sentiment analysis in twitter. In: Proceedings of the 10th International Workshop on Semantic Evaluation (semEval-2016), pp. 1–18 (2016)
16. Newman, N., Fletcher, R., Levy, D.A.L., Nielsen, R.K.: Reuters institute digital news report 2016. Technical report, Reuters Institute for the Study of Journalism, University of Oxford (2016)
17. Pak, A., Paroubek, P.: Twitter as a corpus for sentiment analysis and opinion mining. In: LREc, vol. 10, pp. 1320–1326 (2010)
18. Pawar, P.Y., Gawande, S.: A comparative study on different types of approaches to text categorization. Int. J. Mach. Learn. Comput. **2**(4), 423 (2012)
19. Ratnaparkhi, A.: A simple introduction to maximum entropy models for natural language processing. IRCS Technical Reports Series p. 81 (1997)
20. Recuero, R.: Weblogs, Webrings e Comunidades Virtuais. Revista 404notfound-Revista Eletrônica do Grupo Ciberpesquisa **31**, 1–15 (2003)
21. Sobre as APIs do twitter. https://help.twitter.com/pt/rules-and-policies/twitter-api (2018). Accessed 10 Sept 2018
22. Souza, M.V.d.S.: Mineração de opiniões aplicada a mídias sociais. Master's thesis, Pontifícia Universidade Católica do Rio Grande do Sul (2012)
23. Training spaCy's statistical models. https://spacy.io/usage/training (2018). Accessed 10 Sept 2018

**Clarissa Castellã Xavier**, Ph.D., started to work with Natural Language Processing (NLP) in 1999 at Catholic University of Rio Grande do Sul (PUCRS) NLP Research Group and received her doctoral degree in 2014 in the same institution. Since then, she worked for multi-cultural companies around the world, developing language-processing tools for social media and networks. She accomplished a post-doctoral fellowship with focus on semantic data extraction from social networks for urban traffic analysis at the Federal University of Rio Grande do Sul (UFRGS) in 2018. Her current research focuses on semantic data extraction from social networks and multilingual Open Information Extraction. She is also guest researcher at Federal University of Bahia (UFBA) FORMAS research group.

**Marlo Souza**, Ph.D., received his doctoral degree in 2016 at Federal University of Rio Grande do Sul (UFRGS) and currently is adjunct professor at Federal University of Bahia (UFBA). His teachings and research activities focus on theoretical computer science, knowledge representation, applied logic and NLP. He started working with NLP in 2007 in the context of CoGROO project—Free Grammatical Broker for OpenOffice, moving thereafter to Pontifical Catholic University of Rio Grande do Sul (PUCRS) NLP Research Group where he studied entity identification methods and opinion mining on Twitter. Integrates UFBA FORMAS research group working with semantic information extraction from text.

# Chapter 8
# Data from Multiple Web Sources: Crawling, Integrating, Preprocessing, and Designing Applications

**Natércia A. Batista, Michele A. Brandão, Michele B. Pinheiro, Daniel H. Dalip, and Mirella M. Moro**

## 8.1 Introduction

The Web is under constant evolution to manage the most diverse types of documents that go well beyond the original hypertext (e.g., video, sound, image, and the like) as well as allowing users to create and publish their content. Both academia and industry have explored Web data in a variety of ways and for immeasurable purposes because of its huge volume.

In fact, there are different Web data sources, including sites and applications, media and social networks, and even complete databases. Examples of data sources available in the Web include Excel spreadsheets, Comma-Separated Values (CSV) files, relational and non-relational databases, data warehouses, and different Web platforms (e.g., social sites and applications). Such data sources are generally unstructured, denormalized, inconsistent, duplicate, incomplete, and of varying quality [9, 12, 23].

In this vast context, any Web-oriented search requires establishing a relationship between these data sources to better combine and analyze them [18, 22]. That is, when considering multiple data sources, researchers and developers acquire a greater insight into the context studied, promoting the discovery of complementary

N. A. Batista · M. B. Pinheiro · M. M. Moro
Federal University of Minas Gerais (UFMG), Minas Gerais, Brazil
e-mail: natercia@dcc.ufmg.br; mibrito@dcc.ufmg.br; mirella@dcc.ufmg.br

M. A. Brandão (✉)
Federal Institute of Minas Gerais (IFMG), Belo Horizonte, Brazil
e-mail: michele.brandao@ifmg.edu.br

D. H. Dalip
Federal Center of Technological Education of Minas Gerais (CEFET-MG), Minas Gerais, Brazil
e-mail: hasan@decom.cefetmg.br

© Springer Nature Switzerland AG 2020
V. Roesler et al. (eds.), *Special Topics in Multimedia, IoT and Web Technologies*,
https://doi.org/10.1007/978-3-030-35102-1_8

information, which allows to make more precise inferences or to identify patterns that only become visible when these multiple sources are connected. As a practical and real example, consider two of the largest online social platforms that are independent of one another: Facebook (social networking friend) and GitHub (collaborative software development platform). In order to understand different collaboration profiles, researches can integrate data from both in order to, for example, analyze how personal relationships influence software development; check whether a developer is popular on GitHub by also being on other social media; or if a developer can influence the developers community by creating new development patterns as well as disseminating new patterns in another social network; among many other interesting possibilities.

Another practical and real example is using data from multiple sources to support decision-making, mainly considering the financial aspect [12]. In this context, an e-commerce team can analyze the profile of its users on different social networks to discover interests and then recommend combined sales. However, doing so requires to collect, integrate, and preprocess data and then be able to extract *value* (and then financial gain) from such data.

Overall for both examples (collaborative development and targeted marketing), the solution starts at obtaining the data from the Web. Technically, the first problem is to select or develop the *crawling* strategy defining several aspects such as the seed, crawling periodicity, and/or whether to crawl/navigate from an URL. The strategy to *integrate* data from multiple sources is also important to provide a uniform view for users or applications as well as adequate storage, which also allows to efficiently query the data afterwards. Finally, due to quality issues and other problems, the data may not be ready and may go through preprocessing, either before or after data integration. It involves the resolution of missing and duplicate data, normalization, and other strategies.

In summary, as Fig. 8.1 illustrates, developing any research or application with Web data requires: collect such data from various sources (usually spread around the Web); integrate such data and often applying different preprocessing strategies to, finally, perform analyses and apply any technique which commonly have their

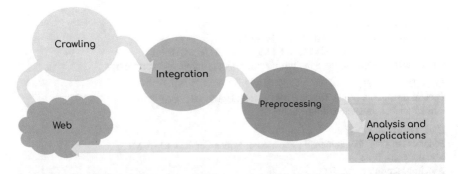

**Fig. 8.1** Web Data from multiple sources analysis process and topics covered in this chapter

results reported or stored again on the Web (closing the cycle). Overall, collecting, integrating, and preprocessing data from various (often heterogeneous) sources represent different challenges, including: collecting data in real time, tunning crawling tools, deciding on privacy issues, standardizing different data, solving duplicate data, working with non-uniform data, useful mining, and quality patterns, among others.

Although known, such tasks are often complex and context-dependent. For example, according to [20] data scientists spend 80% of their time preprocessing data. In practice, not only data scientists, but also programmers, researchers, students, companies, and users can benefit from solving these challenges. In particular, everyone can benefit when such solutions return to the community through the publication or availability of standardized and complete data on the Web.

Hence, the motivation of this chapter is to help researchers and developers who need Web data and reduce the time to obtain such data by presenting existing solutions of several of the challenges previously mentioned. This chapter addresses the three steps in an integrated way: crawling, integration, and preprocessing, and presents solutions that can be applied to the research and development of commercial applications. The organization of this chapter is as follows: Sect. 8.2 presents Web data sources; Sect. 8.3 summarizes the Web data crawling process; Sect. 8.4 presents strategies for data integration; Sect. 8.5 discusses the main problems during data preprocessing; and Sect. 8.6 details a real data application by using GitHub. Finally, Sect. 8.7 presents the final considerations and pointers to other sources of information on the subjects discussed here.

## 8.2  Web Data Sources

Web data processing requires prior knowledge of the available sources. Such knowledge allows to trace a data collection plan and defines strategies that can improve its efficiency and coverage. In this section, we present some of the most common types of data sources on the Web, such as open data, connected data, APIs, and web pages. For each source, we also present existing challenges.

### 8.2.1  Open Data

As the name implies, open data is data made available openly. In 2004, a nonprofit organization called *Open Knowledge Foundation* (OKF)[1] was created to encourage and define a set of policies for publishing open data. It generally states that open

---

[1]Open Knowledge Foundation: https://okfn.org/.

data shall be made fully available, in machine-readable form and without using restrictions. Specifically, the directives presented by OKF include:

- availability and accessibility—define that the open data must be fully available at a cost no higher than the cost of reproduction, and preferably available for download;
- reuse and distribution—define that the data must be distributed with a license that allows its reuse including mixing with other databases, in addition to being in a machine-readable format; and
- universal participation—defines that data must enable universal participation, i.e., they should be capable to be used, reused, and distributed by any person without discrimination, such as restrictions for non-commercial purposes or educational purposes only.

There was also a strong involvement of several countries in the opening of official data as a form of state transparency. Thus, there are great portals of data publication. Examples of these large public data portals are the Brazilian portal,[2] the American[3], and the European.[4]

Publishing such data on the Web has its own challenges, such as indexing, cataloging, and retrieving these datasets. Generally, these challenges are a consequence of the way the data are published—as already mentioned—in machine-readable file formats such as Extensible Markup Language (XML), CSV (Comma-separated Values), and JSON (JavaScript Object Notation). Thus organizing data usually requires metadata that is informed about these files. Therefore, all operations of indexing, cataloging, and retrieval of information are performed in relation to their metadata.

There are different applications for publishing data catalogs. Most allow queries over metadata only, i.e., they do not allow to query the query per se. In the context of general-purpose data applications, stand out tools such as CKAN[5] and Socrata.[6]

On the other hand, there are also databases that have a specific data type such as spatial data. For this type of data, there are specific applications that allow both metadata search and spatial data visualization, and even their joint visualization by composition with stacks of layers. These applications are called Spatial Data Infrastructures (SDIs—Spatial Data Infrastructure). There is a number of alternative implementations of SDIs, including GeoServer,[7] most popularly used,

---

[2] Brazilian Open Data Portal: http://dados.gov.br.

[3] data.gov: https://www.data.gov.

[4] European Data Portal: http://europeandataportal.eu.

[5] CKAN:https://ckan.org.

[6] Socrata: https://socrata.com.

[7] GeoServer: http://geoserver.org.

and MapServer.[8] In case of SDI's, the data is published following the standard's defined by the Open Geospatial Consortium (OGC) for both data formats and service protocols.[9]

## 8.2.2  Linked Data

Linked data is a topic in the Semantic Web area. Therefore, to understand its representation, we first discuss the purpose of the Semantic Web, as well as the contextualization of the key points in its structuring.

The Semantic Web is an extension of traditional Web that includes information about the meaning of the data on your pages or openly published. The meaning of the data is then considered as the way data can be interpreted by applications. Having access to data meaning allows applications to perform more complex tasks in a more autonomous way. Thus, through this type of information, an application that collects Web pages can identify the meaning, for example, of the term "Bertha Lutz" as the name of a person, address (street, avenue, neighborhood, hospital, etc.). Based on this knowledge, the application can then perform more precise actions on these data, such as storing them as spatial data, discarding if it is not the type of data the application is interested in collecting, or connecting a data to other information previously encountered by the crawling process, thus generating a more complex data set with more information about its context.

For representing the context and meaning of the data, the Semantic Web proposes two important concepts: Ontology and Vocabulary. The concept of ontology comes from Philosophy and implies the study of the nature of the existence and property of beings and "things." For Computer Science, ontologies are data models that represent the description of beings, objects, and things that exist in the world. Thus, ontologies in the Semantic Web have the function of describing what a data refers to. In the case of the previous example, on the term "Bertha Lutz," the place can be described by ontologies such as street, avenue, neighborhood, school, hospital. Within the concepts of Semantic Web, languages were also defined for the description of ontologies, as the most commonly used OWL (Web Ontology Language). Through OWL it is possible to describe ontologies using components such as Classes, Attributes, Individuals, Relationships, Functional Terms, Constraints, Rules, Axioms, and Events [19].

---

[8]MapServer: https://mapserver.org.

[9]OGC: http://www.opengeospatial.org.

On the other hand, vocabularies are collections of terms used to describe one area of interest. For example, one of the most commonly used vocabularies for describing "People" is called FOAF (Friend of a Friend[10]), and presents terms that represent classes such as *OnlineAccount*, *PersonalProfileDocument*, properties like *hosts*, and so on. Vocabularies, in general, can be referenced during the publication of data through *namespaces*, which in turn are represented by *"xmlns"* attributes.

In short, the concepts of ontology and vocabulary are similar. Also, according to W3C[11] there is no clear separation between the two. However, Ontologies are usually referred to more complex data description models.

The linked data represents data that is related to each other. They are used in the context of the Semantic Web for expliciting the meaning of the data, as well as the meaning of the relationships represented. Thus, they are able to represent broadly both the data sense and the context of their relationships.

One of the most widely used formats for representing linked data is RDF (Resource Description Framework). This format is able to represent the description of any type of data present on the Web. Therefore, the framework has its own vocabulary that allows describing information about the data like literals, classes, properties, lists, sets, and sequences [19]. RDF is structured with sentences that follow the form subject-predicate-object (or resource-property-value), also known as *RDF triple*. The triples, in this way, are able to express the properties of a content present in the Web, as well as its context. Expressing the properties of a resource is the simplest task, since the triples represent the resource-property-value sentence. Thus, this triple shape can be used to characterize the resource through its properties. On the other hand, RDF can represent a relation between resources present in the Web, using triplets of the subject-predicate-object form, where the object is another resource also available on the Web, and the predicate specifies the meaning of the relation established between both.

Returning to the example of Bertha Lutz, we can create a file with the N-Triple format that describes the information related to the Brazilian biologist, as well as other information related to its context. Code 8.1 shows these two ways of using triples; that is, applied to describe the properties of a resource, and to describe its connection with other resources.

---

[10]FOAF: http://xmlns.com/foaf/spec/.

[11]W3C: https://www.w3.org/standards/semanticWeb/ontology.

**Listing 8.1  RDF example using N-Triple" source code**

```
<https://www.wikidata.org/wiki/Q1264246> <rdf:type>
   <foaf:Person> .
<https://www.wikidata.org/wiki/Q1264246> <foaf:knows>
<https://www.wikidata.org/wiki/Q199652> .
<https://www.wikidata.org/wiki/Q1264246>
   <schema:birthDate> "02-08-1894"^^<xsd:date> .
<https://www.wikidata.org/wiki/Q1264246>
   <foaf:publications>
   <http://memoria.bn.br/DocReader/178691_05/36862> .
<https://www.wikidata.org/wiki/Q10301958>
   <dcterms:title>
   "A Federacao Brasileira pelo Progresso Feminino:
      seus fins" .
<https://www.wikidata.org/wiki/Q10301958>
   <dcterms:creator>
   <https://www.wikidata.org/wiki/Q1264246> .
```

Listing 8.1 utilizes one way to represent RDF known as N-Triples, but there are also other formats that follow the concepts proposed by the RDF as N-Quad and Turtle, which are part of the RDF language family called *Turtle*, as well as RDF/XML, RDFa, and JSON-LD. The detailed description of the usage of these formats can be seen on the W3C's page about RDF.[12]

To understand the relationships established by the RDF triples, the previous example is illustrated in Fig. 8.2. The figure shows how triples connect the Bertha Lutz's resource to its own properties, like date of birth and to other resources, like Bertha Lutz publications'.

The linked data is also called this way because it represents and describes the connections between resources available on the Web. Thus, it is possible to express the links between the content of different contexts, such as people to objects through relations of belonging, interests, etc. In this sense, there is an effort to publish this type of data in an open way. Since these data can be interconnected in different contexts, the combination of these databases has the potential to generate numerous complex applications, since they also carry the semantics of such data and relationships. In this way, there is an effort to standardize the process of publishing these types of data in the form of open data. The open data of this nature has been called Linked Open Data (LOD). There are already several LOD databases,[13] which

---

[12]https://www.w3.org/TR/rdf11-primer/#section-graph-syntax.

[13]LOD Cloud: https://lod-cloud.net/.

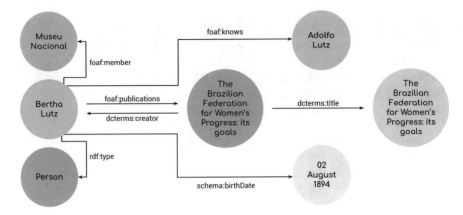

**Fig. 8.2** Graphic representation of the example presented using RDF in N-Triples

began to be published in the mid-2007, with emphasis on DBpedia, GeoNames, and Freebase (Fig. 8.3).

## 8.2.3 Web Pages

Web pages are the most common form of data that can be collected. Such pages were created to allow the dissemination of information on the Web, with the main purpose to display such information to users obeying visual elements defined by their authors. In this way HyperText Markup Language (HTML) was created, which allows the pages to be disseminated while maintaining the formatting stipulated by the content producers.

Due to the initial purpose of the Web, its pages have been developed in a less structured way, because although the visual elements are interpreted, there is no common data model between pages that guarantees a unique structure between them. That is, by disregarding the rendering elements, the Web pages were not developed for their data be interpreted by machines, but instead by humans.

Collecting data from these pages requires knowledge of HTML navigation and query tools such as XPath (a query language for XML documents [18]) that allows navigation in the HTML structure tree. In addition, although there is no well-defined data model for the Web as a whole, it is sometimes possible to find a data model specific to some domains. This occurs when Web pages constitute a way of displaying data that is already structured on a database in which those sites' content relies on. Examples include user profiles on social networks, product sales pages, data from different publications in a digital library, and more.

With the emergence of the Semantic Web, there has also been an advancement in the conventions of using HTML tags and their possible attributes in order to

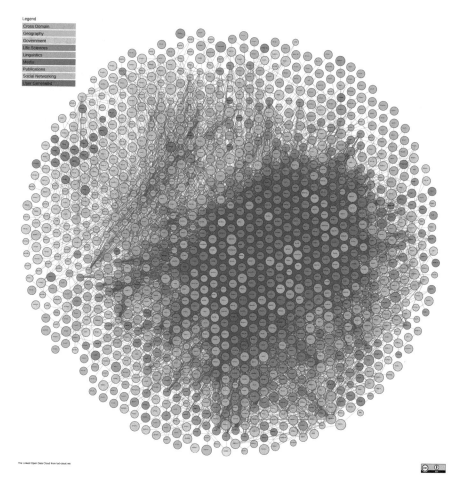

**Fig. 8.3** Distribution of relationships between open connected databases. Source: *Linked Open Databases Cloud*

comprise the description of the shared data. In the case of Web pages, the insertion of semantic annotations allows classic applications to be improved. Examples of such applications are the search engines, which have come to better understand the content of web pages, improving indexing and the quality of query results. Among the main changes of the HTML, should be highlighted the insertion of metadata through microformats, RDFa, *microdata*[14] for HTML5 and JSON-LD.

Microformats are one of the first attempts to include semantic information in web pages and follow ideas such as those of the so-called Plain Old Semantic HTML.[15]

---

[14]HTML Microdata: https://www.w3.org/TR/microdata/.

[15]Plain Old Semantic HTML: http://microformats.org/wiki/posh.

Therefore, they are based on the strategy of reusing some of the attributes of existing HTML tags (such as *rel*, *class*, and *rev*) to annotate the meaning and meaning of the data present on one page. There are also some patterns[16] to describe several entities through the microformats, among the most known ones are the *hCalendar* for the description of events and the *hCard* for personal contact information, companies, and organizations. Back on the example of Bertha Lutz, one can publish data about the founding event of the League for the Intellectual Emancipation of Women, in which she was involved, as well as the personal basic information of the researcher, as can be seen in the Listing 8.2.

**Listing 8.2  Usage example of the microformats pattern *hCalendar* and *hCard***

```
<!-- hCalendar -->
<span class="vevent">
 <span class="summary">
 Fundacao da Liga para Emancipacao Intelectual da
     Mulher
 </span> on <span class="dtstart">1919</span>
 ocorrida no
 <span class="location">Brasil</span>
 organizada por <span class="organizer">Bertha
     Lutz</span>.
</span>

<!-- hCard -->
<div class="vcard">
 <span class="fn given-name">Bertha</span>
 <span class="fn family-name">Lutz</span>
 <div class="adr>
  <span class="type">Nascida em</span>
  <span class="locality">Sao Paulo</span>,
  <abbr class="region" title="Sao Paulo">SP</abbr>
  <span class="country-name">BRA</span>
 </div>
</div>
```

RDFa is another way of annotating semantic information in HTML pages, specifically focused on the concept of linked data. RDFa proposes the implementation of RDF triple's concept through new attributes (*vocab*, *typeof*, *property*, *resource*, and *prefix*) that are inserted in traditional HTML tags. In general, the page containing the RDFa represents the subject of the triples, when it is not highlighted by the *resource* attribute, as presented in the Listing 8.3 by using the attribute in the *div* tag. In case

---

[16]Microformats wiki: http://microformats.org/wiki/Main_Page.

of the predicate, this is annotated by the *property* attribute; and the object to which this predicate refers is the content existing within its tag, as was used in the *h2* tag containing the title of Bertha Lutz's article in Listing 8.3. The other attributes indicate information present in RDF, such as vocabulary, types, and prefix, which is used in RDF to reference a *namespace* or vocabulary, exemplified in *body* tag (8.3).

**Listing 8.3  Usage example of RDFa**

```html
<html>
  <head>
    ...
  </head>
  <body vocab="https://bib.schema.org/Thesis">
   <div
    resource="/bertha_lutz/publications/thesis"
    typeof="Thesis">
    <h2 property="https://schema.org/headline">
     A Nacionalidade da Mulher Casada perante
     o Direito Internacional Privado
    </h2>
    <h3
     property="https://schema.org/author"
     resource="#me">
     Bertha Lutz
    </h3>
    <div property="text">
     <!-- article content -->
    </div>
   </div>
  </body>
</html>
```

Another way to annotate the semantics of data in a Web page is through *Microdata* for HTML5. This approach was developed specifically for HTML5, and therefore is compatible with it (unlike Microformats, for example, which in some cases have incompatibility in reusing some attributes in elements when using HTML5 to encode a page). Microdata also uses the key-value pattern through the attributes introduced by this format, among which includes the ones: *itemscope*, *itemtype*, *itemprop*, *itemid*, *id*, *itemref*. Specifically, *itemprop* should be used to indicate a new object scope, as can be seen in the first *section* tag in Listing 8.4. The *itemprop* attribute must generally be accompanied by the semantic information of this object through the *itemtype* attribute, which can assume values that are a reference to a vocabulary or ontology.

In Listing 8.4, the first *section* tag is followed by the information that it refers to a person, described by the *FOAF* vocabulary, identified with its *itemtype* attribute.

The *itemid* attribute can be used to indicate the identifier of the object described in the context of the Website or application. Therefore, it can be used by sites that display objects that are cataloged in a database, for example. This attribute is used in Listing 8.4 code as an attribute of the *section* tag, with value 3309.

Finally, the attributes *id* and *itemref* are used to establish a relationship between two objects on the same page, when these objects are not nested, for example. The *id* should not necessarily has the same semantic value as *itemid* attribute, but should be consistent with its reference using *itemref*. An example of using such references can be seen in Listing 8.4 when a description of the Bertha Lutz publications is made. The elements that describe the feminist's personal information are presented in the first *section*; this reference is used later, in the second *section*, for the description of Lutz's publications.

**Listing 8.4  Usage example of *microdata***

```html
<html>
 <head>
  <title>Bertha Lutz</title>
 </head>
 <body>
  <section itemscope itemtype="foaf:person"
   id="berthaLutz" itemid='3309'>
   <h1>
    <span itemprop="foaf:firstName">Bertha</span>
    <span itemprop="foaf:surname">Lutz</span>
   </h1>
  </section>
  <section itemref="berthaLutz" itemscope
   itemtype="foaf:publications">
   <div itemprop="schema:article">
    <a itemprop="rdf:resource"
     href="http://memoria.bn.br/docreader/178691_05/36862">
     A Federacao Brasileira pelo Progresso Feminino: seus
        fins
    </a>
    <span itemprop="dcterms:creator">Bertha Lutz</span>
    <span itemprop="dcterms:creator">Carmem de
        Carvalho</span>
    <span itemprop="dcterms:creator">Orminda Bastos</span>
   </div>
  </section>
 </body>
</html>
```

Within the mentioned formats for data publication in Web pages followed by their semantic information, JSON-LD is the most different one. This format uses the *script* tag of the HTML language to specify all objects referenced on the page using JSON (JavaScript Object Notation). For this, the *script* tag is marked with the *type* attribute indicating that it refers to a JSON-LD format code. Following the semantic annotation logic, the *@context* and *@type* keys define the vocabulary or ontology to which the object is addressed. In addition to these keys, *@id* is another key defined by the model and should be used to annotate the identifier of that object in its dataset. Additionally, any other kinds of properties defined by the ontology can be used inside JSON-LD document. An example of this format usage can be seen with the example of Bertha Lutz in Listing 8.5.

**Listing 8.5 Usage example of JSON-LD**

```
{
  "@context":
      "https://json-ld.org/contexts/person.jsonld",
  "@id": "https://pt.wikipedia.org/wiki/Bertha_Lutz",
  "name": "Bertha Lutz",
  "born": "1894-08-02",
  "father": "https://pt.wikipedia.org/wiki/Adolfo_Lutz"
}
```

## 8.2.4 APIs

In the mid-2007, the Web experienced a transformation in the way of organizing its pages. This transformation happened through the emergence of Web 2.0 concepts that change the way data published on the Internet is produced. Specifically, Web 2.0 has brought a new insight into how to best use the features already available on the Web to include the Web page's viewer-only users in the production of content circulating on the network. In this way, the idea of Web applications, which are similar to traditional for *desktop* applications, has arisen and they includes functions for data creation, modification, persistence, and visualization known by the CRUD standard (*Create, Retrieve, Update*, and *Delete*). On the other hand, the Web applications differ from applications in *desktop* because they allow access from any Web browser, being available without the need of installing any other program.

Because it is a different environment from the desktop, there has been the need to develop new architecture concepts for this new kind of application. In this sense, [10] proposes the layered architecture, which is widely adopted in this type of application. This architecture divides applications into components that are distributed across three main types of layers: Application, Business, and Persistence. Figure 8.4 illustrates such architecture. The application layer contains all applications that can be created to manipulate the same dataset present in the Persistence layer. The APIs then appear as components that integrate the Business layer (which is responsible for organizing the entire logic of CRUD operations) and control the users requests permission to manipulate the data present in the Persistence layer, among other security assignments.

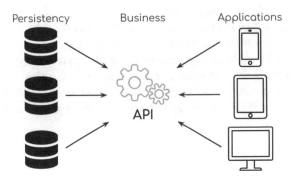

**Fig. 8.4** Web applications' layer architecture

To generate third-party applications that revert to a greater use of their Web applications, the companies commonly grant access to APIs that allow to some extent the manipulation of their data through services requests. This strategy allows these third-party applications to be developed without the companies necessarily having to spend their resources to do so. Through this grant, these APIs become another data source on the Web.

In addition, the APIs have expanded their use with the concept of service-oriented architecture[17] (SOA). In this sense, SOAP (Simple Object Access Protocol) was the first service standard to be formalized. This standard states that service requests must be made through HTTP (Hypertext Transfer Protocol) and Remote Procedure Call (RPC) protocols, and messages must be exchanged using the XML format. Years later, a new service architecture called REST (Representational State Transfer) [10]—also known as RESTful—was proposed. The vast majority of services implemented with the REST pattern also use JSON (JavaScript Object Notation) format for messages exchanged over the HTTP protocol.

Note that access to these APIs is accomplished only with the grant provided by companies like: Google, Facebook, Twitter, etc. Therefore unlike previous unrestricted access data, access to data provided by the APIs requires a prior registration within those companies. This registration usually takes place on behalf of applications that wish to use the API and not on behalf of the developers; and in it, developers ensure that this application will follow the policies of access and use of data with the limitations imposed by companies. After registration, applications receive an access key (or set of keys) that must be used to authenticate requests made to the API. Through this authentication, companies can control which applications request their information and enforce their access policies.

Access policies vary among APIs, but generally they try to ensure that the service is not overloaded by requests, and that part of the user's data can only be accessed if the user has granted that permission to the application. The first access policy case

---

[17]Web Services Architecture: https://www.w3.org/TR/ws-arch/.

is common in almost all APIs, and is defined by measures such as the number of requests per time interval (minutes, hours, days, for example), or by the time interval between requests (seconds, minutes, for example). In some cases, noncompliance with this policy may result in penalties for the applications, usually in the form of the temporary interruption of the response to their requests. Therefore, this policy must be observed by the applications that consume the data of the APIs, so that it does not block its operation.

The second type of access policy is related to applications that manipulate user data with their consent. In this case, these applications usually implement an authentication protocol known as OAuth. This authentication protocol allows users to grant permission to third-party applications to access their data. In some cases, companies require developers to specify what data applications want users to access, so the users are informed about which data the third-party application intends to access when they are granting access to their data.

One of the advantages of data accessible through APIs is that they have a clear and documented requests signatures and data schema. Because these APIs follow a well-defined protocol, the format of their messages is largely XML or JSON. On the other hand, the schema of the data provided is characteristic of each API, and companies generally provide documentation on the schema adopted. In addition to the data format, in the case of the APIs it is important to understand the format of the requests, both to handle the authentication process and to know which *endpoints* are available to be used on data collection and manipulation by the developed applications. The documentation covers all of this information, as well as the usage restrictions of these *endpoints*, such as access policies, which may also vary between *endpoints* in the same API.

## 8.3   Web Data Crawling

There are several ways to collect data from the several types of data publishing on the Web discussed in the previous section. In the first two types of data presented (Open Data and Linked Data), both can be obtained as a dump in the open data sites. These data are made available in a structured way, on machine-readable formats such as XML, CSV, and JSON, for general purpose open data; and in the form of RDF/XML, N-Triples, N-Quad in the case of linked open data (LOD). It is usually possible to get the whole data about a particular subject from a source through download, since those sites already offer this content organized as a dump.

On the other hand, Web pages and APIs maintain fragmented or scattered data, requiring the use of an application to collect and store in the developer desired structure that may include relationships between the fragmented content. In the case of Web pages, the data is scattered in several files, which depending on the intended application for their content, requires to collect them through different domains, like search engines that sweep over tons of different pages and domains indexing these files. In the case of APIs, although the content is well-formatted, the relationship between the information provided is what may not be directly available, such as the relationships of friendship in social networks and the profiles of the users that are part of the relationship of friendship, for example. In addition, the size of the database that these sources cover is very large, and it is possible that not all of the data in these contexts is required for the desired analysis. For these reasons, it is convenient to develop applications to handle the collection in an organized way, with a clear definition of what information will be collected, as well as how they will be stored so that the developer can make use of them. These data collection applications are commonly called *crawlers*.

Crawlers have various applications in several areas such as information retrieval and complex networks. For information retrieval, Baeza-Yates and Ribeiro-Neto [3] lists six types of applications specific to this context: Web browsing in general, search for specific topics, Web page archives, Web characterization, Website analytics, and Web mirrors. For complex networks, crawlers can be used in studies of online social networks (OSNs) involving the analysis of relationships among their users, for example. Finally in the middle of both areas, retrieval of information and complex networks, there is also structure analysis of the graph formed by Web pages.

Baeza-Yates and Ribeiro-Neto [3] also present three aspects that the crawlers explore: updating, quality, and volume. The first aspect is dealt with crawlers which are constantly functioning and keeping the bases up to date. The second value for portions of the Web that have better quality (which the concept may be different among application) in the disseminated data and that quality is homogeneous between pages. Finally, the volume corresponds to the number of pages collected that may be reduced to favor the updating maintenance or better quality.

### 8.3.1 Crawling Challenges

The data crawling also has specific problems that must be observed such as time between requests, soft-404 error, identification of URL patterns of the pages, and extraction of data from the source code. The first challenger is present in both Web pages and APIs. In the case of Web pages, this information is made available by site administrators in a file called *robots.txt*. This file formalizes the general guidelines of good practices that crawlers must follow when collecting their pages. Thus, in these files the requisition time information is present, as well as which sections of the site the administrator allows to be collected, and which sections would like to not be checked.

The second problem is related to the soft-404 error. Error 404 occurs when trying to access a page that does not exist, and usually this response is given directly by the server. There is a small portion of sites (29% are missing page links according to [3]) that instead of returning a the *404 HTTP error* with no content, returns a *200 HTTP ok server* response with a content page informing that the resource requested was not found. This problem increases the complexity of crawlers and worsens the efficiency of collection time since it is only possible to verify that the returned page is valid when it is opened and interpreted.

Identifying URL patterns allows the crawler to be implemented using the trial-and-error technique. In many cases, the sites represent a visualization of the data present in databases. It is common to use a standardization of URLs based on the identifiers of the records present in those databases. Thus, knowing the maximum number of records, it is possible to predict the structure of the record identifiers (such as sequential keys). Based on this information, the crawler can be responsible for checking which of these predicted keys lead to actually existing data.

Finally, extracting source code is another task that depends on the knowledge of parsing tools or in the HTML tree of Web pages. Adding the parsing step during the crawling reduces the amount of data that will be stored, since all HTML code is removed.

## 8.3.2  Main Crawling Strategies

The crawling process is based on two main techniques: graph walk and probabilistic sampling. The first technique collect data by traversing the graph consisting of the objects to be collected (nodes), and the links between these objects (edges). The WWW (World Wide Web) is one example of this type of graph, where the pages are the objects or nodes to be collected, and the links between pages are the relationships or the graph edges. This type of collection is very useful when you do not have prior information about how many objects exist in the dataset to be collected, as well as how to find them, like by the exact address where each object is located or which identifier that can be used to retrieve it. It is only known that these objects are connected over some kind of relationship.

An example of this technique is the crawling of Web pages by search engines. In this case, the size of the dataset is defined by all Web pages, and in general it is not possible to know before start collecting, the Web address of all your pages. It is known that Web pages are linked through hyperlinks, which establish a citation relationship between pages. So it is possible to develop a crawler that starts from an initial page (commonly called a seed) which is able to find new pages in the Web through the mentioned addresses through hyperlinks. In this way, the crawling is made by traversing the graph formed by the Web pages and their hyperlinks, as the generic example illustrates in Fig. 8.5.

There are three main graph-based techniques for data collection: breadth-first search (BFS), snowball sampling, and depth-first search (DFS). BFS and DFS are the simplest techniques to implement. According to the Algorithm 1, at each iteration, BFS has a set of page links that will be collected, the initial set being called seed. At each link, it is checked if its page has already been crawled. After analyzing each page, you get a set of links that can be used to access new pages (also called neighbor pages). This set of links will be used in a new iteration of the algorithm.

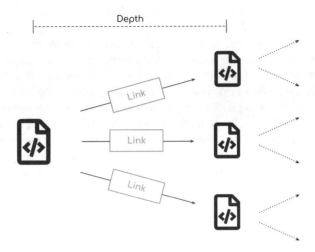

**Fig. 8.5** Web page' graph traversing

---

**Algorithm 1** Breadth-first search algorithm (BFS)
___

1: $L$ set of links on iteration $i$, initially contains the seeds
2: $LNext$ set of links in iteration $i + 1$, initially empty  State $AllLinks$ set of all links obtained
   State $dMax$ maximum height  State $d \leftarrow 0$ current height
3: **while** $d < dMax$ **do**
4:     **for all** $l \in L$ **do**
5:         **if** $l \notin AllLinks$ **then**
6:             $p \leftarrow collect(l)$
7:             $LNext.insert(p.links)$
8:             $AllLinks.insert(l)$
9:     $L \leftarrow LNext$
10:    $LNext \leftarrow \emptyset$
11:    $d \leftarrow d + 1$

___

The Snowball Sampling algorithm is very similar to BFS. The only difference is that it considers only a sample of $k$ links present on each page, thus limiting the maximum width of the tree to $k$ branches [14]. In Snowball, verification is also performed if the new set of links has already been crawled.

Finally, the DFS depth search algorithm, as the name suggests, prioritizes the exploitation of the children before their siblings in the tree graph crawling. Algorithm 2 displays the pseudo-code for DFS using a stack data structure. Again, the algorithm starts with a set of links to seed pages, which are present in the stack $S$. Before crawling a page, the algorithm checks whether this page has already been scanned. The links on the crawled page are then extracted and inserted at the top of the stack. At the next run, the link to be unstacked is the first child of the last collected page. In this way, the algorithm always prioritizes the crawling of the first child of the children sub-tree until the maximum depth is reached. After

**Algorithm 2** Depth-first search algorithm (DFS)

---
1: $S$ links' stack, initially contains only the seeds
2: $AllLinks$ set of all links obtained
3: $dMax$ maximum height
4: $d \leftarrow 0$ current depth
5: **while** $d < dMax \lor P = \emptyset$ **do**
6:     $l \leftarrow S.pop()$
7:     **if** $l \notin AllLinks$ **then**
8:         $p \leftarrow collect(l)$
9:         $S.push(p.links)$
10:        $AllLinks.insert(l)$
11:    $d \leftarrow d + 1$

---

this point, the siblings of the first child in the bottom of the tree are traversed before their ancestor siblings been collected. This process repeats until all pages are crawled.

## 8.4 Data Integration

After collecting data from multiple sources, the next step is *integrate*. In summary, data integration consists of combining data from different sources to obtain valuable information. Such a task has been the focus of many studies because of the large amount of heterogeneous data available on the Web [8, 11, 13]. Integration is important to allow users to have a unified view of heterogeneous data and easily consult different information about them [6]. In addition, this integration allows you to consider multiple definitions/views about an object. For example, [17] use data from multiple sources to identify various drug side effects, and [11] propose a model based on ontologies and data binding (Linked Data) to integrate data sets to calculate the probability of maternal and infant death risk. Thus, users can better discover knowledge from multiple data, and then this integration can provide support for decision-making among many other applications.

However, there are different challenges in integrating data from multiple sources, mainly because most Web data is heterogeneous, unstructured, or semi-structured. In addition, data from various Web sources have distinct models, different representations of real-world objects, and are not always reliable. Another relevant challenge is to keep the data schema consistent after integration, because every change in the data source is necessary to check if the changes need to be propagated by the schema, whether new queries to the data need to be elaborated or if the schema needs to be rewritten [6, 15].

A commonly used approach to data integration is ETL: extraction, transformation/cleanup, and loading [2, 4]. Consider different datasets extracted from different sources and provided as input for conducting a particular study, which needs to be integrated. To do so, there are three main steps: (1) Extraction represents

**Table 8.1** Examples of data integration approaches and their applications

| Approach | Application |
| --- | --- |
| Mediator system | Provides a single view of the data in distinct formats for the user |
| Natural language processing | Process data in text format to allow the standardization and subsequent integration of such data |
| Bayesian approach | Handles incomplete and inconsistent data to ensure that the resulting dataset is reliable |

the acquisition of data from multiple sources; (2) processing and cleaning refer to the standardization and cleaning of the data, which is not always mandatory but is good practice; and (3) loading refers to the insertion of the data into an organization system including, for example, worksheets (although they are not highly recommended for storage and management of large volumes of data), data warehouse, database management systems, etc.

We emphasize that ETL and data integration are distinct concepts. ETL are software tools, while data integration is an architecture.[18] Thus, ETL can be used as part of the data integration step, but not necessarily represent the entire integration. In addition to ETL, the data integration task also includes data modeling, data profiling, structured and unstructured data processing, real-time integration, data governance, among others [8]. Hence, the data integration area is quite broad and comprehensive, and only the main strategies are addressed here.

In practice, you can collect data from each source and store them separately for later integration; or store all of the data in a single location in an integrated fashion as each data collection is performed. There are many advantages and disadvantages of both strategies and different forms of storage. Specifically on the first approach, different volumes of data can be stored in a single repository called Data Lake. Such a store allows users to query the data differently.

Among many strategies for integrating data from multiple sources, we cite: mediator system [6] which is an approach to map different data sources in a global scheme; natural language processing [17] that allows you to convert text from different sources into unique identifier codes; and Bayesian approach [22, 24] which provides a way to integrate reliability information into multiple levels.

An analysis of the definition and application of these approaches reveals that there are different situations in which each of them can best be used to integrate data, as shown in Table 8.1. Indeed, the pros and cons need to be evaluated for a better choice. In addition, such approaches can be used in combination. For example, natural language processing can be used to identify relevant features in the text and enable the storage of such data in a standardized way. Then, the Bayesian approach can be applied to integrate the data to ensure reliability. Finally, the mediator system can be used to ensure a single view of the data.

---

[18]Difference between ETL and data integration: https://www.passionned.com/is-data-integration-becoming-the-new-etl/. Accessed on February 4, 2019.

## 8.5   Data Preprocessing

Web data provide invaluable resources for many researchers and developers. However, this data can come with many problems, especially when collected from multiple Web sources, including missing values, false data (data veracity), duplicate data, reduced data, and lack of standardization. Such problems are usually solved in the data preprocessing step, which requires about 80% of the time of data scientists (as has been pointed out in many studies, such as [20]). Moreover, the representation of the collected data may not be ideal for the processing of the algorithms and analyzes on them. In this way, it is necessary to convert the obtained data into suitable representations.

Data preprocessing strategies vary according to the context and data type. For each type of problem there are some suggestions for solution. However, the application of the solution to the data should be analyzed for each case. For example, in the case of missing values a possibility is to complete them by searching values from some other source (when available) or deleting the records that do not have the complete information. Next, we discuss each of the problems pointed out, presenting solutions suggestions from examples available in the literature.

**Missing Values** They occur when no value is stored for a variable (or attribute) of the database. Missing values may occur in only a few records or they may be important data for the analysis that are not available to any database records. The question then is whether the data should be extracted from some other source or the database must be cleaned to remove such values [1]. In some cases, you can look for another data source that has the specific information available and can be easily integrated with the current database. Assessing the feasibility of data integration is important, since different sources may not present a link binding of records for them to be related. As a third option, a default value can still be found to replace such missing data, when necessary.

**Data Veracity** The problem of data veracity refers to the evaluation and improvement of data accuracy [12]. Usually, the presence of biases, abnormalities, and noise in the data, which are often present in the data collected on the Web, compromise their veracity. When creating and maintaining knowledge bases, one must validate the data and provide its sources to ensure the accuracy and traceability of the information. Because truthfulness is an important issue that directly affects the information and knowledge extracted from the data, there are different strategies for improving or securing this. For example, [12] propose the DeFacto model (*Deep Fact Validation*) that seeks to perform the validation of facts by finding reliable sources for them on the Web.

**Duplicate Data Removal** Duplication of data can occur more simply when there are more copies of the same data on a database. This is an easier case to resolve because you just need to identify identical values and remove them. On the other hand, the case of records that are not completely identical is more difficult, because identifying them requires understanding if indeed those records relate to

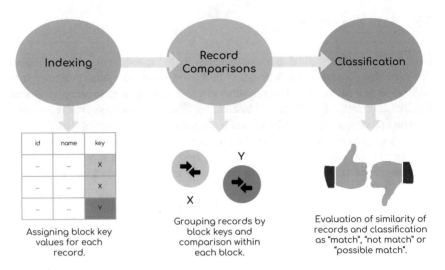

**Fig. 8.6** Data deduplication process [7]

the same information. For example, in proper names with and without abbreviation or omission of any of the surnames: Mirella M. Moro, Mirella Moro, and Mirella Moura Moro. In these cases, you can use context features to identify duplicates, such as user names or e-mail [21], or even other important features [7]. Specifically, [7] present strategies to improve the process of removing duplicates. Figure 8.6 shows the process for identifying duplicates in a database. Initially, the *indexation* of the records is made to divide them into initial groups. Then, comparisons are made between records of the same group, and finally sorting is done to identify duplicate data. The authors identified that in the first step, indexing, the choice of the attribute used is of great impact for the whole process. Then, they proposed a better way to choose this attribute considering aspects such as duplicity, distinction, density, and repetition.

**Data Reduction** Reducing data addresses the problem of minimizing the amount of data that will be stored in the dataset. Depending on the volume of data, storing them in an ordinary database or processing them is a problem related to both space and time. Solutions commonly used include: minimizing data or storing it by considering another form of storage [16], or extracting samples from the complete database without losing most of the analysis [5]. For example, [5] use both strategies to reduce stored data. Specifically, when analyzing the entire GitHub network, some challenges were encountered regarding the volume of data and some context specificities. In this way, the collaboration network was divided in programming languages, selecting the languages with the largest number of repositories. JavaScript, Java, and Ruby languages have been chosen. From the analyzes, the authors realized that the behaviors of the developers within the network of each language are similar, which allowed the results to be obtained in this way.

**Absence of Standardization**  Data standardization is the process of restructuring data into a common format. Having data collected from multiple Web sources can generate a set of data that is not only heterogeneous, but also in a different format. So starting the actual search requires first standardizing all the data. Although the data collected are sufficient for the analyzes to be performed, if they are disorganized or without a standard, they make it difficult to analyze rather than to assist. In this way, it is important to evaluate the database to find the way that this data must be organized to generate the desired results. In some cases, proposing a new modeling for the data collected is a way to organize them formally and standardize them as a whole [5].

## 8.6   Practical Example with GitHub

In order to show an actual application for data crawling, integration, and preprocessing, this section practical examples using GitHub.

### 8.6.1   Preprocessing

On GitHub, we can model the relationship between users when they have collaborated in the same project. Because of this, it is important to know the period when the user is active in the project. However, GitHub API did not provide the date in which the user has left the project. Then, in the preprocessing step, we need to infer when the user left the project by using the last commit of him/her. By doing this, we can create a collaboration social network considering only users who have collaborated in the same time period.

### 8.6.2   Applicability

To show the applicability of this data processing, we here present a collaboration graph $G = (V, E)$ in which $V$ is the set of vertices, representing the developers, and $E$ is the set of edges between two developers which contribute to the same repository. We can assume this contribution of a user considering: (a) if they contributed during the project or (b) when they contributed in the same time frame. Note that, by doing the data preprocessing previously described, we can infer the time which a user contributed to a project.

In order to analyze the impact of using the time frame, we have crawled a JavaScript GitHub repository containing 55 users. This repository started on March 2012 and its last activity was on September 2015. Figure 8.7a shows the graph in

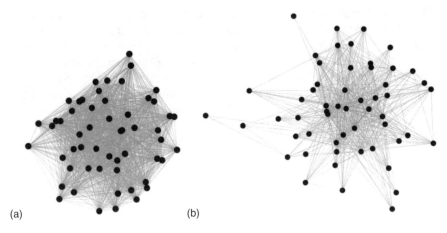

(a)                                                                    (b)

**Fig. 8.7** GitHub collaboration graph in a single repository (**a**) with links between all developers and (**b**) with links between developers contributing in the same time frame

which we did not consider the time frame. By doing this, the graph formed a clique[19] with all the developers and, consequently, the density[20] was equals to 1. On the other hand, by generating edges only between developers who collaborated in the same time frame, we have a less dense graph as shown in Fig. 8.7b (density = 0.385). In other words, the amount of edges in the network is reduced to 571, that is, 38% of the original quantity. Therefore, this new modeling expresses a more realistic scenario of the relationship between developers in a large repository.

In some cases, we want to crawl a more complete sample of GitHub and/or integrate with other social networks. Then, we here present approaches to perform crawling and integration in GitHub.

### 8.6.3  Data Crawler

Here, the goal is to build a collaboration graph by considering a sample from GitHub. To do so, we perform a breadth-first search considering the user and their repositories. Let $Q$ be a queue of users we want to explore. Then, we extract the first user of this queue to extract all the repositories which the user collaborates. After that, we can request the users that collaborate with these repositories and add them to the Queue $Q$. We repeat this process until the Queue is empty or we reached a

---

[19]In graph theory, a clique is a set of vertices in a graph where each vertex is connected to all others by an edge, so it is a fully connected graph.

[20]Density is the ratio between the number of edges in the graph and the maximal number of edges.

limit of users/repositories we want to collect. Finally, we have a graph $G$ where the nodes are the user and there is an edge $(u, v)$ if the user $u$ collaborates in the same repository as the user $v$.

The crawler is performed by using HTTP requisitions and returns JSON files. Listing 8.6 presents how the requisition returns the data for a user. Notice the format of the results of HTTP requisitions for repositories and contributors of repositories are similar to the users.

---

**Listing 8.6 Example of GitHub API to show user information: https://api.github.com/users/lab-csx-ufmg**

```
{
  "login": "lab-csx-ufmg",
  "avatar_url": "https://avatars1.githubusercontent.com/u/15199560?v=4",
  "html_url": "https://github.com/lab-csx-ufmg",
  "followers_url": "https://api.github.com/users/lab-csx-ufmg/followers",
  "Following_url":
      "https://api.github.com/users/lab-csx-ufmg/following{/other_user}",
  "subscriptions_url":
      "https://api.github.com/users/lab-csx-ufmg/subscriptions",
  "repos_url": "https://api.github.com/users/lab-csx-ufmg/repos",
  "type": "Organization",
  "blog": "http://twitter.com/lab-csx-ufmg/"
  "name": "Lab CS+X UFMG",
  "location": "Belo Horizonte, Brazil",
  "bio": "Interdisciplinary Computer Science Lab",
  "created_at": "2015-10-19T16:28:42Z",
  "updated_at": "2018-10-09T15:26:50Z"
}
```

---

## 8.6.4  Data Integration

Each social network is a different social context of a user. On GitHub, the relationships are based on the project which they have done together. On Twitter, the relationship between users are made according to personal interests and whether one user wants to follow other users updates. Then, it can be important to analyze the Twitter social context of GitHub users. By doing this, we can gather more information regarding the user such as their preferences and compare the relationship strength in different social networks. This allows us a thorough analysis of a social network and its influences. GitHub users tend to inform their Twitter account. Thus, we can use the "blog" information in GitHub user profile to obtain their Twitter account. This can be requested through the GitHub API, as can be seen in Code 8.6. Finally, we can use Twitter API to crawl information regarding their interactions in this social network.

## 8.7   Conclusion

In this chapter, we address three issues on the use of data from different Web sources: crawling, integration, and preprocessing. Following, we summarize the main methodologies for each step, as well as we present potential issues that were not covered in this study.

First, the chapter describes four main sources of Web data: open data, connected data, Web pages, and APIs. Considering the first step of processing such data, crawling concepts were presented, mainly discussing the types of data sources and crawling techniques. Specifically, it presents a set of classifications for the crawlers, their main applications, the main challenges, and three simple crawling strategies based on graph search. Among these crawling techniques are Breadth-First Search, Snowball Sample and Depth-First Search.

After that, this chapter discussed how the integration of data from multiple sources can improve an analysis/application. Without such integration, the chances of misinterpreting the data are much greater. Therefore, as presented, different studies were carried out and different strategies were presented for the integration of data, for example, mediation system, natural language processing and Bayesian approach. We also presented the differences between ETL and data integration, as well as examples for two strategies of data integration for relational databases: vertical and horizontal.

After the data integration process, different types of problems identified in data are handled in the preprocessing step. Some of the most common problems were presented, including missing values, data veracity, duplicate removal, data reduction, and lack of standardization. There are several forms of treatment for each of the problems, and ideal solutions vary according to the context and availability of the data. By showing some studies, we have summarized examples of treatment and how to deal with the problem.

To contextualize the three steps, we also presented an application using GitHub going through the processes described in this chapter: preprocessing, to discover when the developer has left a GitHub repository; crawling of repositories using Breadth-First Search; and data integration with Twitter. In addition, we have shown the importance of preprocessing for data analysis in the GitHub collaboration graph.

The treatment of the data until the generation of the results and its analyzes are fundamental processes for several types of research. The accurate generation of knowledge from data depends on the complete process of crawling, integration, and preprocessing to compose information with quality, comprehensiveness and closer to the reality of the subject studied. In this context, several of the studies are conducted by our research group are available on the Apoena[21] page, together

---

[21] Project Apoena: http://bit.ly/proj-apoena.

with the preprocessed databases. Labs that collaborate with these researches are Lab CS+X[22] at UFMG/Brazil and Piim-Lab[23] at CEFET-MG/Brazil.

Finally, it is important to note that this chapter has limitations that are intrinsic to any such work. Specifically, aspects of data storage or types of management systems for such data were not discussed. However, it is necessary to clarify that many variables are involved in these aspects and should be evaluated on a case-by-case basis. We could also better explore other issues inherent in the large volumes of data that are daily transferred on the Web. The other important aspect which can be explored is the processing of strings, images, and videos. In short, researchers and developers who need to use data from the Web have other challenges that are not addressed here and that need to be considered for the execution of their projects.

**Acknowledgements** The research that resulted in the writing of this chapter was funded by CAPES, CNPq and FAPEMIG.

# References

1. Alves, G.B., Brandão, M.A., Santana, D.M., da Silva, A.P.C., Moro, M.M.: The Strength of Social Coding Collaboration on GitHub. In: Simpósio Brasileiro de Banco de Dados (SBBD), pp. 247–252. Salvador, Brasil (2016)
2. Azeroual, O., Saake, G., Schallehn, E.: Analyzing data quality issues in research information systems via data profiling. Int. J. Inf. Manag. **41**, 50–56 (2018). https://doi.org/10.1016/j.ijinfomgt.2018.02.007
3. Baeza-Yates, R., Ribeiro-Neto, B.: Modern Information Retrieval: The Concepts and Technology Behind Search, 2nd edn. Addison-Wesley Publishing Company, New York (2011)
4. Bansal, S.K.: Towards a semantic extract-transform-load (ETL) framework for big data integration. In: Proceedings of IEEE International Congress on Big Data (BigData Congress), Anchorage, AK, USA, pp. 522–529 (2014)
5. Batista, N.A., Brandão, M.A., Alves, G.B., da Silva, A.P.C., Moro, M.M.: Collaboration strength metrics and analyses on GitHub. In: Proceedings of the International Conference on Web Intelligence, Leipzig, Germany, pp. 170–178 (2017). https://doi.org/10.1145/3106426.3106480
6. Bouzeghoub, M., Lóscio, B.F., Kedad, Z., Soukane, A.: Heterogeneous data source integration and evolution. In: Proceedings of International Conference on Database and Expert Systems Applications (DEXA), Aix-en-Provence, France, pp. 751–757 (2002). https://doi.org/10.1007/3-540-46146-9_74
7. de Souza Silva, L., Murai, F., da Silva, A.P.C., Moro, M.M.: Automatic identification of best attributes for indexing in data deduplication. In: Proceedings of the 12th Alberto Mendelzon International Workshop on Foundations of Data Management, Cali, Colombia (2018)
8. Doan, A., Konda, P., Ardalan, A., Ballard, J.R., Das, S., Govind, Y., Li, H., Martinkus, P., Mudgal, S., Paulson, E., et al.: Toward a system building agenda for data integration (and data science). IEEE Data Eng. Bull. **41**(2), 35–46 (2018)

---

[22]Lab CSX: http://www.labcsx.dcc.ufmg.br.

[23]Piim-Lab: http://piim-lab.decom.cefetmg.br.

9. Farnadi, G., Tang, J., De Cock, M., Moens, M.F.: User profiling through deep multimodal fusion. In: Proceedings of the Eleventh ACM International Conference on Web Search and Data Mining, pp. 171–179 (2018). https://doi.org/10.1145/3159652.3159691

10. Fielding, R.T.: Architectural styles and the design of network-based software architectures. Ph.D. thesis, University of California, Irvine (2000)

11. Freitas, R., Rocha, C., Braga, O., Lopes, G., Monteiro, O., Oliveira, M.: Using linked data in the data integration for maternal and infant death risk of the SUS in the GISSA Project. In: Proceedings of the 23rd Brazilian Symposium on Multimedia and the Web, Gramado, RS, Brazil, pp. 193–196 (2017). https://doi.org/10.1145/3126858.3131606

12. Geerts, F., Missier, P., Paton, N.: Editorial: Special issue on improving the veracity and value of big data. J. Data Inf. Qual. 9(3), 13:1–13:2 (2018). https://doi.org/10.1145/3174791

13. Golshan, B., Halevy, A., Mihaila, G., Tan, W.C.: Data integration: after the teenage years. In: Proceedings of the 36th ACM SIGMOD-SIGACT-SIGAI Symposium on Principles of Database Systems, Chicago, Illinois, USA, pp. 101–106 (2017). https://doi.org/10.1145/3034786.3056124

14. Goodman, L.A.: Snowball sampling. Ann. Math. Stat. 32, 148–170 (1961)

15. Laender, A.H.F., Moro, M.M., Nascimento, C., Martins, P.: An X-ray on web-available XML schemas. SIGMOD Rec. 38(1), 37–42 (2009). https://doi.org/10.1145/1558334.1558338

16. Liu, J., Ram, S.: Using big data and network analysis to understand Wikipedia article quality. Data Knowl. Eng. 115, 80–93 (2018). https://doi.org/10.1016/j.datak.2018.02.004

17. Ma, F., Meng, C., Xiao, H., Li, Q., Gao, J., Su, L., Zhang, A.: Unsupervised discovery of drug side-effects from heterogeneous data sources. In: Proceedings of the 23rd ACM SIGKDD International Conference on Knowledge Discovery and Data Mining, pp. 967–976 (2017). https://doi.org/10.1145/3097983.3098129

18. Moro, M.M., Braganholo, V., Dorneles, C.F., Duarte, D., de Matos Galante, R., dos Santos Mello, R.: XML: some papers in a haystack. SIGMOD Rec. 38(2), 29–34 (2009). https://doi.org/10.1145/1815918.1815924

19. Sikos, L.: Mastering Structured Data on the Semantic Web: From HTML5 Microdata to Linked Open Data. Apress, New York (2015)

20. Tyagi, N.K., Solanki, A., Tyagi, S.: An algorithmic approach to data preprocessing in web usage mining. Int. J. Inf. Technol. Knowl. Manag. 2(2), 279–283 (2010)

21. Vasilescu, B., Serebrenik, A., Filkov, V.: A data set for social diversity studies of GitHub teams. In: Proceedings of the 12th Working Conference on Mining Software Repositories, pp. 514–517 (2015). https://doi.org/10.1109/MSR.2015.77

22. Wang, L., Pan, R., Wang, X., Fan, W., Xuan, J.: A Bayesian reliability evaluation method with different types of data from multiple sources. Reliab. Eng. Syst. Saf. 167, 128–135 (2017). https://doi.org/10.1016/j.ress.2017.05.039

23. Wang, R., Ji, W., Liu, M., Wang, X., Weng, J., Deng, S., Gao, S., Yuan, C.a.: Review on mining data from multiple data sources. Pattern Recogn. Lett. 109, 120–128 (2018). https://doi.org/10.1016/j.patrec.2018.01.013

24. Zhao, B., Rubinstein, B.I.P., Gemmell, J., Han, J.: A Bayesian approach to discovering truth from conflicting sources for data integration. Proc. VLDB Endow. 5(6), 550–561 (2012). https://doi.org/10.14778/2168651.2168656

**Natércia A. Batista**, B.S., is a graduate student in Computer Science at the Federal University of Minas Gerais, with Bachelor in Information Systems from the Federal University of Minas Gerais (2017). She is currently working at the CS+X Interdisciplinary Computing Laboratory and her main interests are in the areas of data analysis and management, and social network analysis.

**Michele A. Brandão**, Ph.D., is a Professor at IFMG and recently finished her postdoctoral in the Graduate Program in Computer Science at the Federal University of Minas Gerais (UFMG), PhD and MS in Computer Science at UFMG, Bachelor in Computer Science at the Universidade Estadual de Santa Cruz (UESC, Bahia). Her main research interests are in the areas of data mining, data management, recommendation systems, link prediction, social networks and digital forensics.

**Michele B. Pinheiro**, M.S., is a PhD student in Computer Science at the Federal University of Minas Gerais (UFMG). She has a master (2016) and Bachelor (2013) degrees in Computer Science, UFMG. She has worked with active crowdsourcing/crowdsensing in the context of geographic data. She currently works in interdisciplinary projects leaded by the research groups CS+X (Department of Computer Science—UFMG) and the Indisciplinar (School of Architecture—UFMG).

**Daniel H. Dalip**, Ph.D., is a Professor at CEFET-MG and his research areas are Information Retrieval, Natural Language Processing and Databases. He has a PhD and MSc degrees in Computer Science from Federal University of Minas Gerais and a BSc degree in Computer Science from University Center of Belo Horizonte (UniBH). During his PhD and MSc, he researched the use of machine learning to assess the quality of collaborative content and his thesis has awarded important prizes.

**Mirella M. Moro**, Ph.D., is an Associate Professor in the Department of Computer Science (DCC) of the Federal University of Minas Gerais (UFMG). She holds a Ph.D. in Computer Science from the University of California in Riverside (2007), and a Master's Degree in Computer Science from the Federal University of Rio Grande do Sul (UFRGS). She is a member of the Education Council of ACM (Association for Computing Machinery). She was Director of Education at SBC (Brazilian Computing Society, 2009–2015), editor-in-chief of the electronic magazine SBC Horizontes (2008–2012), associate editor of JIDM (Journal of Information and Data Management, 2010–2012) and coordinator of Special Commission on Databases (CE-BD) of SBC (2015). Her research interests are in the Database area, including topics such as query processing, social networks, recommendation, bibliometry, and NoSQL.

# Chapter 9
# Multimedia Games User Experience Data Collection: An Approach for Non-experts Researchers

**Márcio Maestrelo Funes, Leandro Agostini do Amaral, Renata Pontin Mattos Fortes, and Rudinei Goularte**

## 9.1 Introduction

Game development refers to an area of knowledge that embraces several lines of studies in Computing, Education, Design, Simulation, Entertainment, among others. Because it involves various possibilities of integration of contents and advanced interaction modes, many researches can benefit from its mechanisms to attend specific demands of scientific methodology procedure, especially data collection.

It is believed that scientific research can obtain many advantages from the use of games [5], but this scenario was, for a long time, difficult to access, due to various obstacles that made the immersion of games in the field of scientific researches timid, including exorbitant development costs and inaccurate graphical representations that limited the simulation fidelity. The advances in game engines (for example, Cry-Engine,[1] Unity,[2] and Unreal Engine[3]) have greatly reduced the problems associated with its adoption. Therefore, it is time to seriously consider the utility of serious games for the research area [5].

In the face of the countless domains of knowledge that approach the game as a theme and attending to the segment that holds the entertainment as a background, emerge the name serious games. In general terms, the expression "serious games" means that games of this type have an explicit educational motivation, carefully

---

[1]http://www.crytek.com/cryengine.

[2]https://unity3d.com/pt.

[3]https://www.unrealengine.com/.

---

M. M. Funes (✉) · L. A. do Amaral · R. P. M. Fortes · R. Goularte
University of São Paulo (USP), São Paulo, Brazil
e-mail: marciofunes@usp.br; leandroagostini@usp.br; renata@icmc.usp.br; rudinei@icmc.usp.br

© Springer Nature Switzerland AG 2020
V. Roesler et al. (eds.), *Special Topics in Multimedia, IoT and Web Technologies*,
https://doi.org/10.1007/978-3-030-35102-1_9

thought, and are not intended to be played exclusively for enjoyment or entertainment purposes. However, this interpretation does not mean that the serious games are not, or should not be, funny; on the contrary, the idea is that the serious games possess creative and pleasing elements as their components. The serious games are projected to have an impact on the target audience, which is beyond pure entertainment [12, 17, 29]. One of the most important areas of application is in the field of education, due to its recognized potential, taking into account the continuous necessity for improvement of techniques and update of educational resources [11, 38]. Another more recent initiative for use of serious games is its application with the elderly audience. This public represents a community of potential users who can benefit greatly from digital games [34], as they represent a tool that contributes to the quality of life during the aging process, alleviating the decline of some aspects resulting from this process, such as motor, perceptual, cognitive, and psychosocial aspects [3].

In this context, according to [37], one of the most promising areas for games applications aimed at the elderly public is the neuropsychological assessment. The games can revolutionize the cognitive assessment of the elderly in clinical settings, allowing for more frequent, accessible, and pleased assessments [35]. In a study of different moments and clinical situations of the elderly, studies [13] reveal that serious games have been very important to maintain and develop the cognitive and social skills of the elderly. In the specialized literature, studies point out that the serious games for the elderly may be an option to improve the deterioration of cognitive functions [36], the maintenance of self-image, motor functions [39], and social life (affection and solitude) [24].

In the face of the relevant potential of research involving games, this chapter adds concepts about the use of games; in particular, it is presented the data collection procedure adopting games and practical examples of development.

## 9.2  Terms and Definitions

There are many terms and definitions used in research for game development and application. Therefore, in this chapter we make a clipping, considering the concepts of the area of games most related to the activity of data collection in the research area, both in the production of complete games or in the use of gamification elements, explained later, to contribute in the engagement of the games.

Player engagement is directly associated with the elements of construction of a game, as well as the enriching of the user experience. In the view of the diversity of user's abilities (both limitations and intensified capacities), it is essential to use guidelines that contribute to the inclusion of a greater number of specificities, contributing with their usability and accessibility.

## 9.2.1 Games and Data Collection

The use of games in the research area aims to enrich the end objective of applied researches, especially in the context of data collection, in the obtainment of scientific evidences that promotes confirmation of questioning under investigation. Thus, the use of games by researchers is not only associated with the planning and development of games as finished or complete products, but also in the use of gamification elements in order to offer support to the tasks required during the activities developed in the research.

Gamification is understood as the use of mechanics, ideas, and aesthetic of games to engage people, motivate actions, promote learning, and solve problems [25]. Therefore, when performing gamification, its use the elements and design techniques of games in situations outside the game environment, in order to obtain greater user participation and involvement [31].

In the context of computer aid to researchers, the concept behind the term "game" can be summarized, as defined by [32]: it refers to a system in which players get mixed up in an artificial rule-defined conflict and that has a quantifiable result.

In general terms, the development of games are based on certain elements that can characterize and even generate the user engagement, such as the system, the players, abstraction, challenge, rules, interactivity, feedback, quantifiable results, emotional reactions, and history [25]. These elements defined below should be considered in the ambit of any type of games.

- **System:** set of interconnected elements that occur in the context of the game;
- **Players:** people interacting with the game or with other people;
- **Abstraction:** refers to a mental image of reality to define the context of the game;
- **Challenge:** the game incorporates activities and objectives that instigate players to achieve goals and results at different levels of difficulty;
- **Rules:** contain the fluidity structure of the game, setting the environment for a proper gameplay;
- **Interactivity:** it is the process of relationship of the player with the content, with the game, or with other players;
- **Feedback:** return of the system to the actions performed by the players;
- **Quantifiable results:** the game must clearly reproduce, to the user, the concept of gain or loss, from the interaction with the player;
- **Emotional reactions:** The game should provide feelings of pleasure or frustration, depending on the outcome of the player's activities;
- **History:** The use of the narrative of a story contextualizes the player to the scenario, introducing a meaning to the game.

In particular, in the context of data collection, games propitiate that innovative forms of application of its elements can be used in procedures to collect data in an unbiased and judicious way, according to the rigor prescribed in the scientific investigations. From the perspective of research methods in general, data collection is considered one of the most important stages of a research [6, 27, 28, 30], whether qualitative or quantitative. Among the main tools used during data collection, there are:

1. **Observation:** when the researchers without any mediation directly notice the facts. It must be planned, registered, verified, and checked for validity and accuracy. Among the disadvantages, the behavior of the observed ones can be changed due to the presence of the researcher.
2. **Interview:** requires formulation of questions to the investigated, being a social interaction. It makes it possible to obtain data referring to a spectrum of information. Among the advantages, it provides clarification and capture of interviewee's expressions (body, gestures, voice...). Among the disadvantages, it can be influenced by the interviewer's personal opinions, as well as involve costs for training and application of interviews.
3. **Questionnaire:** set of written questions presented to the interviewees, it allows that a large number of respondents can participate/collaborate. Among the disadvantages, an exclusion of those who cannot read and write, as well as a requirement of differentiated treatment for the visually impaired people. For example, obstruct the knowledge of circumstances of the interviewee when he replied to the questionnaire.
4. **Documents:** are sources in "paper" (archives, statistical records, diaries, biographies, journals, magazines, reports, memoirs letters, newsletters...) that store different data, which enable the acquisition of knowledge represented therein.

Among the disadvantages: it requires meticulous rigor in obtaining and interpreting the assembled material. It is worth mentioning that these instruments can be used in a complementary way, according to the type of research. In any type of survey (data collection) with the target audience of a research, the utmost care is required when collecting information. Among care, in the context of the theme presented in this chapter, game elements must be properly designed, as discussed in the following section.

## 9.2.2 Games and User Experience

Among the definitions to the expression "User experience (UX)", many researchers converge, considering that UX embraces all aspects of user end interaction with a certain system, service, or product [14, 19].

To [14], a relevant aspect to be considered in the game development, related to the user experience, is that it can be boring when very easy, and frustrating when very hard. The majority of single-player games allow to the player just a gross adjustment in the level of difficult, usually making the choice between the modes of the games possible: easy, medium, hard, or expert [22]. This approach is static in the face of the player interaction with the game and may present a divergence between the player's skills level and the general difficulty of the game.

Few commercial game developers have implemented dynamic adjust systems for their games, among these, it can be cited God Hand® (Clover Studio and Capcom, 2006), in which during the game a gauge regulates the intelligence and strength of opponents. This gauge increases whenever the player succeeds in dodging enemy attacks or striking opponents, decreasing as the player is hit. A great reward is offered to the players who beat opponents that, according to the gauge, are very difficult to their skill level.

However, in the commercial games, in the field of serious games, no initiative was identified in this sense. Not so distant from the adaptability of games to the different skills levels, the user experience may also be related to interface issues. These issues are relatively more complex for people (potential players) who present some decline in their cognitive or motor functions, encouraging research into the design of games intended for universal use, to everybody.

It is important to ponder over a perspective of developing traditional software, which is not a game, considering the user experience. The development with UX for traditional software aims to the user removes the problems. On the other hand, in the game development, the user experience refers it to offer "problems"/challenges to the user. In both cases, the users' required reasoning and their cognitive capacity must be examined.

In general, the work of a developer who concern with the user experience of traditional software is forwarded to create an excellent experience to the user when using the product with a purpose. Thus, this developer does his best to make the interface clear (so the user needs to think as little as possible), suggestive (so the user knows what possibilities of interaction he has), flexible (that adapts as the user develops skills), and rich in information and feedback (so the user knows more about something or situations that bring problems).

It is about driving users to build a mental model that will help them do their job. Classic examples: the steering wheel of a car or the metaphor of the entire work area. The steering wheel is hiding from the user the fact that there is a rather complex mechanism between the wheel and the tires. Instead, it is trying to get the user to think "turn the wheel, turn the car". This is an intentional illusion. The work of game developers, usually, is aimed at creating a great experience to the player to play a game. Therefore, they do their best to create the game:

- **Challenging:** the game is often required to make the user think, carefully, using memory and reasoning capacity.
- **Exploration:** it is usually required that the user think that there is always more possibilities to be discovered.
- **Climbing:** for players to learn to play better, while they play.
- **Surprising:** for the players to be captivated by the spectacle that the game presents. With this relation of excitement, there is even an invitation to error, because it is often required that the users learn through their mistakes.

Finally, while the user experience in traditional software aims to clearly conceal all the intricacy of the product, in the UX games the aim is clearly to teach how to deal with the complexity. Still, accessibility in games is requisite of important quality, and in the next section, it is described.

### 9.2.3 Games and Accessibility

Despite the growing interest in using digital games in different areas, many people, including the elderly ones, are often deprived of its use, whether by some decline, visual, motor, auditory, or cognitive restriction [1, 15].

In order to produce an objective reference to game developers, and in order to include as many people as possible, considering the various needs presented by people with disabilities, a collaborative effort among producers, specialists, and researchers was the accessibility guidelines for games [9].

The specialists and end users should not only use the guidelines during the game development, but also in the continuous evaluation of the application. Given the variety of approaches available to the accessibility assessment for digital games, the use of more than one evaluation method is important to obtain better quality results [10].

In order to consider the limitations of individuals who may be affected by the lack of accessibility, it is generally used the classification defined by the World Health Organization (WHO) in International Classification of Impairments, Disabilities, and Handicaps (ICIDH). It covers the following commitments: visual, which is the consequence of a certain degree of loss of vision; auditory, which refers to the partial or total loss of the ability to hear, by one or both ears; motor, which is the loss or limitation of the function of muscle control, movement, or mobility limitation; and cognitive, which represents a mental or psychological illness, from a retardation developed during infancy to Alzheimer's or senility, as a result of the aging process.

As the popularity of technology increases, efforts are intensified to understand those affected by these commitments, as well as making technology accessible to the greatest number of people. A result of this guidance is a worldwide reference and consists of the Web Accessibility Initiative (WAI), which developed the Web Content Accessibility Guidelines (WCAG) document, developed from the World Wide Web Consortium (W3C) process [20]. The WCAG guidelines guide the production of content (texts, images, forms, sounds) for the Web that is accessible to people with different types of disabilities.

With the reality of the increasing popularity of digital games, the focus of work and research to provide accessibility to this type of interactive systems should also increase, but efforts are still limited in this direction [42]. There are neither official guidelines, standards, or global initiatives, comparable to WCAG in the field of digital games, nor related governmental or legislative actions. However, there are two interventions in order to obtain this set of guidelines: one published by Special Interest Group (SIG), of the Independent Game Developers Association (IGDA), which proposed 19 accessibility guidelines in 2004. Updated in 2010, it was obtained from an experiment with 20 games, prioritizing visually impaired users, and another one from the organization Norwegian MediaLT, which also in 2004 published a set of 34 accessibility guidelines.

More recently, in 2012, in order to produce an objective reference to digital game developers, and to include as many people as possible, considering the different needs presented by people with disabilities, it was carried out a collaborative effort between producers, specialists, and academics, emerging the accessibility guidelines for games.

Parallel to the achievement of accessibility guidelines for digital games, formalized internationally, it is evident the progress of game quality, from the creation of a structured process of game design, called Unified Design (DU) [16]. The DU includes as one of its steps, the assessment of technical accessibility, which can verify the use based on the guidelines, but also resort to the participation of experts and end users.

## 9.3 An Approach for Non-experts Researchers

According to [33], it is increasingly important to explore new forms of interaction, in particular, for collecting data from user experiences. According to [40], the games development and the gamification use allow reaching a significant portion of users, especially younger users, since direct contact with games can occur more frequently in their daily lives. The adoption of gamification elements in case studies, not necessarily related to the games area, can provide new perspectives of data collection, new experiences to the users, and new methods to conduct academic research.

However, there is a need for an approach that satisfies the following requirements: (a) offers several possibilities for supporting the development of games, handling of gamification elements intuitively, (b) that is easy to use even for researchers with no previous experience with the area of games and especially (c) enable the design of case studies, as well as the collection and storage of variables for future analysis.

Considering the previously mentioned requirements on the data collection-oriented games context for researchers who do not have experience in game development, the authors have developed an approach that will be presented in detail in this chapter. The approach aims to assist researchers in the development of their own experiments, allowing the adoption of game elements in their research. The approach is represented in Fig. 9.1.

1. **Experiment Design:** refers to the planning of the purpose of the experiment and what is desired to be obtained with such experiment should be performed after the game development in the initial stage and will be the guide on how the game should be developed. In order to assist the researcher in this design of his experiment, the theoretical concepts about games and user experience will be presented in Sect. 9.3.1.

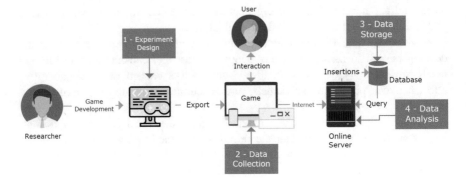

**Fig. 9.1** Approach use example to assist researchers in the development of their experiments involving games and data collection

2. **Data Collect:** occurs during user interaction with the game, which can be designed for multiplatforms (Web, mobile, and desktop). Section 9.3.2 presents the multimedia data collection guidelines and describes the data collection regarding quantitative and qualitative variables. This subsection describes also a case study to exemplify a data collection performed through games using cognitive tests as research base.
3. **Data Storage:** one of the most important parts of game-related research, it is the interaction with users is the way in which the variables will be stored, these topics will be the discussion in Sect. 9.3.3. Such planning guarantees that the data can be analyzed and manipulated in several ways aiming the gain of knowledge related to the objective that the experiment set itself to achieve. Correctly stored data can be later shared and contribute to advancement in the state of the art.
4. **Data Analysis:** after the data collected have been stored in a database, queries to the data can be made by the researcher aiming to knowledge increase. Using statistical methods, several modes of analysis can be performed, on Sect. 9.3.4 will be presented examples of analysis of data collected through games and what results could provide.

Next in this session, each part of the proposed approach will be discussed individually, presenting state-of-the-art examples as well as the practical application of the approach through the Construct 2 tool.

## 9.3.1 Experiments Design

According to [26], the most important activity in Experiments Design is to decide which variables the research needs to collect to reach the established goal. According to the author, thinking about which variables can be obtained during the user interaction and the design of the experiment helps convert generic questions (e.g. Will the user like my game?) to focused and testable research questions (e.g. Can a task get done faster by comparing two interfaces?).

In order to better understand the experiments design process, let us analyze one famous game under the research perspective, the Flappy Bird game. Launched in the year 2013, this game was developed for mobile devices, became very popular mainly because it is very difficult, in the opinion of players, who felt challenged to earn higher scores. Because of the great popularity of this game, several researchers have used this case for better understanding the user experience. As an example of this research's, [23] published one papers named "Exploring Game Space Using Survival Analysis" was conducted with the follow goals:

- To help designers explore game space, like layout, scenarios, and sprites.
- Better understand the relationship between design and player experience.

From the defined focus on the listed objectives, the next step of the research was to delimit the analysis by establishing a research question, in the context of the objectives, which should be discussed and answered. "How can parameters, without changing the rules, affect the game difficulty?". One of the ways found to answer this research question was to conduct a case study containing the following two stages:

- Stage 1—Questionnaire: focus on collecting independent variables: gender, age, game playing experience, and exposure to Flappy Bird games and its clones.
- Stage 2—Ability Measurement: focus on collecting dependent variables: precision, reaction time, and actions per second.

Once the research question is established and what experimental variables will be used in the data collection process, the next step is the development of the game.. Using the case study presented earlier, below we present the approach (Fig. 9.1) to replicate data collection using the Construct 2 tool. To reply the game and apply the approach, a generic Flappy Bird game model that accompanies the free version of the tool will be used. Available as a free Construct 2 template, the development screen for this game is shown in Fig. 9.2, containing the elements needed to develop the data collection mode in the variables.

The first phase of data collection, from the example cited above, used the following independent variables: gender, age, experience as a player, and exposure to the game. It is very common that in case studies, a questionnaire containing questions about users profile and opinions will be applied at some point. To collect the same variables in the game development tool, a new layout must be added to the game, in which will be inserted the fields in which the player must answer the questionnaire.

An advantage of using forms to collect data while playing games is that you can use your own information to change the interaction experience. If a user says he or she is experienced in a certain subject, a possibility (depending on what one wants to collect) lies in the difficulty level that can be adjusted for each user, and thus, at the end of the experiments, the collected data may reflect most loyal, the real user experience.

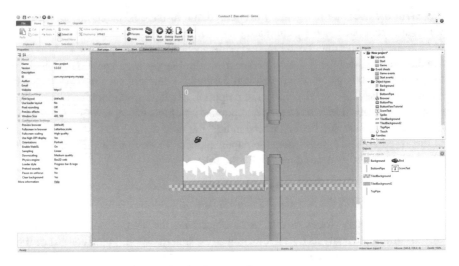

**Fig. 9.2** Flapping bird game template in *Construct 2*

**Fig. 9.3** Graphics elements
created to replicate precision
variable collection

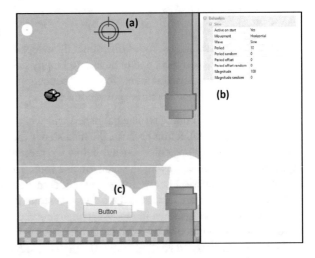

The second stage of data collection, from the example mentioned above, used
the dependent variables: precision, reaction time, and actions per second. For these
variables, quantitative data must be properly collected and clearly presented to
researcher for further analysis.

To collect precision variable, users were instructed to simply click a button
whenever a constantly moving line was horizontally aligned with a target on the
screen. The test was repeated 20 times at three different speeds. To verify the
possibility of the tool replicating the same data collection, the Flappy Bird template
on Construct 2 has been modified as shown in Fig. 9.3.

In Fig. 9.3, the (a) item shows the position of the red target added along with a
black line that performs horizontal movements, and the (b) item shows the setting

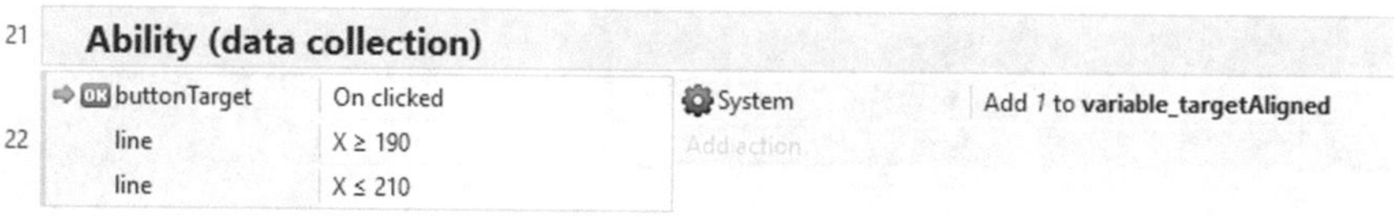

| 21 | **Ability (data collection)** | | | | |
|----|----|----|----|----|----|
| | ⇒ 𝗢𝗞 buttonTarget | On clicked | | ⚙ System | Add 1 to **variable_targetAligned** |
| 22 | line | X ≥ 190 | | Add action | |
| | line | X ≤ 210 | | | |

**Fig. 9.4**  Conditional rule for collect the "Precision" variable on game

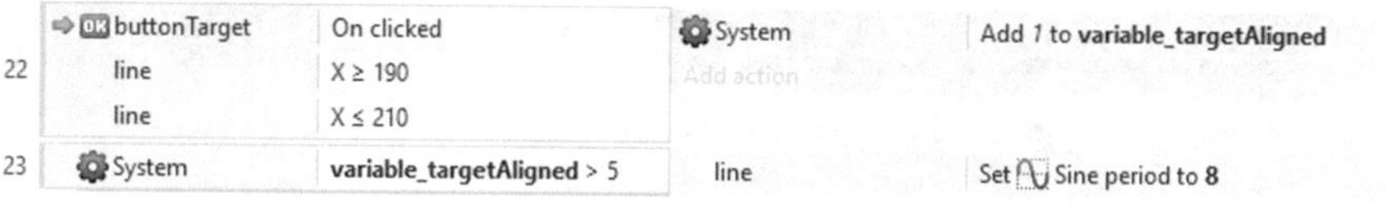

| | ⇒ 𝗢𝗞 buttonTarget | On clicked | | ⚙ System | Add 1 to **variable_targetAligned** |
|----|----|----|----|----|----|
| 22 | line | X ≥ 190 | | Add action | |
| | line | X ≤ 210 | | | |
| 23 | ⚙ System | variable_targetAligned > 5 | line | | Set ⌐⌐ Sine period to 8 |

**Fig. 9.5**  Conditional rule to collect the "Movement Period"

used to assign the line movement behavior. This item is important as it allows for easy line speed change by only indicating a value in the Period field. The (c) item shows the position of the button to be pressed (in the work of which is not specified which name is assigned to the button). These graphics have been added to the game interface using the Construct 2 tool without the need for programming skills, and can be easily repositioned and dragged using the mouse (drag-and-drop), allowing focus on data collection and not in programming these elements by some specific language or method. To verify that the precision rule has been respected, a program has been added to the example as shown in Fig. 9.4.

A condition has been defined on line 22 of the figure, so that a variable called *variable_targetAligned* will only be added to a value when the button (buttonTarget) is clicked and the line is between the values $X \geq 190$ and $X \leq 210$; these values represent the alignment of the target and line in the game interface. This range of values on the X axis can be set for greater flexibility of line alignment with the target. Thus, at the end of the interaction, it is possible to know precisely how many times the user was able to perform the condition of pressing the button in line alignment with the target.

This condition can also be reset during user interaction. For example, on line 23, you can increase line speed by creating the following condition "when variable_targetAligned is greater than 5, the movement period will be 8" as shown in Fig. 9.5.

To measure reaction time, players were instructed to press the button as quickly as they could see the horizontal line on the right side of the game window. The average delay, which allowed the reaction time to be calculated, was obtained using the moment the line was positioned to the right of the window and the moment the user pressed the button. To collect this variable, a schedule has been added, as shown in Fig. 9.6.

In Fig. 9.6, the line 24 contains the rule that only adds one value to the variable "variable_Button_lineRight" and captures the time (seconds) in the variable "variable_Button_lineRight_Time" when the following condition is met: "When the button "buttonTarget" is clicked and the position of the line "line" is greater than or

**Fig. 9.6** Conditional rule to verify the "click" event and the horizontal line position

**Fig. 9.7** Conditional rule to verify the user button touch time

equal to 300" (X axis value $\geq$ 30 indicates if the line is to the right of the game window). In the line 25 rule, the moment (time in seconds) that the line is to the right of the window (X $\geq$ 300) is added to the variable "System_lineRight_Time" by subtracting the two time variables. It is possible to calculate the average delay as objectified in the design of the "Reaction Time" collection.

To collect the data referring variable Actions per Second, users were instructed to keep the button pressed for 10 s. On [23] paper was not specified when users should perform this task. To replicate this collection, the following schedule was added to the example on line 26: "If the buttonTarget button is pressed for 10 s, add a value to the variable 'variable_touchButton'" as shown in Fig. 9.7.

The Construct 2 and other nonprogramming tools have alternative ways of touch-related actions, allowing the researcher, who is not familiar with game development, different alternatives to collect data by performing tasks. By analyzing the [23] work and using the Construct 2 tool, it was possible to understand an example of state-of-the-art experiment design and its alignment with the approach proposed in this chapter. Thus, researchers who do not have prior knowledge of game development have an approach to start their research or experiments to collect user experience data.

### 9.3.2 Data Collection

As presented before, there are many aspects that can be studied in experimental scientific works, as well as their cataloged variables, which can vary widely depending on the test and the objective when performing data collection procedures inside game context. For this reason, sometimes, the unfamiliarity with tools, techniques, and languages used in game development, as well as ignorance of gamification-related elements, may discourage investigators involved in experimental investigations from using alternative forms of data collection in their case studies, for example.

There are currently many tools and resources available related to the game development area. Aiming to help those researchers who do not have expertise with game programming or development, below are some examples of tools that enable the design of games without requiring technical knowledge.

- **GDevelop**: is an open-source, cross-platform game creator designed to be used by everyone—no programming skills required. Site: https://gdevelop-app.com/
- **Construct 2**: is a powerful ground breaking HTML5 game creator designed specifically for 2D games. It allows anyone to build games—no coding required. Site: https://www.scirra.com/construct2/.
- **RPG Maker**: allows you to customize every aspect of your game with an easy-to-use interface, making it perfect for beginners yet powerful enough for experts. Site: http://www.rpgmakerweb.com/.
- **GameMaker Studio 2**: Making games development accessible to everyone means taking away the barriers to getting started. Site: https://www.yoyogames.com/gamemaker.
- **Godot**: completely free and open-source under the very permissive MIT license. Site: https://godotengine.org/.
- **BuildBox**: the power to design, build, and launch 3D and 2D mobile games without coding. Site: https://www.buildbox.com/.
- **GameSalad**: is the revolutionary game development platform that allows anyone to create the game of their dreams with a sophisticated visual programming interface. Site: https://gamesalad.com/.

To exemplify the approach, this session will present and discuss an example of multimedia game development for data collection. For this example, the Construct 2 tool was selected because it does not require programming language knowledge, is intuitive and easy to use, and allows the user to collect multimedia data. More information about the use of the tool can be found at [8] and [2].

One of the main features of the Construct 2 tool is not to impose the knowledge of any programming technique or language, making it an ideal tool for researchers with no previous experience in game development. Its programming occurs through events that tell the system what the relationship and behavior that all elements in the game should/can do, as well as the interaction with variables and controls. With this tool, it is also possible to export the game to multiple platforms, such as Web, mobile, and desktop, in addition to communicating with database for variable storage. Figure 9.8 shows an example of logic event rules shown in the Construct 2 tool; it is possible to find this same logic structure in other game development tools.

Due the focus of this chapter is provide ways for user experience possibilities oriented data collection through an approach, will not be discussed basic elements as the download and installation tools. Thus, a set of examples will be presented below, which, from an approach to assist researchers in the development of their own experiments, enables the adoption of game elements.

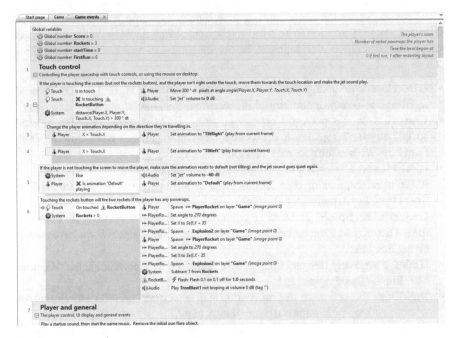

**Fig. 9.8** Conditional rule interface required for game development in Construct 2

### 9.3.2.1 Speech Recognition Data Audio Collection

In Sect. 9.2.3, accessibility guidelines are described that should also be used to improve the user experience. Among them, using as an example the "Speech" skill, a W3C [20] intermediate category guideline recommends: "speech recognition should occur on the basis of individual words from a small vocabulary (e.g., 'yes,' 'not,' 'open') instead of long sentences or multi-syllable words." In order to collect data related to the "Speech" skill, the following events can be programmed in the Construct 2 tool as shown in Fig. 9.9.

After the game project receives the object named "UserMedia," the events listed in Fig. 9.9 can be created and handled. In line 1, the "UserMedia is recognizing speech" event defines that the microphone should be accessed whenever the game is run in the browser and provides user feedback which exemplifies the text "Currently recognizing speech …"; the text content can be changed or replaced by an image, for example. Between lines 2 and 4 events are defined the exception in case the microphone or the browser does not support multimedia access.

Between lines 5 and 7 is defined the main speech recognition event; there is a condition to click a button to start or pause recognition. In line 7, the "Request speech recognition (Continued mode, Interim results)" setting defines the language used for recognition, and the "Continuous mode" setting complies with

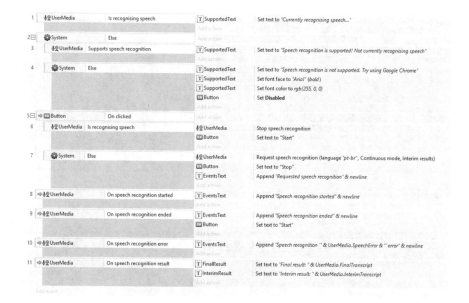

**Fig. 9.9** Conditional rule to speech recognition

the aforementioned guideline of recognizing individual words (For recognition of whole sentences the setting "Single phrase mode" should be used).

### 9.3.2.2 Video Screen Recorder Data Collection

Capturing the screen during gameplay can be a valuable resource when it comes to analyzing the user experience. According to [26], screen record is a creative approach to collecting data, especially when there is interaction with some software. One problem related to screen record use, as a data collection feature, is the software availability in this segment. In some cases, specialized software required license for use or because the game frame rate does not perform the correct screen record.

The Construct 2 tool allows to record the screen during entire gameplay or record special moments related to user actions and, as output, generate a video that can be exported in several formats. Figure 9.10 shows the logic rules used for this purpose.

In line 1 of Fig. 9.10, the browser compatibility test is defined and the feedback generated in the example is given on interface by text display, but can be changed. Line 2 tells the system that when the game starts ("On start of layout") and the browser supports screen capture, the record button will be active. In line 3, the event that starts recording is configured, which is conditioned at the click of a button. In line 4, the action of interrupting the recording by means of a button is foreseen, and in line 5, the immediate download of the result of the capture in video format that can have its format (AVI, MP4, etc.) is changed.

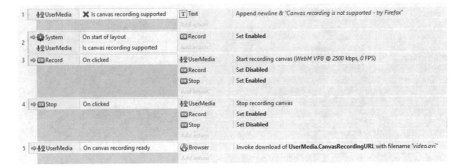

| 1 | UserMedia | ✖ Is canvas recording supported | T Text | Append *newline & "Canvas recording is not supported - try Firefox"* |
|---|---|---|---|---|
| | | | Add action | |
| 2 | System | On start of layout | Record | Set **Enabled** |
| | UserMedia | Is canvas recording supported | Add action | |
| 3 | Record | On clicked | UserMedia | Start recording canvas (*WebM VP8 @ 2500 kbps, 0 FPS*) |
| | | | Record | Set **Disabled** |
| | | | Stop | Set **Enabled** |
| | | | Add action | |
| 4 | Stop | On clicked | UserMedia | Stop recording canvas |
| | | | Record | Set **Enabled** |
| | | | Stop | Set **Disabled** |
| | | | Add action | |
| 5 | UserMedia | On canvas recording ready | Browser | Invoke download of **UserMedia.CanvasRecordingURL** with filename *"video.avi"* |
| | | | Add action | |

**Fig. 9.10** Conditional rule to video screen recorder

| | Global number **userPoints_variable** = 0 | | | |
|---|---|---|---|---|
| 1 | UserMedia | ✖ Is canvas recording supported | T Text | Append *newline & "Canvas recording is not supported - try Firefox"* |
| | | | Add action | |
| 2 | System | On start of layout | Record | Set **Enabled** |
| | UserMedia | Is canvas recording supported | Add action | |
| 3 | System | **userPoints_variable** = 20 | UserMedia | Start recording canvas (*WebM VP8 @ 2500 kbps, 0 FPS*) |
| | | | Add action | |
| 4 | System | **userPoints_variable** = 30 | Browser | Invoke download of **UserMedia.CanvasRecordingURL** with filename *"video.avi"* |
| | | | Add action | |

**Fig. 9.11** Conditional rule example to video screen recorder according user interaction

Another feature on Construct 2 tool that can be used to collect more accurate data is that it allows data screen recording during a specific moment of interaction on gameplay, using user action as a condition. In Fig. 9.11, for example, recording only occurs when the user gets 20 points and will stop when the user reaches 30 points.

In line 3 of Fig. 9.11 is setting the system condition that will only start recording when the value of the variable "userPoints _variable" is equal to 20 and line 4 indicates the end of record occurs when the same variable reaches the value 30. Programming such as this permits greater flexibility and case studies can be performed more precisely to collect expected data defined in design of the experiment.

### 9.3.2.3  User Photos Data Collection

During user's game interaction, the Construct 2 tool also offers the ability to capture photos before, during, and after the game is running. User video recording in the currently available version does not yet offer such support. Figure 9.12 shows an example of the programming required for webcam access.

**Fig. 9.12** Conditional rule to user photos data collection

For photo capture, the following logic rules defined in the Construct 2 tool, shown in Fig. 9.12, show the main definitions to be made:

1. Line 1: Checks if one webcam is connected and properly installed when the game is loaded.
2. Lines 2 and 3: Allow listing and selection of detected webcams.
3. Line 4: Using a button allows the previously selected webcam to be started; also displays the detected webcam resolution. With this logic rule it is already possible to view in-game webcam footage in real time.
4. Line 5: If the webcam is recognized, the buttons that allow you to take a picture are activated, and stop using the webcam.
5. Line 6: Displays the status if the selected webcam is not working.
6. Line 7: Required for the system to display the capture content at all times.
7. Line 8: Provides an action in the event that the button that stops recording is triggered.
8. Line 9: One action if the browser does not have multimedia support.
9. Line 10: Allows the capture of the user's photo using one button. It also allows you to configure image quality and store it in memory.
10. Line 11: Allows to download the previously captured photo.

It is possible also to take user's photo under conditions associated with an action. This possibility enables the capture of a moment (or sequence of moments) when the user performs determination action or any condition is reached. In Fig. 9.13, for example, the user photo is taken when the variable "userPoinst_variable" is equal to the value 10.

**Fig. 9.13** Conditional rule to user photos data collection according user interaction

### 9.3.3  Data Storage

A very important step in research involving user experience data collection is developing strategies for data storage generated during the interaction. Such strategies should ensure the correct analysis in search of knowledge and allow research reproducibility through data sharing. The data should therefore be stored in such a way as to allow easy manipulation, subsequent consultation, and reproducibility of analyses.

In this section we describe an example of data collection in real time and storage inside one online database following the approach described in Fig. 9.1, developed using the Construct 2 tool. The possibility of data storage in an online database aims to ensure all user interactivity data is secured, accessible, and be analyzed from anywhere. Section 9.2.3 discussed the relationship between accessibility guidelines and game aims including as many people as possible, considering the diverse needs presented by people with disabilities. The guidelines should not only be used during the game development process, but also in the ongoing application evaluation by experts and end users. Given the variety of approaches to assessing accessibility for digital games, the use of more than one assessment method is important to achieve higher quality results [10].

According to [9] the guidelines for games can be divided into three types: basic, intermediate, and advanced. These categories include differences in the number of people benefited, the impact provided to users, and the cost of implementation. The guidelines are also grouped into subcategories related to the different skills: motor, cognitive, visual, auditory, and speech. Using the "Motor" skill guideline as an example, it is recommended: "make interactive elements that require stationary precision (e.g., cursor/touch controlled by menu options)." Using this guideline as a base, Fig. 9.14 shows a game interface in which users must drag the apples to the basket with the mouse, allowing them to collect two variables: the "amount" of apples and the exact "time" in that the apple was put in the basket.

The game demonstrated in Fig. 9.14 has been developed using the Construct 2 web tool and can be accessed locally or hosted on a web server. To store the data variables "amount" of apples in the basket and "time" in which the apple is collected an online server was necessary, following the LAMP[4] scheme, a code in PHP language to perform access and insertion in the database.

In Listing 9.1 is presented the logical rule to create the table called "apples" that will receive the user interaction data. In line 3, the "score" variable will receive the

---

[4]Linux, Apache, MySQL, and PHP.

**Apples in the Basket: 3**
**Current Time: 0:38**

**Fig. 9.14**  Game interface example for collecting Motor skill data

amount of apples placed in the basket and in line 4, the "time" variable will receive the times (seconds since the beginning of the gameplay) of each apple was placed in the basket.

---

**Listing 9.1   SQL code used for database table development**

```
1 CREATE TABLE 'apples' (
2   'id' int(11) NOT NULL,
3   'score' int(11) NOT NULL,
4   'time' time NOT NULL
5 ) ENGINE=InnoDB DEFAULT CHARSET=utf8
     COLLATE=utf8_unicode_ci;
```

---

In order to store variables inside the database, a code as shown in Listing 9.2 in the PHP language was hosted on the web server. The game programming makes a request using the POST method to the PHP source code. In line 2, a header was added to allow the game to access the database, from line 4 to 7, the database connection variables were created and in line 9, the variable *$dblink* makes the connection with the database using the previous PHP variables. Finally, lines 11 and 12 contain the PHP variables "score" and "time" that will receive the values sent by the game via the POST method. Line 13 executes the query to insert data into the database, and in line 15, the connection is terminated for security reasons. This PHP source code exemplifies only a simple way to insert data into the database, other structures in the database area can be used for better data storage results.

---

**Listing 9.2  PHP code used for insert values in game database**

```
1  <?php
2     header('Access-Control-Allow-Origin: *');
3
4     $db = "database";//Your database name
5     $dbu = "username";//Your database username
6     $dbp = "password";//Your database users' password
7     $host = "localhost";//Your host
8
9     $dblik = mysqli_connect($host,$dbu,$dbp,$db);
10
11    $score = $_GET('score');
12    $time = $_GET['time'];
13    $sql mysqli_query($dblink, "INSERT INTO
          '$db','apples' ('id','score','time') VALUES
          ('','$score','$time');");
14
15    mysqli_close($dblink);
16  ?>
```

---

Figure 9.15 shows a logical rule for sending data to an external database. To make this send process, the Construct 2 tool uses AJAX[5] that must be added beforehand in game development.

In Fig. 9.15 line 1, one condition has been created and triggered every time when a collision occurs between the "basket" and "apple" sprites; the "apple" sprite disappears (apple Destroy function) from the game interface so that the user understands that the apple has been placed in the basket. The value 1 should also be added up to the current value of the variable "variable_Basket." The most important part of the programming still occurs on line 1 which makes AJAX

**Fig. 9.15** Conditional rule to external database storage

---

[5]Asynchronous JavaScript and XML.

call as follows: *variable_Url* & *"savescores.php?score="* & *variable_Basket* & *"&time="* & *variable_Time*, where:

- *variable_Url*: a global variable that contains the online server address ("http://www.youraddress.com.br" or IP address can be used). An important detail, at the end of the address assigned to this variable, "/" must be included so that concatenation using the symbol "&" can be performed.
- *"savescores.php?score="*: this is the continuation of the address that will be concatenated with the server address global variable. In it should be placed the name of the file containing the PHP code hosted on the server. In this example, the web page file has the name "savescores.php," as the request will use the POST method. The continuation of the request sends the score and time variable value will be received in the database.
- *variable_Basket*: this variable has the value of which apple was placed in the basket. Since researcher desired to know the time when the apple is placed in the basket, every time an apple is placed, a new database entry is made. In this way, it will be possible know how much time has passed between the user placing apple number 1 and apple number 2 in the basket.
- *"&time="* & *variable_Time*: the second value sent to the bank will be the variable "time" which, in this example, is concatenated with the variable "variable_Time." This variable gets the exact time an apple is placed in the basket.
- *(method "POST", tag "PostScore")*: configures which request method the AJAX call should perform and assigns a tag to this call. This feature allows to verify if the call was made successfully.

The line 2 as shown in Fig. 9.15 tells the game system that at all times ("Every Tick") the value of the _Basket variable must be updated in the interface. A text box named Score has been created on the basket in the game interface to inform the user the quantity of apples inside the basket.

In line 3 the system updates the text box on the interface, labeled "Clock," every 1.0 s with the current time since the game started. By default, the tool works with milliseconds and needs to be converted to minutes and seconds, using the expression: zeropad(int (time / 60 % 60), 1) & ":" & zeropad (int (time % 60), 2). Also in this line, the time value is added to the variable "variable _Time" every 1.0 s the value is displayed in the interface and the value that will be added to the database is always the same.

In line 2 as shown in Fig. 9.15, the system checks if the AJAX call named "PostScore" was executed successfully (it is also possible to assign actions if the call is not executed successfully). The action assigned in the example adds the value 1 to the variable "variable_Save" and displays this value in the interface through a text box called "save," this variable was created to inform that the data is being successfully saved to the database.

In Fig. 9.16, the result of the stored data query is presented. The first apple was placed in the basket at 3 s and the third apple was placed at 30 s. Thus, it is possible to verify the speed that each user, using their motor skills, is interacting with the

```
SELECT * FROM `apples`
```

| ←T→ | | | | id | score | time |
|---|---|---|---|---|---|---|
| ☐ | Edita | Copiar | Apagar | 1 | 1 | 00:00:03 |
| ☐ | Edita | Copiar | Apagar | 2 | 2 | 00:00:09 |
| ☐ | Edita | Copiar | Apagar | 3 | 3 | 00:00:30 |

**Fig. 9.16** Query in Apples table returning stored values

game. As a possibility of collecting new data, it would be feasible to also control the speed at which new apples appear on the screen, check the order in which users place apples in the basket, and change the position of the basket, for example.

Through the game example described here, using accessibility motor skills concepts and the Construct 2 development tool, it was possible test one example to store the data generated during user interaction on online database follow the approach described in Fig. 9.1. There are other ways to store data using the tool, but among those currently available, this mode proved to be efficient for further analysis.

### *9.3.4 Data Analysis*

The case study described here exemplifies a data collection performed through games. In this example, the data collection performs an important role in research and it was made as a part of an investigation about the conversion of cognitive tests batteries for the digital medium. The test app was developed in the form of a game. The digital cognitive test was submitted to an experiment with users, based on usability heuristics [7]. Heuristics are processes that seek to find problems that recurrently occur, and in general, the possible solutions are recognized.

Due to the end user of the cognitive test is the elderly public, accessibility issues have been considered since its planning. An example was the choice of the color palette, which was made respecting its appreciation by colorblind individuals, more specifically in the three possible situations[6]: Tritanopia, Protanopia, and Deuteranopia.

The tool Color Oracle[7] was used to inquire the palette in the three situations and then the colors that in one or more cases were very close to each other were eliminated, becoming almost indistinguishable. Even so, caution is still needed when designing the game's assets. Feedback and objectives cannot rely exclusively on color to differentiate objects. Sounds and shapes should also be used.

[6]The kind of color blindness analyzed here were Tritanopia—insensitivity to short waves (the blue ones); Protanopia—insensitivity to long waves (the red ones); Deuteranopia—insensitivity to medium waves (the green ones).

[7]https://colororacle.org/.

In the battery of cognitive tests, eight aspects related to the intellectual requirements of the users were treated, namely: (**Test 01**)—Visual Perception, Incidental Memory and Immediate Memory, (**Test 02**)—Praxis, (**Test 03**)—Abstraction, (**Test 04**)—Digits Extension Test (Direct), (**Test 05**)—Digit Extension Test (Inverse), (**Test 06**)—Attention, (**Test 07**)—Verbal Fluency Test, and (**Test 08**)—Facial Recognition. From the definition of these aspects, a correlation was sought between them, in order to identify/verify the level of reach that the portability for the digital medium would allow, without there being a significant change in the context.

The data collections in the Case Study were carried out having a set of cataloged variables, referring to the aspects related to the cognitive loads required of the users. Then, cataloged variables are listed, which exemplify how the experiment was planned with users using the game (playing).

1. (**Test 01**)—Visual Perception, Incidental Memory, and Immediate Memory:

   (a) Number of objects: it is the number of objects that show up in the screen simultaneously. This variable can have a direct impact on the relative performance of the same player. For example, an interaction with fewer objects on the screen may have better results.

   (b) Amount of Shapes: it is the number of different shapes that show up on the screen. This variable can have a direct impact on the relative performance of the same player. For example, a test where triangles and squares appear may have fewer results than one in which only squares appear.

   (c) Elements of Confusion: it is the number of objects that will be inserted to create confusion, relevant only in the previous version of the test, in which the player needed to mark which objects were different from the memorized matrix. This variable can have a direct impact on the relative performance of the same player. It is expected that in a scenario with more elements of confusion the player makes more mistakes.

   (d) Score: player's score from 0 to 100. This data only stores how many of the spaces were filled correctly, ignoring spaces that were filled unnecessarily. To circumvent the possibility of the player filling the entire array the number of objects that can be placed was limited to the same number as the variable "Amount of Shapes." This data is important to compare the matrix inserted by the player and the original matrix, evaluating if the player actually memorized the original matrix.

   (e) Total Time: it is the sum of the time since the player started the test until completing it. This may be indicative of difficulty in interacting with the tablet screen, difficulty in understanding the test as well as motor limitations or distractions.

   (f) Clicks:

   - Clicked form: it is the data that stores how the screen was touched by the user, relevant only in cases with more than one available way. This may indicate difficulty in interacting with the tablet screen, difficulty in understanding the test as well as motor limitations.

- Color: it is the data that stores the color of the touched object, relevant only in cases where there will be more than one object color. This data may indicate difficulty in distinguishing colors or difficulty in understanding the test.
- Time: it is the time between the current and previous clicks. This data may indicate difficulties in interacting with the tablet screen, difficulty in understanding the test as well as motor limitations.
- Click type: it is the data that marks if the player touched a button, an object of interest or none of the previous two, thus setting a miss click. This may indicate difficulties in interacting with the tablet screen, very small objects, and motor limitations.
- Accuracy: it is the data that marks whether the touch made was a hit or an error, within the test hit and error settings. This data may indicate difficulties in interacting with the tablet screen, difficulty in understanding the test as well as motor limitations.

2. (**Test 02**)—Praxis

   (a) Score: player's score from 0 to 100, marking how many objects were fitted in correctly. This data stores the evaluation of the connections two by two, with a small margin of error for each connection, dividing the maximum score by the number of total connections that will be verified. This may indicate difficulties in interacting with the tablet screen, difficulty in understanding the test as well as motor limitations.

   (b) Total time: it is the sum of time since the player started the test until completing it. This may be indicative of difficulty in interacting with the tablet screen, difficulty in understanding the test as well as motor limitations or distractions.

   (c) Clicks:

   - Shape: it is the shape touched by the user. This data may indicate that the player has more difficulty interacting with a certain piece of the Tangram, whether its size or format.
   - Color: it is the color of the shape played by the player; it is important because there is more than one copy of some shapes, but different colors and/or rotations. This data may indicate that the player has difficulty in distinguishing certain colors.
   - Time: it is the time between the current and previous clicks. This may indicate difficulties in interacting with the tablet screen, difficulty in understanding the test as well as motor limitations.
   - Click type: this data indicates whether the player touched a button, an object of interest, or none of the previous two, setting a miss click then. This may indicate difficulties in interacting with the tablet screen, very small objects, and motor limitations.

3. (**Test 03**)—Abstraction

   (a) Score: player's score from 0 to 100, marking how many interactions of the abstraction test were properly answered. This may indicate difficulty in interacting with the tablet screen, difficulty in understanding of the test as well as motor limitations.

   (b) Total time: it is the sum of time since the player started the test until completing it. This may be indicative of difficulty in interacting with the tablet screen, difficulty in understanding the test as well as motor limitations or distractions.

   (c) Clicks:

   - Time: it is the time between the current and previous clicks. This may indicate difficulties in interacting with the tablet screen, difficulty in understanding the test as well as motor limitations.
   - Click type: this data indicates whether the player touched a button, an object of interest, or none of the previous two, setting a miss click then. This may indicate difficulties in interacting with the tablet screen, very small objects, and motor limitations.
   - Accuracy: it is the data that marks whether the touch made was a hit or an error, within the test hit and error settings. This data may indicate difficulties in interacting with the tablet screen, difficulty in understanding the test as well as motor limitations.

1. Sequence Size: it is the variable that stores how long the sequence on the screen is. This variable can have a direct impact on the relative performance of the same player. For example, longer sequences can cause more confusion by repositioning the various numbers on the screen.

2. Total errors: it is the data that stores how many times the player touched a number that was not next in the sequence. This data may indicate difficulties in interacting with the tablet screen, difficulty in understanding the test as well as motor limitations.

3. Total time: it is the sum of the time since the player started the test until completing it. This may be indicative of difficulty in interacting with the tablet screen, difficulty in understanding the test as well as motor limitations or distractions.

4. Clicks:

   (a) Pressed Number: it is the data that stores which digit was pressed. This data may indicate difficulty in understanding the test and confusion with the numbers shown on the screen.

   (b) Time: it is the time between the current and previous clicks. This data may indicate difficulties in interacting with the tablet screen, difficulty in understanding the test as well as motor limitations.

   (c) Accuracy: it is the data that marks whether the touch made was a hit or an error, within the test hit and error settings. This data may indicate difficulties in interacting with the tablet screen, difficulty in understanding the test, distraction as well as motor limitations.

For each of the tests, the data set represented by the cited variables was captured during the interaction process with the elderly. These measures were used in the convergence analysis phase, with the tests validated according to [7] guidelines. The main objective in the use of these variables was to represent the result of each test and to allow the computational analysis, without the human perception.

### 9.3.5 Others Data Collection Possibilities

As technology advances new forms of interaction can be offered to users creating other experiences for new applications or exploring new possibilities. For example, the 2006 published work [18] proposes virtual environment interaction to reduce time and unify the exploration and analysis of qualitative and quantitative volumetric data. The study case described in this work that the user should use a 3D glasses, a flat screen, and a pen control to interact with the projected 3D objects. Although there were not many hardware resources at the time, researchers were looking for ways to provide users with new experiences for collecting and interacting with data. As mentioned earlier, currently new possibilities can be used for data collection during user interaction with new experiences in multimedia games, one of these possibilities is the use of Extended Reality (XR).

XR is a new terminology recently adopted in both market and state-of-the-art applications. According to [21], XR encompasses a wide spectrum of the reality continuum including virtual reality (VR), augmented reality (AR), and mixed reality (MR). In simple words, XR comprehends the three immersive technologies (VR, AR, and MR) on the same "umbrella" terminology aiming to unify technology and people. Because it offers new possibilities in game development and data collection, we selected the Virtual Reality area to better understand the user experience data collection potential.

As an example of the use of state-of-the-art VR games, the paper [4] proposes a virtual reality (VR) interactive game to offer an experience themed around racially motivated police brutality. The users comes face to face with the characters of the story, filmed with live action, and interacts in the space with them directly using gaze interaction and voice recognition aimed at.

To achieve the goal of exploring the emotional impact of VR space versus traditional film, during user interaction head movement data is collected (gaze interaction) to indicate options in the game's UI and also the user's own voice for action selection. Another example of user data collection generated by physical interactions with games in virtual reality is discussed in the work of [41] which aims a qualitative study with seven people, so that we could demonstrate how our visualization could represent the individual differences in the nature and level of physical activity for each game. For the data collection of use the paper describes Microsoft Kinect V2 use which allowed data collection about what specific part of the body players used during each VR game and a head-mounted display for Virtual Reality game viewing and heart-rate data collection for each participant. For data comparison users were asked to rest for 2–5 min to get a resting heart-rate and after each game, there was a 2–10 min break, to collect recovery heart-rate. With this data it was possible to create body maps to illustrate how the body maps provide a compact representation that can enable people to know what interactions and muscle groups each game involves, how much exertion they can expect, and how to make a set of games in a session a valuable part of their broader physical activity.

In order to investigate the possibilities that the potential use of Virtual Reality technology and gesture-based interaction may provide, we conducted an exploratory research using the technologies mentioned above and the approach proposed in Fig. 9.1, below our used methodology:

**Experiment Design:** identify the technical feasibility required for user data collection through the use of Virtual Reality and Gesture-Based Interaction technologies. The following hardware and software resources were used to conduct the exploratory research:

- **Lenovo Mirage Solo:** for Virtual Reality tests, the Lenovo Mirage Solo[8] has been selected. This head-mounted display allows the mobile app installation for the Android Operating System. This device does not require external sensors for use; another interesting feature of this headset is the light weight, which helps usability of users.
- **Senso Glove:** for interaction through gestures, the Senso Glove[9] was selected. Similar to a regular glove, it allows gesture capture made by the user's hands for interaction in the virtual environment.
- **Software:** for a prototype development Unity engine was selected because it possesses several features for Virtual Reality development and Senso Glove support. The C# language was used with Unity and as a development SDK we used the Senso Glove SDK[10] which allows the raw data collect generated from the users hand gestures. Lastly, the Google Daydream SDK indicated by the manufacturer for development was used for import Lenovo Mirage Solo capture movement features.

Figure 9.17 shows a user example testing the Lenovo Mirage VR headset and Senso Glove interaction.

**Data Collection and Storage** For technical feasibility tests, the research of a Virtual Reality application was started. Firstly, an application was developed in VR through Unity that can be seen in Fig. 9.18.

In the application on Fig. 9.18, the users should simulate assembling and disassembling hardware components of a hardware server using their own hands. The participants were was not properly informed about how they should make

---

[8]https://www.lenovo.com/us/en/daydreamvr/.

[9]https://senso.me/.

[10]A software development kit (SDK or DevKit) is typically a set of software development tools that allows the creation of applications for a certain software package.

**Fig. 9.17** Gesture-based
interaction applied to Virtual
Reality elements interaction
for data collection
exploratory research

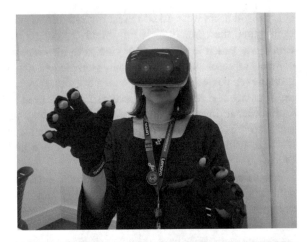

**Fig. 9.18** User making
gestures through a glove to
interact with a virtual
environment

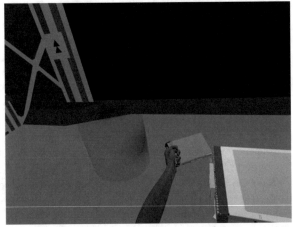

the procedures hold the server pieces in front of them; this intentional lack of information was adopted in order to verify the strategies used by users while learning a new means of gesture interaction.

After some initial observations, some cases made it impossible for gestural interaction to occur satisfactorily because was not possible directly communication between the glove and the headset due driver incompatibility problems. Because of these technical restrictions, it was necessary to use one laptop to mediate the communication between user generated data, using Senso Glove, and Lenovo Mirage Solo headset; for tests Lenovo ThinkPad T460 laptop was selected but for study replicability it is possible if user has another laptop with the same hardware specifications. This new hardware arrangement (Glove → Laptop → Headset) caused some delay on communication impacting the user experience.

**Data Analysis** Through this simple exploratory research using gloves and VR headset, with some difficulty, it was possible to capture raw data from the sensors present in Senso Glove. For future research, such data could verify the correct positioning of the hand of the users in certain virtual games that require hand gestures precision.

## 9.4 Conclusions

This chapter covered the topic of game development for researchers in areas related to experiments that consider user experience. In particular, the games adoption in scientific research is discussed to assist data collection and case studies. This chapter serves a wide range of researchers, even those who encounter difficulties or are unfamiliar with game element development. The use of games in research presents itself as a topic of great relevance for professionals and researchers involved with user experience, especially for those who want alternative ways of acquiring knowledge and conducting research through experiments and case studies.

The authors experience has shown that game development can be both a challenge and an innovation for research in various fields of science. Researchers have the knowledge to develop experiments containing data collection from user interaction. However, their lack of familiarity with the tools, techniques, and languages used in game development can often discourage them from adopting innovative strategies in existing experiments or in devising new ways to gain knowledge through experience analysis of the user involving gamification elements.

Finally, in this chapter, we present a game development approach using the Construct 2 tool that allows several possibilities to support game development and, mainly, enables the experiment design of case studies, data collection, and storage for future analysis. For better use of the approach, an overview of the gaming area was presented aiming at data collection, containing references about the user experience, considering the topics of usability, accessibility, and related studies examples.

**Acknowledgements** We would like to acknowledge Lenovo Tecnologia LTDA with the support from Brazil IT Law no 8248/1991 for supporting this research, CAPES (Coordination of Improvement of Higher Level Personnel) and FAPESP (São Paulo Research Support Foundation) for financial support (process no. 2016/01009-0).

## References

1. Atkinson, M.T., Gucukoglu, S., Machin, C.H.C., Lawrence, A.E.: Making the mainstream accessible: what's in a game? In: Miesenberger, K., Klaus, J., Zagler, W.L., Karshmer, A.I. (eds.) Computers Helping People with Special Needs, pp. 380–387. Springer, Berlin (2006)
2. Bura, J.: Construct 2 Game Development by Example, 1st edn. Packt Publishing, Birmingham (2016). ISBN-10: 1849698066

3. Chen, S.T., Huang, Y.G.L., Chiang, I.T.: Using somatosensory video games to promote quality of life for the elderly with disabilities. In: 2012 IEEE Fourth International Conference on Digital Game and Intelligent Toy Enhanced Learning (DIGITEL), pp. 258–262. IEEE, Piscataway (2012)
4. Cho, J., Won, Y., Kothari, A., Fawaz, S., Ding, Z., Cheng, X.: Injustice: interactive live action virtual reality experience. In: Proceedings of the 2016 Annual Symposium on Computer-Human Interaction in Play Companion Extended Abstracts, CHI PLAY Companion '16, pp. 33–37. ACM, New York (2016). https://doi.org/10.1145/2968120.2968121
5. Coovert, M.D., Winner, J., Bennett Jr., W., Howard, D.J.: Serious games are a serious tool for team research. Int. J. Serious Games 4(1), 41–55 (2017)
6. da Costa, M.A.F., da Costa, M.d.F.B.: Research Methodology: Concepts and Techniques, 2nd edn., Interciência (2009)
7. de Lima Salgado, A., do Amaral, L.A., de Mattos Fortes, R.P., Chagas, M.H.N., Joyce, G.: Addressing mobile usability and elderly users: validating contextualized heuristics. In: International Conference of Design, User Experience, and Usability, pp. 379–394. Springer, Cham (2017)
8. Dillon, R.: HTML5 Game Development from the Ground Up with Construct 2, 1st edn. A K Peters/CRC Press, Boca Raton (2014). ISBN 9781482216615
9. Ellis, B., Ford-Williams, G., Graham, L., Grammenos, D., Hamilton, I.: Game Accessibility Guidelines. http://www.gameaccessibilityguidelines.com (2012)
10. Fortes, R.P.M., de Lima Salgado, A., de Souza Santos, F., do Amaral, L.A., da Silva, E.A.N.: Game accessibility evaluation methods: a literature survey. In: International Conference on Universal Access in Human-Computer Interaction, pp. 182–192. Springer, Cham (2017)
11. Frederik, D.G., Peter, M., Jan, V.L.: Uncharted waters?: exploring experts' opinions on the opportunities and limitations of serious games for foreign language learning. In: Proceedings of the 3rd International Conference on Fun and Games, pp. 107–115. ACM, New York (2010)
12. Gee, J.P.: What video games have to teach us about learning and literacy. Comput. Entertain. (CIE) 1(1), 20–20 (2003)
13. Gonçalves, C.: Cognitive stimulation program in institutionalized elderly. O Portal dos Psicólogos 18, 1–18 (2012)
14. Goodman, E., Kuniavsky, M., Moed, A.: Observing the user experience: a practitioner's guide to user research. IEEE Trans. Prof. Commun. 56(3), 260–261 (2013)
15. Grammenos, D.: Game over: learning by dying. In: Proceedings of the SIGCHI Conference on Human Factors in Computing Systems, CHI '08, pp. 1443–1452. ACM, New York (2008). https://doi.org/10.1145/1357054.1357281
16. Grammenos, D., Savidis, A., Stephanidis, C.: Unified design of universally accessible games. In: Proceedings of the 4th International Conference on Universal Access in Human-computer Interaction: Applications and Services, UAHCI'07, pp. 607–616. Springer, Berlin (2007). http://dl.acm.org/citation.cfm?id=1757148.1757218
17. Greitzer, F.L., Kuchar, O.A., Huston, K.: Cognitive science implications for enhancing training effectiveness in a serious gaming context. J. Educ. Res. Comput. (JERIC) 7(3), 2 (2007)
18. Griffith, E.J., Koutek, M., Post, F.H., Heus, T., Jonker, H.J.J.: A reprocessing tool for quantitative data analysis in a virtual environment. In: Proceedings of the ACM Symposium on Virtual Reality Software and Technology, VRST '06, pp. 212–215. ACM, New York (2006). https://doi.org/10.1145/1180495.1180538
19. Hassenzahl, M., Tractinsky, N.: User experience – a research agenda. Behav. Inf. Technol. 25(2), 91–97 (2006). https://doi.org/10.1080/01449290500330331
20. Henry, S.L.: How WAI develops accessibility standards through the w3c process: milestones and opportunities to contribute https://www.w3.org/WAI/standards-guidelines/w3c-process/ (2018)

21. Huh, S., Muralidharan, S., Ko, H., Yoo, B.: XR collaboration architecture based on decentralized web. In: The 24th International Conference on 3D Web Technology, Web3D '19, pp. 1–9. ACM, New York (2019). https://doi.org/10.1145/3329714.3338137
22. Hunicke, R.: The case for dynamic difficulty adjustment in games. In: Proceedings of the 2005 ACM SIGCHI International Conference on Advances in Computer Entertainment Technology, pp. 429–433. ACM, New York (2005)
23. Isaksen, A., Gopstein, D., Nealen, A.: Exploring game space using survival analysis. In: FDG (2015)
24. Jung, Y., Li, K.J., Janissa, N.S., Gladys, W.L.C., Lee, K.M.: Games for a better life: effects of playing WII games on the well-being of seniors in a long-term care facility. In: Proceedings of the Sixth Australasian Conference on Interactive Entertainment, p. 5. ACM, New York (2009)
25. Kapp, K.M.: The gamification of learning and instruction: game-based methods and strategies for training and education. Wiley, San Francisco (2012)
26. MacKenzie, I.: Human-Computer Interaction: An Empirical Research Perspective. Elsevier Science, Waltham (2012). https://books.google.com.br/books?id=k0kBgyCaokAC
27. Marconi, M.A., Lakatos, E.M.: Methodology of Scientific Work, 6th edn. Atlas, São Paulo (2001)
28. Marconi, M.A., Lakatos, E.M.: Research Technique, 5th edn. Atlas, São Paulo (2002)
29. Michael, D.R., Chen, S.L.: Serious Games: Games that Educate, Train, and Inform. Muska & Lipman/Premier-Trade, New York (2005)
30. Pádua, E.M.M.: Research Methodology: Theoretical-Practical Approach, 6th edn. Papyrus, Smythesdale (2000)
31. Pedro, L.Z.: Uso de gamificação em ambientes virtuais de aprendizagem para reduzir o problema da externalização de comportamentos indesejáveis. Ph.D. thesis, Universidade de São Paulo (2016)
32. Salen, K., Zimmerman, E.: Rules of Play: Game Design Fundamentals. MIT Press, Cambridge (2004)
33. Samodelkin, A., Alavesa, P., Voroshilov, A.: A platform for pervasive games for research. In: Proceedings of the 15th International Conference on Mobile and Ubiquitous Multimedia, MUM '16, pp. 335–337. ACM, New York (2016). https://doi.org/10.1145/3012709.3016066
34. Souza, G.R., Trevisan, D.G.: Investigative study on the elderly, games and their motivations. Cadernos de Informática 8(3), 35–40 (2014)
35. Tong, T., Chignell, M., Tierney, M.C., Lee, J.: A serious game for clinical assessment of cognitive status: validation study. JMIR Serious Games 4(1), e7 (2016)
36. Torres, A.C.S.: Cognitive effects of video games on old people. Int. J. Disabil. Hum. Dev. 10(1), 55–58 (2011)
37. Valladares-Rodríguez, S., Pérez-Rodríguez, R., Anido-Rifón, L., Fernández-Iglesias, M.: Trends on the application of serious games to neuropsychological evaluation: a scoping review. J. Biomed. Inform. 64, 296–319 (2016)
38. Van Eck, R.: Digital game-based learning: it's not just the digital natives who are restless. EDUCAUSE Rev. 41(2), 16 (2006)
39. Wiemeyer, J., Kliem, A.: Serious games in prevention and rehabilitation – a new panacea for elderly people? Eur. Rev. Aging Phys. Act. 9(1), 41 (2011)
40. Wood, M., Wood, G., Balaam, M.: Sex talk: designing for sexual health with adolescents. In: Proceedings of the 2017 Conference on Interaction Design and Children, IDC '17, pp. 137–147. ACM, New York (2017). https://doi.org/10.1145/3078072.3079747
41. Yoo, S., Kay, J.: Body-map: visualising exertion in virtual reality games. In: Proceedings of the 29th Australian Conference on Computer-Human Interaction, OZCHI '17, pp. 523–527. ACM, New York (2017). https://doi.org/10.1145/3152771.3156170
42. Yuan, B., Folmer, E., Harris, F.C.: Game accessibility: a survey. Univ. Access Inf. Soc. 10, 81–100 (2010)

**Márcio Maestrelo Funes** senior researcher at Lenovo, received M.S. (2018) in Computer Science at University of São Paulo. Currently conducts research in user data collection with games, Virtual Reality, and accessibility. Works on the following subjects: Human–Computer Interface, Ubiquitous Computing, Natural Interfaces, and Virtual Reality.

**Leandro Agostini do Amaral** Ph.D. candidate at University of São Paulo (USP), received M.S. (2014) and B.S. (2010) in Computer Science at USP. Responsible Researcher in a PIPE / FAPESP project that uses games for cognitive training aimed at the public over 50 years. Since 2010 research subjects were related to Human–Computer Interaction, prioritizing accessibility issues.

**Renata Pontin Mattos Fortes** professor at the Department of Computer Sciences at the University of São Paulo, São Carlos campus. Graduated in Bachelor of Computer Science from the University of São Paulo (1982), Master's degree in Computer Science and Computational Mathematics from the University of São Paulo (1991) and PhD in Physics from the University of São Paulo (1996). Currently associate professor at the University of São Paulo, consultant at the Ministry of Education, and ad hoc consultant at the São Paulo State Research Support Foundation. Has experience in Computer Science, focusing on Software Engineering, acting on the following subjects: web engineering, free software projects, web accessibility, and software process.

**Rudinei Goularte** associate Member of the Brazilian Computer Society (SBC) and the Association for Computing Machinery (ACM). Graduated in Computer Science from the Federal University of Mato Grosso do Sul (1995). Master's degree (1998), a doctorate (2003), and a teaching degree (2011) from the University of São Paulo [São Carlos], all in Computer Science. Currently an associate professor at ICMC/USP under full dedication to teaching and research and a full masters and doctoral advisor. Ad hoc consultant to the São Paulo State Research Support Foundation (FAPESP) and the National Council for Scientific and Technological Development (CNPq). Develops Multimedia research in the following lines: Digital Video Coding, 3D Video, Content Based Retrieval, Multimodal Analysis, Multimedia Big Data Analytics.

Printed in the United States
By Bookmasters